37.50

Approaching Eden

Approaching Eden

ADAM AND EVE IN POPULAR CULTURE

Theresa Sanders

ROWMAN & LITTLEFIELD PUBLISHERS, INC.
Lanham • Boulder • New York • Toronto • Plymouth, UK

Published by Rowman & Littlefield Publishers, Inc.
A wholly owned subsidiary of The Rowman & Littlefield Publishing Group, Inc.
4501 Forbes Boulevard, Suite 200, Lanham, Maryland 20706
www.rowmanlittlefield.com

Estover Road, Plymouth PL6 7PY, United Kingdom

Excerpt from "The Tree" by Martin Buxbaum in *Rivers of Thought*. Published 1958 by The National Publishing Company, 1958. Reprinted with grateful permission by the family of Martin Buxbaum.

British Library Cataloguing in Publication Information Available

Library of Congress Cataloging-in-Publication Data

Sanders, Theresa, 1963–
  Approaching Eden : Adam and Eve in popular culture / Theresa Sanders.
    p. cm.
  Includes bibliographical references and index.
  ISBN 978-0-7425-6333-9 (cloth : alk. paper) — ISBN 978-1-4422-0063-0 (electronic)
  1. Adam (Biblical figure) 2. Eve (Biblical figure) 3. Eden. 4. Popular culture—
Religious aspects. 5. Bible. O.T. Genesis II–III—Influence. I. Title.
  BS580.A4S36 2009
  222'.11092—dc22   2009017941

Printed in the United States of America

Contents

Preface and Acknowledgments

As I discovered shortly after deciding to embark on this project, there is a vast amount of material in popular culture that springs, either directly or indirectly, from the story of Adam and Eve as found in the Bible's book of Genesis. In an attempt to make the project more manageable, I decided early on to focus exclusively on works that make a recognizable reference to the story or to its well-known interpretations. Sometimes that reference occurs in the names of the characters in a particular book or movie: for example, Adam, Ad, Eve, Eva, Evelyn, Lilith, Lil, or a similar variant. Other times the reference is to an iconic element of the story as it has come to be known in culture, for example, a serpent, a fig leaf, or an apple tree.

In restricting my scope in this way, I have largely ruled out works that deal with themes that are similar to those found in Genesis 2–3 but that make no reference to that text. For example, many movies and books deal with the ideas of temptation and sin. However, unless they do so in ways that recognizably refer to Adam and Eve, I have not included them here. Likewise, I have for the most part not dealt with works about paradise or utopias unless they make a reference to the Garden of Eden.[1]

There is one exception to the above rules, as I did include discussion of an episode of the sci-fi television series *Star Trek: Deep Space Nine* entitled "Paradise." The episode is one of very few in which the temptation to leave an Edenic environment is resisted, and so I have included it in the chapter called "Back to Nature" even though it makes no reference to the story of Adam and Eve.

Another way of restricting the focus of this project was to look only at cultural expressions that arose in the past hundred years. Though the book includes discussion of the long history of interpretations of Genesis 2–3, I have included pre-twentieth century works only insofar as they shed light on the television shows, movies, songs, and other artwork of more recent decades.

In attempting to decide what, exactly, constitutes "popular culture," I turned to what is probably the single most popular source of information in contemporary culture: Wikipedia. By its nature, Wikipedia (www.wikipedia.org) is a medium of the masses. An online encyclopedia, it is constantly being added to and edited by thousands of contributors. It is one of the top-ten most-visited websites in the United States and one of the top five most-visited sites in the world.[2]

According to Wikipedia, popular culture is "the culture—patterns of human activity and the symbolic structures that give such activities significance and importance—which are popular, well-liked or common."[3] As the site recognizes, however, this definition requires significant explication and nuance, and for that it turns to cultural studies expert John Storey.[4] Storey explores at length what popular or "pop" culture is. First, it can be defined quite simply as culture that is popular, or culture that is encountered by a large number of people. In this book several sources fit that criterion, including the television show *Desperate Housewives*, which is routinely watched by tens of millions of viewers, and the movie *The Passion of the Christ* (2004), which was one of the top-grossing films of all time (though it fared better in the United States than in the rest of the world).

Another approach to defining pop culture is to contrast it with "high culture"—though as Storey points out, precisely what that latter term means is equally difficult to determine. It seems safe to say that Michelangelo's frescoes in the Sistine Chapel are "high culture" rather than pop culture. At the same time, however, given that reproductions of those frescoes routinely show up in advertisements, parodies, and cartoons (see, for example, the *Time* magazine cover from August 15, 2005, or posters for the 1988 movie *And God Created Woman*, or the 2007 episode of *The Simpsons* entitled "The Homer of Seville"), the contrast is blurrier than one might think.

Storey offers another approach to popular culture, which is to define it in terms of how it is made. Popular culture can be defined, he says, as something that is "mass produced for mass consumption." By this definition, nearly every television show, movie, or advertisement ever made would qualify, from the 2004 horror flick *Adam and Evil* to the cartoon strip *Frank and Ernest*, which routinely uses the Garden of Eden as a setting for its gags.

However, this definition is countered by another of Storey's approaches, which holds that popular culture is culture produced by "the people," as opposed to by large conglomerates. For example, the "Fall of Man" woodcarvings of Kentucky artist Edgar Tolson were created by hand and were first exhibited through an organization called the Grassroots Craftsmen (see fig. 00.1).

Figure 00.1

Tolson, Edgar (1904–1984). Paradise, 1968. Carved and painted white elm with pencil, 12 7/8 × 17 × 10 in.

Reprinted with permission of Smithsonian American Art Museum, Washington, DC, Hemphill / Art Resource, NY

They are "popular" in the sense of representing an Appalachian style of carving that is practiced by nonprofessional artists and has been around for centuries. In a similar vein, Rita Denenberg—whose quiltwork entitled "We Are All Connected to One Rib" features Eve standing with Mother Teresa, Maya Angelou, Sally Ride, Pocahontas, Florence Nightingale, and other women of note—is a self-taught artist.[5] Though her works are available for sale, they are not mass-produced.

By and large, this book will focus on cultural phenomena that are both widely distributed and widely recognized. However, at times it will examine works that have appealed to or been seen by smaller audiences.

I confess that I have at times adopted whatever definition of popular culture allows me to highlight works that seem particularly interesting or significant. By necessity, my choices have been eclectic. One of the things that quickly became apparent as I began writing the book is the sheer mass of material from which to choose. Invariably, whenever I mentioned the project in conversation, I would be asked, "Have you seen. . .?" or "Have you read. . .?" or "Do you know about. . .?" After a while, I wanted to put my fingers in my ears and hum loudly whenever it looked like someone was going to suggest yet another movie to watch or another work of fiction to track down!

As always, many people contributed to the completion of this work, though all mistakes are, unfortunately, my own. First I would like to thank the students in my "Problem of God," "Systematic Theology," and "Adam and Eve" courses for their many insights. Traviss Cassidy in particular did essential work as a research assistant. Several colleagues deserve special mention for their assistance, including John F. Haught, Joseph Murphy, Elizabeth McKeown, James Walsh, Jonathan Ray, Ariel Glucklich, William McFadden, Ori Soltes, Diane Apostolos Cappadona, and Diane Yeager. Ervin and Mary Catherine Sanders read early drafts of the work, and several members of my family provided me with the names of works that should be included. The online community at the website of Turner Classic Movies (tcm.com) was quite helpful as well.

This book would not have come about had my colleague Tod Linafelt not brought to my attention an excellent volume entitled *Eve and Adam: Jewish, Christian, and Muslim Readings on Genesis and Gender*, edited by Kristen E. Kvam, Linda S. Schearing, and Valarie H. Ziegler.[6] Their book contains a selection of nearly two millennia's worth of interpretations of Genesis, as well as explication of those interpretations, and it is an invaluable resource for anyone interested in the topic. Many of the sources that I refer to in this book I first encountered in *Eve and Adam*.

Unless otherwise noted, all biblical quotations are from the New Revised Standard Version (1989).

References to the Talmud are taken from the Soncino Press translation edited by I. Epstein (1969). The information contained in parentheses following the references indicates the Tractate and folio where the original may be found.

Martin Buxbaum's poem "The Tree" first appeared in *Rivers of Thought* (National Publishing Company, 1958) and appears here with the permission of his daughter, Ms. Kate Prado.

CHAPTER ONE

In the Beginning

You don't have to be religious to know the story of Adam and Eve. Nearly everyone has heard the tale, or at least heard about it. And nearly everyone has absorbed something of its symbolism. That is why it is no accident that the mascot of Harry Potter's foe, Lord Voldemort, is a snake; after Eden, we all know that snakes cannot be trusted. It is no accident that the wicked queen in Walt Disney's *Snow White* (1937) tempts the innocent girl with an apple; we know that apples are forbidden fruit and that biting into one can be dangerous. This lesson is so deeply embedded in our culture that an advertisement for Beech-Nut baby food could feature an apple with the simple caption "The permitted fruit" and everyone would get the joke.

The English language is full of references to Adam and Eve. For example, the phrase "forbidden fruit" has come to signify not just what the first two people were warned to avoid but all sorts of temptations ranging from love affairs to alcohol to Cuban cigars. The term "Edenic" signifies something that is delightfully restful, and a "fig leaf" means a flimsy disguise that conceals something shameful. As boys grow into men they develop an "Adam's apple," since legend holds that the fruit that Adam ate got stuck in his throat. If you have never met a particular person, then you "don't know him from Adam"—or from Adam's brother or his housecat or his foot or his hatband or his off-ox or his old fox or his pet monkey, depending on where you grew up. The plant species *Aplectrum hyemale* is also known as "Adam-and-Eve root" and was once believed to have been grown by witches for their brews. If you are in a diner and order "Adam and Eve on a raft," you will be served poached eggs on toast. If you order "Adam's ale" you will be served water.[1]

The story of Adam and Eve is everywhere, and there is something about it that fascinates. What seems on the face of it to be a simple morality tale has managed to generate thousands of paintings, songs, movies, television shows, and cartoons. The Bible passage takes only about five minutes to read, but it would take a lifetime to read all of the poems, plays, and novels that make reference to it, and several lifetimes to read all of the sermons and scholarly commentaries that it has generated. It is as if the story holds the same allure that the forbidden fruit held for the first couple. We keep coming back to it time and again.

But though the story is everywhere, one must immediately be cautious in approaching all of these references. It is true that uses of the biblical tale are ubiquitous: an online gift company advertises "Forbidden Fruit Baskets" containing chocolates, and a fragrance company advertises a perfume called "All About Eve." And yet one of the points this book will make is that the cultural memory of the story frequently differs—sometimes quite dramatically—from the story as it is found in the Bible in Genesis 2:4–4:1.[2] As we will explore in more depth in chapter 2 of this book ("And God Said"), the gap between what the text says and what traditions *say* that the text says can be wide and deep.

For example, consider an episode of the original *Star Trek* series which frequently refers to the story of Adam and Eve.[3] The episode begins with the crew of the Starship Enterprise beaming down to a planet that they have been instructed to investigate. The planet is idyllic and filled with lush foliage and exotic flowers; it is, as the character Dr. McCoy observes, "like the Garden of Eden." What the Enterprise's Captain Kirk and his officers discover, however, is that the planet and its inhabitants are controlled by a computer that the natives call Vaal and that they think of as a god. Vaal has absolute power over the planet's life-forms and has arranged matters so that nothing has changed for thousands of years. There is no birth and there is no death, and the servants of Vaal know neither suffering nor love. As Kirk observes, "These people aren't living, they're existing. They don't create, they don't produce, they don't even think. They exist to service a machine."

By the end of the episode, the crew of the Enterprise has destroyed the computer and freed the people from the rule of Vaal. In the process, however, they have introduced both violence and sexuality to the planet, and First Officer Spock is not convinced that they have done the right thing: "Captain, you are aware of the biblical story of Genesis," he says. When Kirk affirms that he is indeed aware of the story, Spock states that "in a manner of speaking we have given the people of Vaal the apple—the knowledge of good and evil, if you will—as a result of which they too have been driven out of Paradise." At this point Captain Kirk inquires, "Are you casting me in the role of Satan?" A bit of good-natured humor then follows, as Kirk and McCoy imply that, with his pointed eyebrows and ears, Mr. Spock looks more like Satan than does anyone else on the ship.

There are several things to notice about this science-fiction use of Genesis. First, the episode is called "The Apple," and several characters bite into apples during the course of the story. As noted above, the apple as a symbol of temptation is deeply ingrained in the popular imagination; and yet, the biblical text itself makes no reference to apples. The Bible says only that the first couple ate the fruit of the tree of knowledge of good and bad and does not specify what sort of fruit it was. Various rabbinic sources identify the fruit as a fig, a citron, a carob, a nut, and wheat.[4] The Jewish Talmud suggests that the fruit was a grape. It has God scold Noah, who according to Genesis 9:21 became so drunk that he passed out, "Noah, Noah, shouldst thou not have taken a warning from Adam, whose transgression was caused by wine?" It then adds, "This agrees with the view that the [forbidden] tree from which Adam ate was a vine" (Sanhedrin, 70a). Other theories state that the fruit was a pomegranate or an apricot.[5] The most likely reason for tradition to portray the fruit as an apple is that the Latin words for "evil" and "apple" are identical (malum), and after the Christian saint Jerome translated the Bible from Hebrew to Latin, the connection was easy to make.[6] In any case, however the association may have come about, by the Middle Ages European artists nearly always portrayed the fruit of the tree as an apple, and it is this symbol that pervades Western popular culture.

The second thing to notice about the Star Trek episode is the association it makes between eating the forbidden fruit and sexuality. When Captain Kirk first asks the people of Vaal where their children are, they do not understand his question. Kirk tries to explain, and finally one of the men informs him that "replacements" have been forbidden by Vaal, as has touching between men and women. (At this point Dr. McCoy comments, "Well, there goes Paradise.") As it happens, two of the Enterprise crew are in love with each other, and their kissing is observed by two of the followers of Vaal. The Vaalians imitate what they have seen and conclude, "It is pleasant." By the end of the episode, after Vaal has been destroyed, Kirk tells the people that they will now have the chance to "learn something about men and women—the way they're supposed to be. Caring for each other. Being happy with each other. Being good to each other. That's what we call 'love.' You'll like that too, a lot, you and your children." When someone asks again, "What are children?" Kirk smiles slyly and advises them simply to keep learning more about each other and that eventually they will "find out." Now that they have been given the apple of knowledge, sex will come naturally to them.

This association between the forbidden fruit and sexuality does not occur in the Genesis text itself, at least not explicitly. In the story, Eve eats the fruit of the forbidden tree not because she wants to experience sexual pleasure but because "the tree was good for food, and . . . it was a delight to the eyes, and . . . it was to be desired to make one wise" (Genesis 3:6). It is true that once they have eaten, the man and woman realize that they are naked and cover themselves with fig leaves; however, it is not clear whether this gesture is to hide their sexuality or if it is simply because they suddenly understand that they are different from all the other creatures in the garden and require clothing.

Why then is the story so often associated with sex? The fifth-century Christian Saint Augustine probably bears most of the responsibility for this; in his *City of God* he attributes the advent of lust in the world to the sin of our first human parents: "[T]hat their disobedience might be punished by fit retribution, there began in the movement of their bodily members a shameless novelty which made nakedness indecent" (14:17). In other words, spontaneous sexual arousal is, for Augustine, a form of punishment. Moreover, all sexual activity, even if it takes place within the noble institution of marriage, is now in his eyes "accompanied with a shame-begetting penalty of sin" (14:18).[7]

On the topic of relations between men and women we will have much more to say in chapter 3 ("A Helper Fit for Him") and chapter 4 ("Fig Leaves"). For the moment, however, it is enough simply to note that the association between Adam and Eve's transgression and sexuality occurs over and over again in popular culture.

A third point of interest in the *Star Trek* episode is the connection made between the serpent in the Garden of Eden and Satan. There is no indication in the Genesis text that the snake is a devil. On the contrary, the reptile is identified as one of God's creatures: "Now the serpent was more crafty [Hebrew: *arum*] than any other wild animal that the Lord God had made" (3:1). Though crafty, it is God's creature. Nor should we assume that being crafty is a bad thing; in the Bible's book of Proverbs, one who is "clever" (*arum*) is praised as being superior to a fool (12:23). Why, then, when Mr. Spock compares Kirk's actions to those of the serpent in Eden, does Kirk assume that he is casting him in the role of Satan? And why do viewers understand the reference?

The association between the snake and the devil goes back at least to the first century. A Jewish text probably written around the year 100 C.E. and entitled the "Life of Adam and Eve" says that when God first created Adam, the angel Michael called all the other angels to worship the newly made image of God. The angel Satan, however, refused to bow down to Adam, saying, "He ought to worship me." Later, when telling of this incident to Adam, Satan recalls, "And the Lord God was angry with me and sent me with my angels out from our glory; and because of you, we were expelled into this world from our dwellings and have been cast onto the earth. . . . So with deceit I assailed your wife and made you to be expelled through her from the joys of your bliss, as I have been expelled from my glory."[8] Here Satan plainly tells Adam that it was he who spoke to Eve in the voice of the serpent.

Christian writers made the same connection between devil and snake. The second-century theologian Theophilus, like the author of the "Life of Adam and Eve," also identified Satan as the one who tempted Eve in the Garden, and his contemporary Tertullian thundered that since Eve had listened to the reptile, every woman is now "the devil's gateway."[9]

In the seventh century, the Muslim Quran told a story similar to the one found in the "Life of Adam and Eve." According to the Quran, the *jinn* Iblis (also called Satan) rebelled against God's command. As the Quran testifies, "And behold, We [God] said to the angels: 'Bow down to Adam': and they bowed down; not so Iblis: he refused and was haughty: he was of those who reject Faith" (Surah 2:34). Iblis explains to God why he did not want to bow down to Adam: "I am better than he: Thou didst create me from fire and him from clay" (Surah 7:12).

Given how widespread the tradition is that the serpent in the Garden of Eden was a devil, it is not surprising that snakes are almost always seen in popular culture as emblems of evil. Think, for instance, of the opening scenes of Mel Gibson's movie *The Passion of the Christ* (2004). As Jesus prays in the Garden of Gethsemane, he is approached by a pale, demonic-looking figure who wears a black hood. The figure taunts Jesus by telling him that God's grandiose plans for saving humanity are impossible to achieve: "Do you really believe that one man can bear the full burden of sin? No one man can carry this burden, I tell you. It is far too heavy. Saving their souls is too costly." Tormented by fear that the demon might be right, Jesus huddles on the ground and prays that God might spare him from his impending crucifixion. The demon then turns its eyes to the ground, and from where it stands a serpent crawls out and slithers towards Jesus. For a moment it looks as if Jesus might lose his nerve and give in to the temptation of the devil. Just as the snake reaches him, however, Jesus stands and crushes it with his foot.

The allusion here is to Genesis 3:15, in which God tells the serpent, "I will put enmity between you and the woman, and between your offspring and hers; he will strike your head, and you will strike his heel." Jesus in Gibson's movie plays the role of the New Adam, the one who is made in the image of God but who, unlike the first Adam, does not listen to the serpent/devil and thus does not sin. Rather than giving in to the reptile, Jesus uses his heel to strike its head.

We should not be surprised by this conflation of Adam and Jesus, as the linkage between the two goes back as far as the first century. In one of his letters to the followers of Jesus in Corinth, the New Testament writer Paul compared the two men: "For since death came through a human being, the resurrection of the dead has also come through a human being; for as all die in Adam, so all will be made alive in Christ" (1 Corinthians 15:21–22). The same comparison is drawn over and over again in art. Many medieval paintings, for example, show the cross of Jesus raised upon the very spot where Adam lies buried. A medieval legend says that the cross of Jesus was made of the same tree that Adam and Eve ate from, and a fifteenth-century fresco by Giovanni da Modena makes the same point by showing Jesus crucified on a tree around which a serpent is coiled and from which Eve is plucking fruit.[10] The message, which we will explore in chapter 5 ("The Curse of Adam"), is that the first Adam brought death and sin, but the second brings life and salvation. Thus, when looking for allusions to Adam in popular culture, we must at the same time be on the lookout for allusions to the story of Jesus. As we will see in chapter 6 ("The Curse of Eve"), the same applies to Mary and Eve; over and over again, Mary is portrayed as the Second Eve who, unlike her biblical predecessor, refused to sin and thus conquered Satan.

It is clear, then, that the story of Adam and Eve stands at the center of a tangled web of allusions, interpretations, and reinterpretations. Perhaps what is most fascinating about the text is the widely divergent and often contradictory readings it has received throughout history. For example, the tale has been seen as both an endorsement of celibacy and an exhortation to marriage. How is this possible? How can the same story give rise to such different interpretations? Part of the answer lies in the cultural situation of the interpreter, and part of it lies in which section of the story the interpreter chooses to emphasize.

Thus some early Christian readers saw Genesis 4:1 ("Now the man knew his wife Eve, and she conceived and bore Cain") as evidence that until they had been driven out of the Garden, Adam and Eve had not had sex. These interpreters concluded that intercourse was something that took place only after Adam and Eve had sinned and was therefore a manifestation of humanity's fallenness. It did not help matters that Cain, a few verses after 4:1, murdered his younger brother Abel. If we can judge an action by its results, the sexual union of Adam and Eve was not exactly a great success. The fourth-century theologian John Chrysostom agreed, and he saw the first couple's mistakes as an endorsement of celibacy: "You see, before their disobedience they followed a life like that of the angels, and there was no mention of intercourse." He concluded, "Accordingly, consider, I ask you, dearly beloved, how great the esteem of virginity, how elevated and important a thing it is, surpassing human nature and requiring assistance from on high."[11]

On the other hand, some interpreters focus on the part of the story in which Adam says of Eve, "This at last is bone of my bones and flesh of my flesh" (2:23). Commenting on this passage, Rabbi Eleazar says in the Talmud, "This teaches that Adam had intercourse with every beast and animal but found no satisfaction until he cohabited with Eve" (Yebamoth 63a).

So. Either Adam had no sex in the Garden at all, or he had sex with every animal and then with Eve. Which is it? Just as scholarly commentators give different answers, popular culture does as well. The Mexican film *El Pecado de Adán y Eva* (also known as *The Sin of Adam and Eve*, 1969) portrays the first couple as having no interest in sex until after they have eaten the forbidden fruit. Pre-transgression, the two cavort naked in their lush environment, but they show no sexual desire at all for each other. On the other hand, the 1980 movie *The Blue Lagoon* takes great pleasure in lingering over the sexual awakening of its adolescent protagonists on their Edenic island. The 1920 novel on which the movie was based makes the point clearly. In a chapter entitled "The Sleep of Paradise," Henry De Vere Stacpoole describes the moon looking down upon the postcoital young couple as they lie "naked, clasped in each other's arms, and fast asleep." He explains, "The thing had been conducted just as the birds conduct their love affairs. An affair absolutely natural, absolutely blameless, and without sin."[12]

The diversity of interpretations is perhaps most marked when it comes to the question of whether or not Adam and Eve were literally the first human beings. As we will see in chapter 7 ("Monkeyshines"), debate between those who hold that humans evolved from other species, on the one hand, and those who say that God created humans exactly as described in Genesis, on the other, is alive and well. The opening in 2007 of the Creation Museum in Kentucky, which advertises itself as "The only place with tickets to the Garden of Eden," has thrust the issue into the spotlight once again.

However, other divergences in interpretation are just as interesting. For example, the contemporary Christian Nativist movement sees the Genesis text as a justification for nudism, but other Christians are horrified by this reading and see the story instead as a prohibition against public nakedness. This, and controversies about vegetarianism and ecological stewardship, will be taken up in chapter 8 ("Back to Nature").

One of the most important recent scholarly interpreters of the Adam and Eve story, Elaine Pagels, shows that a diversity of readings is nothing new. Even in the ancient world, and even within a single religious tradition, exegeses clashed. For Saint Augustine, as Pagels points out, Adam and Eve were the source of original sin, a condition which they passed on to their offspring and which manifests itself in the evils of lust and death. For Christian thinker Julian of Eclanum, on the other hand, the sin of Adam and Eve affected only them and not their descendants;

moreover, sexual desire and death were natural phenomena rather than punishment for sin. As Pagels also shows, many ancient Christian readers saw the Genesis text as a testimony to the goodness and justice of God; some, though, saw it as evidence of the pettiness of God.[13]

The list of divergences could go on and on. The story is either an endorsement of slavery or an argument against slavery;[14] a justification for racism or a bulwark against racism;[15] a rejection of sex in anything other than the missionary position,[16] a rejection of homosexual sex, a rejection of birth control—or it is an endorsement of all non-hurtful erotic activity.[17]

A key question in all of this debate is whether one focuses attention on the "before" or the "after" part of the story. That is, if one takes the condition of Adam and Eve in the Garden as normative, then one is more likely to adopt a utopian vision in which the job of humans is to strive for perfection. On the other hand, if one sees the last part of the story as explicating the will of God, then one is more likely to accept suffering as the consequence of sin. For example, when anesthesia was first invented in the nineteenth century, some doctors argued that it should not be used by obstetricians because to do so would violate God's order (see Genesis 3:16) that women would bring forth children in pain.[18] Most, of course, saw withholding anesthesia as immoral.

Do we accept life as it is, or do we try to improve it? Chapter 9 ("Paradise Regained") will consider utopian visions as they have been depicted in movies such as *Pleasantville* (1998) and in children's novels such as Lois Lowry's *The Giver* (1993). One of the most interesting things to observe is how "perfection" is portrayed in popular culture and how frequently it is rejected as something desirable. As chapter 10 ("The Final Frontier") observes, even versions of the Genesis story in science fiction are reluctant to accept a future in Eden. They are more likely to suspect such portrayals to be nightmares rather than pleasant dreams.

In sum, there is perhaps no biblical story that has received as much attention as the story of Adam and Eve. References to it appear in sources as diverse as Louis Armstrong's 1925 recording of "Adam and Eve Had the Blues"; advertisements for faucets, cars, and condoms; a ballet in the 1960 movie *Can-Can*; *Mother Goose and Grimm* comic strips; computer logos; Japanese anime; songs by Elvis Presley. . . . Again, the list could go on and on. This book hopes to make sense of this bewildering array by giving background about the history of Jewish and Christian interpretations of the story, and then by showing how these interpretations find new life in popular culture. At times, Muslim insights into Adam and Eve will also be incorporated; however, because the account of creation in the Quran is somewhat different from that found in the Bible, references to Muslim interpretations will be far fewer in number.

CHAPTER TWO

And God Said

How we see something often depends on the context in which we observe it. For example, a few years ago, workers at the National Air and Space Museum were making renovations that required the use of a forklift. In order to keep children from climbing on the equipment when it was not in use, the museum staff placed exhibit ropes around it. Soon afterward, a young visitor to the museum observed the forklift and asked his father why it was there. The father, making the best sense that he could out of what he was seeing, answered that astronauts had taken it to the moon with them, and that the forklift was being preserved in the museum now as part of the history of space exploration.[1]

Changing the context in which we encounter something can radically alter our perception of it. A forklift on a construction site is a tool. In a museum, it is an exhibit. Or, to use another example, a photograph of Adolf Hitler in a history book means one thing. The identical photo at a neo-Nazi rally means something quite different.

The same dynamic applies when we interpret a text. When James Frey published *A Million Little Pieces*, the story of his recovery from alcohol and drug addiction, the book became a best-seller and was featured on the *Oprah Winfrey Show*. Soon afterward, Frey confessed that parts of the story were fiction rather than history. In a note to his readers, Frey wrote, "I believe, and I understand others strongly disagree, that memoir allows the writer to work from memory instead of from a strict journalistic or historical standard. It is about impression and feeling, about individual recollection. This memoir is a combination of facts about my life and certain embellishments."[2] In response, Winfrey told the author, "I feel that you betrayed millions of readers . . . that bothers me greatly. . . . I feel that you conned us all."[3] Read one way, the book was an inspirational story about overcoming impossible odds. Read another way, it was a lie.

When approaching the story of Adam and Eve, as when approaching any text, we must consider all sorts of different questions. What genre are we reading, and in what context should the story be understood? Where does tale begin, and where does it end? Who wrote it and why? Should we focus on the details of the story or just get a sense of what we think the author is trying to say? And finally, is the story about our past, our present, or our future?

History or Myth?

For many interpreters, the story of Adam and Eve is a scientifically and historically accurate account of the origin of human beings. Christian creationist Ken Ham asserts that the validity of all Christian beliefs depends on Genesis's being "true history."[4] In a segment of Alexandra Pelosi's HBO documentary *Friends of God* (2007), Ham addresses an audience of children and asks them, "Has any human being always been there—yes or no? No. Has any scientist always been there? No. Who's the only one who's always been there? God. Who knows everything? So, in a big loud voice, who should you always trust first? God or the scientist?" As the children shout "God!" an image appears on the screen behind Ham that shows a cartoon man holding a Bible. The caption says, "God said it, I believe it, that settles it!"[5] For Ham, if the Bible says that people were made on the sixth day of creation, then that is what happened.

For interpreters like Christian theologian Paul Tillich, on the other hand, the narrative about Adam and Eve is not history but rather myth. By the term "myth," Tillich does not mean something that is false. Instead, he means a symbolic story that expresses people's faith. Genesis is not a literal account of what happened but is instead a poetic articulation of the meaning of human life in relation to God.

More precisely, it is a story about how our passion for God is constantly being thwarted by our own finitude. We are, says Tillich, in a state of estrangement: "Man is estranged from the ground of his being, from other beings, and from himself."[6] This estrangement is expressed in the Bible as a narrative about an event that happened long ago, though really the story is about who we are now. In Genesis, the characters Adam and Eve represent all of humanity, and the character God is a symbolic representation of what Tillich calls Being Itself or the Ground of Being.[7] The character God in the story, in other words, is a symbol for God, the God who transcends all symbols.

In Tillich's view, to read the story as a literal description of what happened is to misread it. Tillich asserts, "The presupposition of such literalism is that God is a being, acting in time and space, dwelling in a special place, affecting the course of events and being affected by them like any other being in the universe. Literalism deprives God of his ultimacy and, religiously speaking, of his majesty."[8] God, in this interpretation, is not a being who literally walks and talks. God transcends finite categories, but since we are human we can only talk about God using finite language. The key, for Tillich, is to remember that our language always has to point to the "more" that is God. If we think that our myths literally describe God, then we risk turning God into something less than God.

In Tillich's thought, there is no real conflict between historical or scientific accounts of creation, on the one hand, and religious myths on the other. History tells us what happened, and science tells us how the world works, but myth does something quite different. History and science might tell us that humans evolved over a period of millions of years, rather than appearing whole and entire on a single day. This claim can be judged only by the standards of history and science; religion has no basis for evaluating them. Myths, though, tell us about the meaning of life. They are the language of faith. They can be neither proved nor disproved by history and science.

Tillich is far from the only Christian thinker to accept both a scientific account of the origins of human existence and a myth that also talks about those origins. In 1996, Pope John Paul II gave an address in which he stated that there is "no opposition between evolution and the doctrine of the faith about man and his vocation," so long as one keeps in mind "several indisputable points." For example, one must emphasize that "the spiritual soul is immediately created by God," that people are made in the image of God, and that people are therefore qualitatively different from animals.[9]

Is Genesis history or myth? Quite a bit is at stake in the answer. If one decides with Ken Ham to eschew the findings of scientific inquiry, then one is essentially choosing faith over reason, and this removes any rational basis for religious life. The only justification for worship then is obedience to authority. Ken Ham is unapologetic about this: "Unfortunately, too many people have started with the word of men and then judged what the Bible states. What an arrogant position this is! We cannot tell God what He should say. We must be prepared to come totally under His authority and listen to what He says to us."[10]

This position can cause considerable distress, as one must deliberately suppress rational doubts in order to obey the demands of one's faith. One is forced to choose between the ability to think (which is often described as humans' most precious quality and what distinguishes us from most other animals) and the desire to worship. The exhibits at the Creation Museum in Kentucky, which was founded by Ham, make this clear. Again and again, they contrast human reason with God's word. Human reason, one display says, teaches that galaxies, the solar system, the earth, the moon, and the continents all developed through the slow process of cosmic development. God's word, in contrast, teaches that all creation took place in six days at the beginning of time, and that that word should be believed. The museum contends that questioning the Bible is an assault on God and is the work of Satan.

If one does not accept a literal interpretation of Genesis, one can more easily reconcile the biblical story with one's reason. However, the risk then is that one opens the door to the possibility that none of what the Bible teaches has any basis in history. As Ken Ham asserts, "If the events of Jesus Christ's birth, death and resurrection didn't happen in history, then how can we be saved? If we all don't go back to one man in history, a literal man in a literal garden . . . then who are we?"[11]

The answer, for Tillich, is that the accounts of Jesus's birth, death, and resurrection as they appear in the New Testament are, like the story of Eden, in fact not to be taken at face value. He writes, "It is not a matter of faith to decide how much legendary, mythological and historical material is amalgamated in the stories about the birth and the resurrection of the Christ." For Tillich, the issue is not what literally happened; the issue is whether or not "the reality which is manifest in the New Testament picture of Jesus as the Christ has saving power for those who are grasped by it, no matter how much or how little can be traced to the historical figure who is called Jesus of Nazareth."[12] In other words, the important question is whether or not the Bible's stories about Jesus capture the deepest meaning of life. Not everyone, though, is quite so willing to let go of the assurances of history in deciding how to live their lives.

For the purposes of this book, it matters less how one answers the question of genre than that one become aware of exactly why one or the other answer is persuasive and what the implications are for one's intellect, faith, and religious life.

Text and Context

Tied up with the question of to which genre the story of Adam and Eve belongs is the question of the context in which we should read the story. Should we compare it to other ancient Near Eastern stories such as the *Epic of Gilgamesh* or the *Enuma Elish*? As long ago as 1895, a German scholar named Hermann Gunkel argued that Genesis 1 was, as he put it, "merely the Judaic reworking of much older traditional material that originally must have been considerably more mythological in nature." Among the similarities that Gunkel cited between the biblical story and Babylonian creation accounts were the primordial existence of water and darkness; a process of separation wherein a divine power creates the horizon; creation via divine proclamation; and the creation of animals according to the categories of domestic animals, wild animals, and creeping things.[13]

If in fact there are similarities between the biblical tale and the stories told in other ancient civilizations, what would that mean for a reading of Genesis, or for faith? Should one attribute the parallels to the historical influence of one culture on the other? Should one say that the similarities are simply the result of a coincidence? Should one say that God has revealed the same story to many different cultures? Is the truth of Genesis dependent on its being unique? Or is it possible that truth is best expressed in the symbols and stories already present in a culture—that these are the language through which God speaks to people, and that this explains the similarity of creation stories?

As if these questions were not complex enough, we must also contend with the fact that the Genesis text and its ancient Near Eastern cousins are only a few of the many creation stories found throughout the world. The Bantu people of the Congo River region speak of a creator named

Bumba who vomited up the world. The Ainu of Japan tell a story in which the world began as slush until a little bird trampled it down to create dry land. The Yami of Indonesia speak of a big stone that fell upon the ground, out of which burst a man.[14] These stories may sound quaint or far-fetched. However, when the Genesis story is placed in their midst, it can suddenly seem just as unlikely.

For an example of how this change in perspective can take place, we might turn to Tony Hillerman's detective novel *The Shape Shifter*. The protagonist of Hillerman's book is a Navajo tribal policeman named Joe Leaphorn. The case that Leaphorn must solve centers on an old Navajo rug that was woven shortly after the "Long Walk"—the forced relocation of Navajo people by the United States government in the 1860s. In the course of his investigation, Leaphorn meets a Hmong man who came to America as a refugee from Vietnam. The Hmong people traditionally lived in the hills of southern China, but for various reasons they migrated to other countries that included Vietnam, Laos, and Thailand. In an effort to get to know the man and to win his trust, Leaphorn asks him about Hmong creation stories: "For example," he says, "in the Judeo-Christian culture—the Europe-based white culture—in that one God created the universe in a series of six days, and then said we should rest on the seventh one." The man replies, "Adam and Eve. I've heard about that." Leaphorn then recounts his own Navajo clan's account of their origins. According to his story, the Creator made a group of pre-humans, but these beings did evil things, and so the Creator destroyed the world. The pre-humans escaped to a second world, which was likewise destroyed, and then to a third: "The way my clan teaches the story, a sort of super-version of Coyote kidnapped the baby of another of these primal beings—one we call Water Monster—and he [the Creator] was so enraged he produced a terrible flood and drowned the third world as punishment. So we climbed up through a hollow reed and escaped into this world."[15]

It might feel a little disorienting to have Genesis 2–3 placed alongside Leaphorn's Navajo account of creation. When the Vietnamese man says that he has "heard about" Adam and Eve, the effect is to make us realize that the Eden story is only of marginal interest to him and his people. He does not say that he disagrees with Genesis or that he does not believe that it is true. He simply conveys the sense that it is not part of his own worldview. When Leaphorn goes on to tell his Navajo story, the Genesis story suddenly appears not as universal, timeless, and immutable truth, but rather as the particular tale of a particular people from a particular time and place.

Of course, one can reject this recontextualization. One can assert that Genesis is the unique and sacred word of the one true God and that no comparisons to other literature are valid. Again, the important point is to know why one does this and what the implications of the choice are.

Beginnings and Endings

A third difficulty that arises in reading the story of Adam and Eve is determining where the narrative begins and ends—or in what frame we should view it. One might interpret it in light of the biblical creation story that precedes it in Genesis 1. Or, one might say that it cannot really be understood unless one takes into account the whole of the Tanakh (what Christians often call the Old Testament). Or, perhaps one might believe that the story did not truly end until the death and resurrection of Jesus, whom Christians describe as the New Adam. Or maybe it did not end even then; maybe we must wait until the Second Coming of Jesus at the end of time in order to really understand the significance of humanity's origins. Or perhaps the story as it is told in Genesis should be seen as merely the forerunner to the version that can be found in the Muslim Quran.

Or maybe one should read the story on its own, apart from its relation to any other texts. As Harvard professor Gary A. Anderson points out, scholars have in recent decades tended to see the Bible not as a unified whole but rather as an amalgamation of various compositions written by an unknown number of authors in various places and at various times. Anderson observes, "It is hard to find scholars committed to the notion of scripture's narrative unity. Indeed quite the opposite view is more often the rule—that the Bible is a collection of fragmentary and self-contradictory pieces."[16]

Many scholars believe, for example, that the book of Genesis itself was not written by a single author. Tradition says that the first five books of the Bible (that is, the Torah or the Pentateuch) were composed by Moses. However, the famous biblical scholar Julius Wellhausen proposed a century ago that the books were actually compilations of texts written by four different authors whom he named the Jahwist (J), the Elohist (E), the Priestly writer (P), and the Deuteronomist (D). Wellhausen's theory is now referred to as the Documentary Hypothesis and is more or less taken for granted by most contemporary scholars, though there are many disagreements about which portions of the books should be assigned to which authors and about exactly how many authors there may have been. By and large, though, scholars believe that the story of Adam and Eve found in Genesis 2:4b–3:24 was written by the author designated as J, the Jahwist.[17] The J author tends to portray God using human imagery (for example, in Genesis 3:8 God goes walking in the cool of the evening) and tells colorful stories about God's interactions with humans (for example, God tells Noah to build an ark, and God destroys the Tower of Babel).

By contrast, the story of creation found in Genesis 1:1–2:4a is thought to have been written by the P or Priestly author. This Priestly account describes in considerable detail how God created the entire cosmos (including the sky, the sun, the moon, and the stars), but it passes over the creation of human beings in a single sentence. There is no Garden of Eden in Genesis 1, no forbidden tree, and no talking snake. The focus is less on people and more on the vastness of God's creation.

What should we do with these two accounts? Should we see them as complementary presentations of the same event and thus read them together? Should we see them as presentations of two entirely different events that should be read together but sequentially? Should we choose one over the other? Or should we see them as two myths that express the human understanding of God in different ways? Let us briefly explore each option.

Two Stories, Same Event

If you are committed, as Gary Anderson says, to "the notion of scripture's narrative unity," then you must find a way to reconcile the creation account in Genesis 1 with the account in Genesis 2–3. This is not as easy as it might seem. At first glance, Genesis 1 gives the "big picture" of creation, and then the story of Adam and Eve gives details about the creation of human beings. However, the matter is not quite so simple. In Genesis 1, God creates plants before animals, and animals before people. In contrast, in Genesis 2:4b–3:24, God creates people before plants, and plants before animals. How can these two accounts be reconciled?

Interpreters who believe that the Bible must be read as presenting one consistent coherent message—that otherwise it cannot be considered true, or truly the word of God—must translate the text so as to make the two stories cohere. Consider, by way of illustration, these two renderings of Genesis 2:8 and 2:18–19:

New Revised Standard Version (NRSV):

And the Lord God planted a garden in Eden, in the east; and there he put the man whom he had formed. . . Then the Lord God said, "It is not good that the man should be alone; I will make him a helper as his partner." So out of the ground the Lord God formed every animal of the field and every bird of the air, and brought them to the man to see what he would call them.

New International Version (NIV) with italics added:

Now the Lord God *had* planted a garden in the east, in Eden; and there he put the man he had formed. . . The Lord God said, "It is not good for the man to be alone. I will make a helper suitable for him." Now the Lord God *had* formed out of the ground all the beasts of the field and all the birds of the air. He brought them to the man to see what he would name them.

In the NRSV, God creates the man first and then plants a garden in which to put him. The NIV, a translation which is favored by many who hold that the Bible cannot and does not offer conflicting messages, says that the garden had already been planted before the man was created. In other words, vegetation was created before people were, just as Genesis 1 says.

Likewise, in the NRSV, the man is created before the animals. In the NIV, the animals had already been created prior to the man, and thus the order of creation matches the order in Genesis 1.

True, the translation of the verb in the second version is not very satisfying from a literary perspective. Putting the verb into the pluperfect ("had planted" rather than "planted"; "had formed" instead of "formed") disrupts the narrative flow of the story. Moreover, the second translation does not explain why God would say that it is "not good for the man to be alone" if the animals had already been created. However, if one holds to the principle that the two stories must complement each other and must not contradict, then narrative structure and literary style are irrelevant.

What matters most is simply that one discern the one true account of how the world began.

Holding to the narrative unity of the Bible necessitates not just that one reconcile the Adam and Eve story with the account in Genesis 1. One must also reconcile the story with other texts in the Bible. For example, in Genesis 3:9, when God is walking in the garden, God calls out to Adam, saying, "Where are you?" When Adam answers that he has hidden himself because he is naked, God asks, "Who told you that you were naked?" (3:11). Taken at face value, the story seems to indicate that there are things happening in the Garden of Eden of which God is unaware. If one reads the story on its own, this does not present a problem: the character God simply does not know everything. However, if one reads the story in light of other biblical texts, then one must reconcile the God who asks "Where are you?" with the God of, say, Psalm 139, whom the author of the song addresses in this way: "O Lord, you have searched me and known me. You know when I sit down and when I rise up; you discern my thoughts from far away. You search out my path and my lying down, and are acquainted with all my ways. Even before a word is on my tongue, O Lord, you know it completely" (139:1–2, 4). How could it be that on the one hand God does not know what the only two people on earth have been doing, but on the other hand God can read people's minds and know what they are going to say before they ever say it?

Some early Jewish commentators saw this problem and remedied it by adding details to the Genesis story. They said that when Adam was first created, he was as tall as the heavens. After he ate of the fruit, however, he shrank; thus, God's asking Adam "Where are you?" was not an indication of God's ignorance. It was rather a way "to bring home to Adam the vast difference between his latter and his former state—between his supernatural size then and his shrunken size now; between the lordship of God over him then and the lordship of the serpent over him now."[18] In other words, God's question was rhetorical and was meant to impress upon Adam that nothing that he did could ever escape the divine gaze. It was the equivalent of asking a child who has chocolate smears all over her face, "Have you been in the cookie jar?" The answer is clear, but the question forces the guilty party to acknowledge her wrongdoing.

As we have seen, some interpreters attempt to reconcile all of the different passages of the Bible for theological reasons; in their view, if the Bible is true, then it must cohere in every aspect. One might, however, decide to read the Bible as a seamless text less for theological reasons than for artistic ones. For example, John Huston's movie *The Bible . . . In the Beginning* (1966) portrays the creation of the world and of human beings as one uninterrupted narrative; it gives no hint that there are any problems with merging the two stories together. The film opens with a dramatic reading of Genesis 1. As vague unfocused colors appear on the screen, a deep male voice intones, "In the beginning, God created the heaven and the earth, and the earth was without form, and void, and darkness was upon the face of the deep." The voice then recounts the events of the first five days of creation as the amorphous swirls take more definite shape. Clouds appear, and then oceans, volcanoes, rivers, trees, mountains, and plains. Next the sun, moon, and stars take shape, and finally the creatures of the oceans, the birds, and the land animals appear.

The next thing that we see is a desolate landscape in which a sandstorm blows. Gradually the wind uncovers a male human form while the narrator recounts,

> And God said, "Let us make man in our own image, after our likeness." The Lord God formed man of the dust of the ground and breathed into his nostrils the breath of life, and man became a living soul. And God brought unto Adam every beast of the field and every fowl of the air to see what he would call them.

Most viewers will not be aware that the narrator has just skipped from Genesis 1:26 ("Let us make man . . .") to Genesis 2:7 (The Lord God formed man . . .). Nor will they realize that after the creation of the woman on screen, the narrator doubles back. At that point, the voice says, "So God created man in his own image. In the image of God created he him. Male and female created he them" (1:27). Here the interest of the filmmaker seems to be less theological and more artistic. The aim is to construct a narrative that includes both the cosmic vision of Genesis 1 and the human story of Genesis 2–3, without bothering with the messy conflicts and contradictions between those two accounts.

Two Stories, Different Events

There is another approach to making sense of the two Genesis stories. In the seventeenth century, Isaac La Peyrère published a treatise entitled *Men Before Adam* in which he argued that the first creation story described only the creation of the Gentiles; the second story, though, told about the creation of Adam, ancestor of the Jews.[19] This solved several apparent problems in the biblical text, including a question that had long vexed biblical interpreters: who was Cain's wife? The Bible says that Adam and Eve had two sons named Cain and Abel. Cain killed Abel and then settled in the land of Nod, east of Eden (Genesis 4:16). Cain then impregnated his wife, and she gave birth to a son named Enoch. But who was Cain's wife? Where did she come from? The answer offered by Isaac La Peyrère solved the dilemma. Cain's wife was a member of the group that had been created in Genesis 1—those who preceded Adam.

One problem with this approach is that it opens the door to the kind of racist theories that have plagued the history of the United States. If people are not all descended from the same ancestor, then it is possible to claim that one group or another is inferior. In 1890, the American geologist Alexander Winchell divided people into "lower" and "higher" races and then argued that the lower groups were descended from what he called "preadamites." The preadamites, as their name suggests, existed before Adam and were the "primitive stock" out of which Adam and his offspring eventually emerged. But while Adam's line evolved into the Anglo-Saxons, the other lines, in Winchell's opinion, made far less progress. According to Winchell, some indigenous Indonesians, Africans, and South Americans (to name just a few groups) were possible representatives of these stunted family trees.[20] Some contemporary racist interpreters agree that the Bible is the history of the "white race" only and that non-whites are descended from pre-Adamic stock. [21]

One Story is True and the Other Is Not

According to nineteenth-century feminist Elizabeth Cady Stanton, readers of the Bible are under no obligation to accept both of the creation accounts as true. Stanton, like many interpreters, noticed that there appeared to be discrepancies between Genesis 1 and 2. In the first story, for example, God gives the human beings "every tree" for food (1:29), and in the second story one tree is forbidden. In the first story, male and female are created simultaneously, but in the second story, the man is created before the woman. Based on her observations, Stanton declared that it was "manifest that both of these stories cannot be true; intelligent women, who feel bound to give the preference to either, may decide according to their own judgment of which is more worthy of an intelligent woman's acceptance." For her part, Stanton believed that the first story, in which both male and female are created in the image of God, was "in harmony with science, common sense, and the experience of mankind in natural laws." The second story, in which God tells the woman that her husband will rule over her, was not sacred scripture but was merely something made up by a man in order "to give 'heavenly authority' for requiring a woman to obey the man she married."[22] Stanton thought therefore that any attempt to reconcile the two stories was misguided.

Both are Myths
Indeed, many interpreters agree with her. In the view of these readers, what we have in the Bible is two different stories written by two different authors to express two different understandings of God. The apparently mixed messages in the Bible are simply the result of people's divergent experiences of the divine, just as siblings at a family reunion might tell different stories about what it was like to grow up together. One child might describe a parent as warm and supportive while another might perceive the same parent as intrusive and oppressive. Both are correct in that both are telling the truth as they lived it. The differing nature of the stories does not then constitute a contradiction but simply reflects the complexity of human nature and of human history.

Can conflicting stories both be "divine revelation"? That depends on how one defines revelation. If revelation consists of a body of knowledge that is fixed and immutable, then contradictory accounts cannot both be considered revelatory. One account might be correct and the other incorrect, or both might be incorrect. But both could not deliver correctly and divinely inspired knowledge.

There is another way to think about revelation, however. One can define it instead as an ongoing process in which God reveals God's self and God's will for the world in very human terms. Those terms will differ as much as humans themselves do, and they will be shaped by the often messy details of history. Revelation, in this view, is less a body of pronouncements than it is experience itself, understood as ever-fuller participation in the life of God.[23] If one accepts this model of revelation, then differing stories could both be properly described as divinely inspired because they both reflect people's experience of God.

As biblical scholar Gary Anderson notes, there is no way to prove that one should read the Bible as a whole or that one should read each text instead as a discrete unit. The decision is, as he says, "an act of faith."[24] It is also an act that will change how one thinks about the story of Adam and Eve.

Who Wrote It?

Yet another pair of questions must be considered as we approach the biblical text. First, is it possible to determine who wrote the story of Adam and Eve? And second, does the human authorship matter?

As to the first question, we have already seen that scholars generally agree that the story of Adam and Eve was written by someone designated as the J author. However, scholars frequently disagree about when this author might have lived. Some speculate that J resided in Jerusalem in the tenth century BCE.[25] Others date the Garden of Eden story to four hundred years later, in the sixth century.[26] Still others place J somewhere between those dates, in the ninth or eighth century BCE.[27]

If we do not know when J might have lived, we also do not know how the author came to write the story of Adam and Eve. Some scholars think that the Jahwist was simply compiling myths and folktales that had been circulating for centuries. Others believe that J was consciously incorporating stories from both Israelite and Babylonian sources in order to create a new theological vision.[28]

And who was this Jahwist? Again, scholars disagree. Several years ago, literary critic Harold Bloom wrote a book in which he argued that J was a woman. Recognizing that he could not prove his theory, he nonetheless contended that J's worldview was quite different from that of other Hebrew authors, so much so that the author of the texts also must have been unusual. J's writing, according to Bloom, was distinct in its use of irony and humor and also in its focus on the activities of women. Wrote Bloom, "I think it accurate to observe that J had no heroes, only heroines."[29] The book caused quite a stir, and it soon appeared on the *New York Times* list of best-sellers. However, for our purposes, the important question is not so much "Was the J author a woman?" as "What difference would it make?" Does it matter who J was or when he or she lived?

To some interpreters, it would not matter in the least who actually wrote down the story of Adam and Eve. What matters is only that God inspired the writer and that J wrote down exactly what God said. At the Creation Museum in Kentucky, a display proclaims that "God's Word is True." The sign asserts that all of the biblical authors give the same message, that the original words of the Bible have been preserved throughout history, that the Bible's historical details have been confirmed as accurate, and that not one biblical prophecy has failed. The sign concludes, "Above All, the God of Truth, the Creator of heaven and earth, inspired the men who penned the words."[30] As long as whoever wrote Genesis 2–3 recorded exactly what God inspired, it would not matter to the Creation Museum who exactly J was or when J lived.

Others, though, are not so sure. If J was a man who lived in a patriarchal culture, then perhaps Elizabeth Cady Stanton was right that the Genesis story's agenda was to keep women in their place. (A slogan that can be found on innumerable bumper stickers and T-shirts makes this point: "Eve was Framed!") Alternatively, if J was a woman living among the elite of a tenth-century king's court, as Harold Bloom suggests, then perhaps the story of Adam and Eve reflects the concerns of the wealthy and powerful and should be read as representing a particular economic agenda. Or perhaps the story emerged among the poor but then was written down by an educated scribe. The point is that we simply do not know when or where Genesis 2–3 was written. For some, that fact is irrelevant. For others, it means that we are missing a crucial piece of information that could help us understand what the author's intention might have been.

Word for Word

This brings us to yet another question: how much does the exact wording of the Genesis text matter? Should we pay close attention to precisely which words the Bible uses and try to mine them for clues about what the author had in mind? Or would such close reading constitute nitpicking—putting too much emphasis on details rather than looking at the story as a whole? As we will see repeatedly throughout this book, scholars differ quite a bit when they try to discern the meanings of particular Hebrew terms.

One point of contention, for example, is how to interpret the Hebrew word *tsela*. According to Genesis 2:21, when God realized that it was not good for the first human to be alone, God took a *tsela* from the *adam* (a word usually translated as "man") and fashioned it into a woman. But what does tsela mean? The word is frequently rendered as "rib." However, tsela can also mean "side." Some ancient rabbis thought that the adam was both male and female and that God made an incision in the creature's side that split the two halves apart, rather like separating conjoined twins.

More recently, biblical scholar Ziony Zevit has argued that tsela should be translated as "baculum" or what in animals is the penis bone.[31] Most male primates, and many other male mammals as well, have a baculum; human males, though, do not. It would make sense that ancient observers might have wondered why men lacked what so many of their animal cousins had, and that they would tell a story that took the difference into account. One can almost hear a child in the ancient world asking, "Why don't men have a penis-bone like all the other animals?" and an adult answering, "Well, a long time ago, God used the first man's baculum to create the first woman." It would also make sense that the woman was fashioned from a part of the body associated with fertility and generation, rather than from a rib. Of course, if the tsela is really a baculum, that would give a whole new meaning to country-western singer Kenny Chesney's lament that he wants his "rib" back![32]

What difference does it make how we translate the word? Perhaps none. On the other hand, readers have at times made much of the idea that Eve was taken from Adam's rib. Some have said that God created Eve from a rib in order to show that women are neither above men nor below them, but side-by-side with them. Others have observed that ribs are curved rather than straight, and that therefore women are crooked and not to be trusted. Individual words can make quite a difference in the meaning of a text.

There are many such words in the story of Adam and Eve that are similarly difficult to translate. For example, after the couple has eaten the forbidden fruit, God says to the woman, "I will greatly increase your pangs in childbearing; in pain you shall bring forth children, yet your desire shall be for your husband, and he shall rule over you" (3:16). However, scholars disagree about what several of those words mean. In some translations, "pangs in childbearing" is rendered instead as "your sorrow and your conception" (American King James Version) or "your pains and your conceivings."[33] The meaning then would be not simply that God would magnify Eve's pain in childbearing but that Eve would both bring forth children in pain and have an increased number of pregnancies. The 19th-century American reformer John Humphrey Noyes interpreted this to mean that in the Garden of Eden, Adam and Eve would have had sex, but Eve would have gotten pregnant only rarely. Noyes therefore advocated that in order to overcome God's curse, men and women should enjoy sex but should stop before ejaculation took place. That way they could prevent the dangers that pregnancy poses for women. As Noyes put it, this method of birth control "secures woman from the curses of involuntary and undesirable procreation."[34]

There is disagreement as well about what it means to say that the woman's desire will be for her husband. It might mean that she will desire him sexually despite the fact that sexual relations will lead to painful pregnancies. Or perhaps it means that she will desire to control her husband despite the fact that he will rule over her. Or that she will desire whatever it is that her husband desires because he rules over her. Interpreters, of course, disagree with each other.

Decisions about translation and interpretation can affect everything from how one imagines men and women ought to relate to each other, to how one thinks we ought to interact with the natural world, to what one believes to be God's will for the world. We can choose to ignore the complexities, or we can choose an authority to guide us to the proper translation, or we can choose not to settle on just one interpretation but to experiment with different readings. The decision, as always, is up to us.

Past, Present, Future?

Finally, is the Genesis story about our past, our present, or our future, or about all three? For the Creation Museum, the story is quite clearly about our past; Genesis describes literally and accurately an event that happened long ago. Of course, that event continues to affect us, as we have now inherited the corruption that Adam and Eve brought on themselves. One display in the museum shows several large photographs of the consequences of sin. Some of the photos depict violence and death: a wolf standing over its prey, a mushroom cloud billowing up from an atomic explosion, a stack of skulls and bones (perhaps from the genocide in Rwanda), and a tornado sweeping across a field. Another shows a woman in the throes of labor. Still another depicts the illness of a drug addict who is shooting narcotics into his arm. The effects of sin are made perfectly clear. And yet, the museum believes, the causal event itself occurred in the past, and the Genesis story is a story about that past.

For other interpreters, Adam and Eve are not ancestors who lived long ago but rather are literary or mythic figures who symbolize and illuminate our lives here and now. Writes Paul Tillich, "Theology must clearly and unambiguously represent 'the Fall' as a symbol for the human situation universally, not as the story of an event that happened 'once upon a time.'"[35] In Tillich's view, the story offers us deep insight into ourselves and into the nature of humanity.

If Neil LaBute's movie *The Shape of Things* is an accurate portrayal of that nature, then humans are in sad and sorry shape. *The Shape of Things* is a dark comedy starring Rachel Weisz as Evelyn Thompson and Paul Rudd as Adam Sorenson. Adam is a student at Mercy College, where Evelyn is studying art and preparing for her Master's-level thesis project. Adam and Evelyn first meet at the art museum where Adam, a nerdy young man who appears rather unkempt, works part-time as a museum guard. As the movie opens, Evelyn is wearing a T-shirt with a picture of an apple on it, and she is taking a photograph (something forbidden by museum rules) of a nude statue that has been adorned with a fig leaf. In order to get closer to the statue, she steps over the ropes that surround it, and this prompts Adam to confront her and to tell her that she has broken the rules. Eve replies, "That's why I tried it. To see what would happen."

Evelyn then tells Adam that she is preparing to break another of the museum's rules by spray-painting a penis onto the statue. She explains that the fig-leaf was installed by the museum because the shape of the statue's "thing" was too lifelike, and she says that she does not like art that is not true. The two students begin to flirt, and Evelyn tells Adam that he is cute but that he should change his hair. As soon as Adam goes off-shift, Evelyn defaces the statue.

As the movie progresses, Adam becomes more and more intrigued with and besotted by Evelyn. Soon, at Evelyn's suggestion, he begins jogging in order to lose weight, and he has his hair restyled. He abandons his eyeglasses and takes to wearing contact lenses instead, and he buys a new and more stylish wardrobe. Finally, Adam even agrees to get a nose job because Evelyn tells him that the procedure will improve his appearance.

At this point, it is clear that Adam is far too eager to please Evelyn and that he has lost his sense of himself as existing apart from her. When his friend Phillip notices the bandage on Adam's nose and asks him what caused his injury, Adam tells him, "I fell." The statement rings true in two ways. First, he had the plastic surgery against his better judgment, and so he has allowed Evelyn to tempt him into betraying himself. Second, his action has caused him to be ashamed and thus to lie about what he has done. His "fall" thus reflects the biblical Adam's tasting of the forbidden fruit and his attempt to hide that fact from God. Soon afterwards, Evelyn asks Adam to stop spending time with his friends Phillip and Jenny, and Adam agrees. His fall thus causes him to turn his back on the people who, prior to his encounter with Evelyn, were the closest to him.

What we as viewers do not know, and what Adam comes to discover only toward the end of the film, is that Evelyn's professed love for Adam has been a sham. Her entire campaign to literally re-form Adam has been, in fact, her final art project. We discover this at the same time as does Adam: when Evelyn presents her thesis to an audience consisting of friends, fellow students, and the art school's professors. There she shows slides of Adam before his transformation and after her work had been finished. The project was, she explains, a systematic makeover or sculpting of "the human flesh" and "the human will." Her subject, Adam, was "a living, breathing example of our obsession with the surface of things. The shape of them," she explains.

As commentator Duane Olson points out, *The Shape of Things* uses the story of Adam and Eve in order to present the Fall of humanity "into a world of unreserved individual and social depravity."[36] Neither Evelyn nor Adam comes across as particularly attractive. Evelyn is shown to be a scheming manipulative person who remains unrepentant even when she knows the pain that she has caused to Adam. "I have no regrets, no feelings of remorse for my actions," she says. "I am an artist—only that." Adam, who is in many ways the victim of Evelyn's machinations, gradually loses our sympathy, as he seems more and more desperate to please Evelyn, even to the extent of dropping his best friends.

As Olson also points out, however, there is also a glimmer of hope for redemption in the film. During one scene, Adam allows Evelyn to tape their lovemaking. As the tape continues rolling, Adam and Evelyn exchange whispers, and whatever Evelyn says to Adam causes him to laugh and to embrace her. This video then appears in Evelyn's thesis presentation, much to Adam's humiliation. When he confronts her after the show and demands to know if anything she ever said was true, she at first says no. As Adam turns to leave, however, Evelyn tells him, "That one time. In my bed one night when you leaned over and whispered in my ear, remember? And I whispered back to you, I said that I . . . I meant that. I did." Perhaps, then, despite the fallenness of Adam and Evelyn, and despite the fallenness of the humanity whom they represent, we may still hope for some loving connection in our lives.

In *The Shape of Things*, the story of Adam and Eve is the story of humanity here and now. For biblical literalists like Ken Ham, the story is a historical account of the past. As we will see in subsequent chapters, the story is also frequently understood as a portrayal of how life ought to be and how it will be in the future.

This book does not seek to persuade readers to one position or the other on any of the issues discussed above. Instead, it lays out the options and, more importantly, shows exactly what is at stake in each. Ultimately, the author herself sides with those who see the story as a classic myth rather than as literal history. However, even if readers don't agree with this assessment, it is still possible for them to engage *Approaching Eden* as a commentary on contemporary uses of the story.

CHAPTER THREE

A Helper Fit for Him

The influence of the Adam and Eve story affects how we see ourselves and the others around us. Nowhere is this more true than in our culture's ideas about gender. What does it mean to be a real woman or a real man? How should men and women interact? How should they apportion the various tasks necessary to keep a society running, such as raising children, growing and preparing food, protecting people from harm, and cultivating art? Who should wield political power? Who should control a household's economy? How should men and women dress, speak, and gesture?

Often, the answers to these questions depend on unspoken (and perhaps unconscious) assumptions, many of which trace their roots to interpretations of Genesis 2–3. Consider, for example, Martin Buxbaum's poem "The Tree" [1] and its view of why men and women were created:

> The Tree
> If man were made perfect. . .
> complete as could be . . . then God
> would have never . . . created the "she."
>
> For man is the trunk and the branch
> and the root . . . while woman's
> the blossom, the leaf and the fruit.

The first thing to notice about the poem is that in this view, man (that is, the first man, the primal "he") is created before the woman. God creates the man and yet finds something lacking in him, and so God supplements the he with a "she." The she is an afterthought, however; if the first try had gone better, she would never have been created.

The second thing to notice is the role of the she in procreation. Women are blossoms and fruit, which are both parts of a plant associated with reproduction. Blossoms attract the insects that pollinate trees, and fruits bear the seeds that grow into future trees. Without these "female" aspects, the tree could not reproduce itself.

The third point of interest is the respective roles that men and women play in the poem's view. Man is the anchor and sustainer of the tree: its roots. He is also the bulk and strength of the tree, both its trunk and its branches. Woman, on the other hand, grows out of the man. She is the more delicate portions of the tree, the parts that bloom and then wither with the passing of the seasons. Blossoms, leaves, and fruit cannot endure the rigors of winter; they are beautiful, to be sure, but they depend on the kindness of the climate and the support of the sturdier boughs for their survival, and they die at the end of the growing season.

Why begin this chapter with this small poem? The answer is that the verse encapsulates so many of the assumptions that contemporary culture makes about what it means to be a man or a woman and what the proper relations between the sexes ought to be. Many of these assumptions grow straight from the story of Adam and Eve. And yet, as we have already seen, that story is much more complex than it first appears. It is not at all clear from Genesis 2–4 that man is created before woman. Nor is it clear that the woman is created solely or even primarily for reproductive purposes. And it is certainly not clear that the woman in the story is more delicate or even more decorous than the man.

Sojourner Truth, the great African-American abolitionist and worker for women's rights, made this same point when she addressed the Women's Convention in Akron, Ohio, in 1851. Responding to a male speaker who opined that women were too fragile to be entrusted with the responsibility of voting, Truth, who had been born into slavery, declared,

> That man over there says that women need to be helped into carriages, and lifted over ditches, and to have the best place everywhere. Nobody ever helps me into carriages, or over mud-puddles, or gives me any best place! And ain't I a woman? Look at me! Look at my arm! . . . I could work as

much and eat as much as a man—when I could get it—and bear the lash as well! And ain't I a woman?

Truth then concluded her speech by referring to the story of Adam and Eve:

> If the first woman God ever made was strong enough to turn the world upside down all alone, these women together ought to be able to turn it back, and get it right side up again! And now they is asking to do it, the men better let them. Obliged to you for hearing me, and now old Sojourner ain't got nothing more to say.[2]

In Truth's portrayal, Eve was strong enough to "turn the world upside down all alone." In other words, she was hardly a delicate blossom.

The question "Ain't I a woman" in Truth's speech is therefore more than just a rhetorical device. It cuts to the heart of what one's physical characteristics have to do with the role that one plays or is expected to play. In this chapter we will try to unravel these difficult and thorny issues, showing both how they are influenced by the story of Adam and Eve and how they manifest themselves in popular culture.

First, however, a few points of clarification are required. The terms "sex" and "gender" are the subject of considerable controversy.[3] In this book the word "sex" will be used to talk about biological categories. People with XX chromosomes will be referred to as females or women, and people with XY chromosomes will be called males or men.

As medical research shows, however, these distinctions are hardly adequate. Some people, for example, are born with a condition called adrenal hyperplasia, in which, though they have XX chromosomes and thus are biologically female, they may have ambiguous external genitalia and may eventually develop characteristics usually associated with men, such as a deep voice or facial hair. Likewise, some babies are born with a condition known as Klinefelter Syndrome, in which most of their cells contain an additional X chromosome that results in an XXY pattern. Though they have most of the characteristics associated with males, they may develop less facial and body hair and may be less muscular than average. (The 2007 Argentinean movie XXY, directed by Lucía Puenzo, explores this phenomenon.) Other conditions that complicate the biological categories of "male" and "female" include one in which a person is born with both XX and XY chromosomes, and a condition called Turner

Syndrome, in which a girl is born with only one X chromosome instead of the more usual XX pattern.[4]

If biological categories are complex, the meanings associated with them, or "genders," are even more difficult to map.[5] In this book, the terms "feminine" and "masculine" will refer to culturally influenced notions of what it means to be a woman or a man. Nearly all of us are taught at some point that dolls are feminine and that trucks are masculine, that dresses are feminine and that power tools are masculine, that flowers are feminine and that hunting is masculine. We learn to choose clothing, postures, tones of voice, and countless other behaviors in order to conform (whether more or less) to the expectations that society has for our sex or, at times, in contrast to them, or even to subvert them.

Sometimes, it should be noted, the gender expectations professed by a culture are glaringly at odds with what that culture actually practices. When Sojourner Truth asked "Ain't I a woman?" she was not doubting her own sex; she was rather pointing out the fundamental hypocrisy of a society that expected women (most particularly African-American women) to labor long hours under strenuous conditions but then dismissed them as too fragile to vote.

Many people find that their sex and their gender match up fairly well. Others, though, experience such a marked discrepancy between biological fact and sociological meaning that they opt to change one or the other. They may choose a medical approach and use hormones or surgery to bring biology more into line with gender identity. Or, they may simply present themselves consistently as members of the other gender by changing their names, for example, or their wardrobes or hairstyles. The recent documentary *Sworn Virgins* (2007) explores the lives of twelve women in Albania, most of whom are now quite elderly, who chose to live as men and who thus were accepted as men by their society. The women wear baggy clothes made for men, and they take jobs usually associated with men, such as truck driver or shepherd. For some, the decision to change genders was practical; in the mountainous region of northern Albania where they lived, women could not buy land, so adopting a masculine persona was a reasonable solution to an economic problem. For others, though, the decision seems to have come more from inside: "I had always wanted to be a boy," one says. "I didn't want to be a girl, absolutely not!" Even here, though, the situation is complex; the same person, when asked if she would have felt restricted in a marriage, replies, "Absolutely! More like squashed than restricted. . . . Even when there's love and harmony, only men have the right to decide. I want total equity or nothing."[6] It is possible that if the woman in the film had been presented with opportunities equal to those given to men, she would not have felt compelled to live as a man. Clearly, the norms and expectations of a culture affect what roles we choose for ourselves.

Decisions about how we define ourselves and how we present ourselves in society are deeply personal, but they sometimes meet with religiously based disapproval. When *Newsweek* magazine featured a story about transgendered people on its cover, it received the following letter from a reader in Brentwood, Tennessee: "What a grievous commentary on the fall of American morals. Have we strayed so far from the Bible that we have forgotten God created Adam and Eve? . . . When we walk away from the order God provided, we reap confusion, and boy, are we confused. Please don't ask me to rethink gender. God had it right the first time."[7]

What exactly did God get right? What does Genesis 2–4 tell us about the nature of sex and gender? What does the Bible say is the difference between the first man and the first woman, and how were those two people meant to relate to one another? Finding answers to these questions is the subject of this chapter.

Who Came First?

According to the little poem with which we began this chapter, the first man was created before the first woman. Virtually every presentation of the Adam and Eve story seems to accept this premise. A *Speed Bump* cartoon, for example, portrays Eve criticizing a manuscript written by Adam, and Adam responding, "Well, of COURSE everything I write is in first person." A *Frank and Ernest* cartoon shows two angels looking down at Earth and saying gleefully to God, "This should be good—Adam just pulled his seniority on her" (see fig. 3.1). Another has Eve introducing herself to Adam (see fig. 3.2), saying, "Hi, I'm version 2.0!"[8]

To say that Adam was not created before Eve is to contradict the Bible story. Right?

Well, maybe. And maybe not. In her essay entitled "Eve and Adam: Genesis 2–3 Reread," biblical scholar Phyllis Trible argues that in the story of Adam and Eve, man is not in fact created before woman. Instead, in her reading, one can say that "sexuality is simultaneous for woman and

Figure 3.1

Frank and Ernest

"*This should be good—Adam just pulled his seniority on her.*" *Frank and Ernest cartoon. 12/13/2004.*
© 2004 Thaves. Reprinted with Permission. Newspaper dist. by NEA, Inc.

Figure 3.2

Frank and Ernest

Hi, I'm version 2.0!" *Frank and Ernest cartoon. 10/29/2007.*
© 2007 Thaves. Reprinted with Permission. Newspaper dist. by NEA, Inc.

man."[9] To make her case, Trible focuses on the meaning of the word that is usually translated as "the man." The Hebrew word is *ha-adam*, which is a pun on the word for dust or earth, *ha-adamah*; hence *ha-adam* is taken from *ha-adamah*. Trible interprets *ha-adam* not as "the man" but rather as "the earth creature." She is not alone in translating the passage so as to highlight the pun. Other scholars have described the first creature as a "human, humus from the soil," or a "groundling, soil of the ground."[10] According to Trible, the earth creature in the story is androgynous, that is, both female and male (though in a revised and expanded version of the essay, she uses the term "sexually undifferentiated" rather than "androgynous").[11] Only in Genesis 2:23, after a second person has been created, do the Hebrew words for "man" and "woman" first occur in the text. At that point the *adam* says, "This at last is bone of my bones and flesh of my flesh; this one shall be called Woman [*ishah*], for out of Man [*ish*] this one was taken." Thus Trible concludes, "Man as male does not precede woman as female but happens concurrently with her."[12]

To support her interpretation, Trible points to ancient Jewish commentary that likewise saw the first creature as both male and female. Samuel ben Nachman (third century CE), for example, asserted, "When the Lord created Adam He created him double-faced, then He split him and made him of two backs, one back on this side and one back on the other side."[13] To the objection that in Genesis 2:21 God created the woman from one of Adam's ribs, the rabbi answers that the word for "rib" also means "side." Therefore, the woman was created not by the extraction of a rib but by the cutting of one of *ha-adam*'s sides.

If indeed sexual biology is simultaneous for the first man and woman, then man can have no primacy over woman simply based on his first place in the birth order. Of course, such primacy would be suspect anyway, since it is not always clear in biblical writing that being first is better. If being first means being best, then animals must be superior to humans since they are created before people in Genesis 1. Rabbinic commentary makes this point, warning humanity, "Let him beware of being proud, lest he invite the retort that the gnat is older than he."[14] A *Rhymes with Orange* cartoon agrees. In the cartoon, a cat, who is identified as a "Guest Theology Professor," explains who should be subservient to whom: "The conservative paradigm goes that because woman was created after man, it is her role to accommodate him," says the cat. "The problem with this argument is not its logic, it is in its scope. Humans, if you recall, were created [in Genesis 1] a *full day* after cats. Accommodating *us* should be their primary role."[15]

Adam's Helper

Even if birth order cannot justify the superiority of men over women, that is, if women and men were created simultaneously, still it would seem that since the woman is created as a *helper* for the man (see Genesis 2:18—"Then the Lord God said, 'It is not good that the man should be alone; I will make him a helper as his partner'"), she is inferior to him. Again, however, Trible uses careful attention to the Hebrew text to argue otherwise. She notes that in the Bible, the word for helper (*ezer*) is sometimes used to describe God; one of the psalms, for example, says,

"Our help [*ezerenu*] is in the name of the Lord, who made heaven and earth" (124:8). Thus being a helper does not necessarily imply inferiority, since God is not considered to be inferior to humans. Trible concludes that "God is the helper superior to man; the animals are helpers inferior to man; woman is the helper equal to man."[16]

There are, in fact, any number of interpretations of the term "helper" in Genesis 2:18, only some of which imply inferiority. Scholars translate the passage's description of Eve's role in ways that range from "a partner suited to him" to "a power equal to him" to "a power against him." Adding to the difficulty of translation is the fact that the word *kenegdo* (which the New Revised Standard Version translates as "fit for him") is found nowhere else in the Hebrew Bible. It is related to words meaning "in front of," "opposite to," and "parallel to," which, depending on context, might take on a positive or negative meaning.[17] That duality was captured by an ancient Jewish commentator who, reflecting on 2:18, opined that if a man is fortunate in his mate, then "she is a help; if not, she is against him."[18] The medieval Jewish scholar Rashi put responsibility for the woman's role on the man, commenting, "If he is worthy she shall be a help to him; if he is unworthy she shall be opposed to him, to fight him."[19]

Perhaps we should not wonder that a description of how women and men relate to one another should be so fraught with ambiguity. The "battle of the sexes," it seems, is as old as humanity itself and shows no signs of being resolved any time soon. One of the smartest and most amusing rehearsals of this battle is the 1949 comedy *Adam's Rib*, which starred Katharine Hepburn and Spencer Tracy and was written by husband-and-wife team Garson Kanin and Ruth Gordon. In the film, Hepburn and Tracy play Amanda and Adam Bonner, lawyers who wholeheartedly enjoy being married to each other. The two are attractive, sophisticated, and witty, and their affection for one another is obvious. Adam and Amanda read the newspaper together over breakfast, drive to work together, and cook dinner together on the maid's day off. They even give each other massages after a hard day's work.

All goes well for the couple until the two end up on different sides of the same trial. The case involves a woman who shot her husband when she found him in the arms of his mistress. Amanda has herself appointed as counsel for the defense and argues that her client is being unfairly punished. After all, contends Amanda, if the roles were reversed and a man had shot his adulterous wife, society would merely shrug its collective shoulders and not bother prosecuting, thinking that the unfaithful woman deserved what she got. Why then is there a double standard? Why is it more acceptable for a husband to avenge his spouse's infidelity than for a wife to do so? Why are men held to lower standards when it comes to the use of violence, and women held to higher standards when it comes to sexual purity? Declares Amanda, "For years, women have been ridiculed, pampered, chucked under the chin. I ask you, on behalf of us all, be fair to the fair sex."

Adam, on the other hand, does not buy his wife's argument that justice discriminates against women: "The law is the law, whether it's good or bad," he counters. Predictably, as the trial progresses, it begins to disrupt the Bonners' happy household. What had seemed a marriage of equals is now tested by hidden assumptions about the roles of husband and wife. When an irritated Adam slaps Amanda's backside while he is giving her an evening rubdown, she takes offense:

> Amanda: I'm not so sure I care to expose myself to typical, instinctive masculine brutality.
> Adam: Oh come now.
> Amanda: And it felt not only as though you meant it, but as though you felt you have a right to. I can tell.
> Adam: What have you got back there, radar equipment?

Amanda then begins to cry, and Adam accuses her of using typically feminine wiles to get what she wants. At this point she kicks him in the knee and adds this parting shot: "Let's all be *manly!*"

The trial continues, and at one point Amanda calls to the stand several female witnesses, who include a scientist, a factory supervisor, and a circus performer, in order to show that women can be just as intelligent, hardworking, and strong as men. That evening, irritated by his wife's courtroom strategies, Adam complains, "Just what blow you've struck for women's rights or what have you, I'm sure I don't know. But you certainly have fouled us up beyond all recognition." He continues, "I'm old-fashioned. I like *two* sexes! Yeah, and another thing, all of a sudden I don't like being married to what is known as a new woman. I want a wife, not a competitor. Competitor! Competitor! If you want to be a big he-woman, go and be it—but not with me!"

Adam's Rib is a comedy, and so a happy outcome is guaranteed from the start. Toward the end of the film, just when divorce seems imminent,

Adam uses tears to win Amanda's sympathy and to convince her to give the marriage another chance. When he later reveals that his crying was a ruse ("Oh yes. There ain't any of us don't have our little tricks, you know!"), Amanda takes this as evidence that she was right all along: "What I said was true. There's no difference between the sexes. Men. Women. The same." Adam demurs, and so Amanda concedes, "Well, maybe there is a difference, but it's a little difference." At this point Adam puts on a roguish smile and, drawing the bed-curtains closed around himself and his wife, says, "Well, you know as the French say . . . *Vive la difference!* . . . Hurray for that little difference!"

Thus the movie ends without really solving the riddle of how men and women ought to negotiate the tricky and treacherous path between them. It asserts an equality without specifying how that can be achieved and without pretending that it can be easily maintained. Indeed, in the last scene, when Adam announces with pride that he has been asked to run for a county-court judgeship on the Republican ticket, Amanda congratulates him but then asks slyly, "Adam—Have they picked the, uh, Democratic candidate yet? I was just wondering." Amanda, it seems, is an *ezer kenegdo* in all of that term's senses; she is a helpmeet for Adam, a partner suited to him, a power equal to him and, at times, a power against him.

It is significant that *Adam's Rib* never raises the question of why Adam and Amanda do not have children. In 1949, as the postwar baby boom was in full swing, their childless status would have been unusual. And yet the movie does not allude to the subject of offspring. In all of Adam and Amanda's arguments about the proper roles for men and women, there is no discussion of pregnancy, motherhood, or fatherhood. What commands the couple's attention is not their children but their jobs and their dogs.

This omission seems odd given that the movie is named after the presumptive father of all humankind. However, if *Adam's Rib* is reluctant to define gender roles based on reproductive ones, not everyone shares the same reticence. Numerous commentators have read the story of the first couple in Genesis as primarily a tale about sex and procreation. For example, Augustine concluded that Eve must have been produced by God solely to bear children, because for any other purpose a male companion would have been more suitable: "How much more agreeably could two male friends, rather than a man and woman, enjoy companionship and conversation in a life shared together."[20] The thirteenth-century Christian philosopher Thomas Aquinas agreed: "It was necessary for woman to be made, as the Scripture says, as a *helper* to man; not, indeed, as a helpmate in other works, as some say, since man can be more efficiently helped by another man in other works; but as a helper in the work of generation."[21]

But perhaps the focus of *Adam's Rib* on the man and woman themselves, rather than on their progeny, is actually closer to the intent of the Genesis story. Contemporary writer David M. Carr argues that Eve was in fact created not in order to propagate but so that she and Adam might enjoy erotic intimacy. Carr draws a sharp distinction between the concerns of Genesis 1 and the vision of Genesis 2–3. While the former emphasizes reproduction, with God telling the first people to "be fruitful and multiply" (1:28), the second creation story, according to Carr, "emphasizes the intimate aspects of sexual eros, its role in overcoming the primal isolation of the first human." The focus is not on fertility but rather "on intimacy, an intimacy grounded in the bodily joining of two embodied creatures whom God has so carefully made for shared work as equals."[22]

And He Shall Rule Over You

Equals? But what about that passage at the end of the story, the one where God says to Eve, "I will greatly increase your pangs in childbearing; in pain you shall bring forth children, yet your desire shall be for your husband, and he shall rule over you" (3:16)? If the man is to rule over the woman, then it is difficult to see in what sense the two are equals. And indeed, numerous interpreters of Genesis hold that the man and woman are *not* equal, at least not in power. The author of the First Letter to Timothy in the Christian New Testament advises, "Let a woman learn in silence with full submission. I permit no woman to teach or to have authority over a man; she is to keep silent. For Adam was formed first, then Eve; and Adam was not deceived, but the woman was deceived and became a transgressor" (2:11–12). Contemporary Christian writer Susan T. Foh, lamenting the fact that women have refused to submit to their husbands, observes, "Sin has ruined the marital dance, the easy, loving lead of the husband and the natural following of the wife."[23]

Biblical scholar Phyllis Trible, on the other hand, reads the passage about Eve's submission to Adam as a description of how the world *is* rather than as a prescription of how it *ought* to be: "The . . . narrative tells us who we are (creatures of equality and mutuality); it tells us who we have become (creatures of oppression); and so it opens possibilities for change, for a return to our true liberation under God."[24] In other words, men ruling over women is not a good thing; it is sinful. The ideal would be to return to the state of mutuality and equality found in Eden.

Another way to think about the issue is to turn to the verses that immediately follow 3:16. There God says to the man, "[C]ursed is the ground because of you; in toil you shall eat of it all the days of your life; thorns and thistles it shall bring forth for you . . . By the sweat of your face you shall eat bread until you return to the ground" (3:17–19). One might use this passage to argue against the use of tractors or weed killers or irrigation pumps in farming since those inventions ease the toil of workers and thus defy God's will. And yet, most people find it perfectly sensible and indeed desirable to use technology to reduce the labor and sweat of farmers. Why, then, should we accept that women should be ruled by men? Should not we try to overcome that burden just as we work to overcome the burdens involved in growing food?

The Apple Tree (1966)

Obviously, scholarly interpretations of this passage differ dramatically, and movies, music, and television shows have been similarly diverse in their interpretations of the proper relations between the sexes. Consider, for example, the 1966 Broadway musical *The Apple Tree*, a loose adaptation of Mark Twain's *The Diaries of Adam and Eve*.[25] The play, which has recently enjoyed a revival on Broadway, portrays Eve as unsure of herself and as eager to win approval from Adam. Eve considers changing her hair, cooking enticing food, or changing her style of clothing so as to please her man. When the serpent in the garden attempts to convince Eve to eat from the forbidden tree, he knows just what to promise her in order to get her to disobey God: knowledge with which she can impress Adam. The serpent assures Eve that her mind will expand, her perceptions will grow more acute, and she will have newfound skills in plumbing, philosophy, glazing pottery, and even first aid. The serpent here is playing on Eve's fear that Adam will one day grow tired of her and reject her or, even worse, replace her with someone else.

The inspiration for this scene most likely comes from the most famous retelling of the story of Adam and Eve, John Milton's *Paradise Lost*. Milton's epic poem, published in 1667, is a complex and psychologically astute portrayal of Adam and Eve that explores the characters' motives as well as the cosmic significance of their actions. In Milton's version of the story, after Eve has eaten from the forbidden tree, she considers whether or not she should share the fruit with Adam. On the one hand, she is reluctant to do so. After all, the fruit has given her new-found knowledge and thus gives her an edge when dealing with Adam: "A thing not undesireable/ . . . for inferior who is free?" she muses. On the other hand, however, now that she has eaten from the fruit, she will die: "[T]hen I shall be no more,/ and *Adam* wedded to another *Eve*,/ Shall live with her enjoying, I extinct." This fear of Adam replacing her with another woman convinces Eve to act: "Confirm'd then I resolve,/ *Adam* shall share with me in bliss or woe."[26] For Milton, as for *The Apple Tree*, the woman's fear of being rejected or superseded is paramount in her decision to eat from the tree as well as in the choice to give the fruit to Adam.

In *The Apple Tree*, Eve is so afraid of Adam's disapproval that she does not even care if he loves her in return. She admits that she would devote herself to Adam even if he were to abuse her. All that matters is that she has her man—or, perhaps, any man. This fact is curious, given that Eve actually prefers the company of her own reflection. Not realizing that she is seeing herself when she looks into a pond, she declares that the image she gazes at there is her best friend. When Adam is surly or taciturn, she can turn to the woman in the pond to find comfort. This scene in *The Apple Tree*, though it draws on Twain's *Diaries*, also seems to have its deepest roots in Milton, wherein Eve is entranced by her own reflection and declares that Adam is "Less winning soft, less amiablie milde,/ Then [sic] that smooth watry image."[27]

The reason that Eve describes her life in *The Apple* Tree as "awful" at times is that Adam apparently has little regard for her. Though he acknowledges that she is beautiful and declares that she is interesting, he also describes her as too intrusive, a nuisance, and a numbskull, and he wishes that she would stop talking now and then. Small wonder that Eve prefers her own company. And yet, at the same time, she is desperate to please Adam. Her desire is for her husband, and he rules over her.

This is perhaps the sort of portrayal that Alix Olson had in mind when she composed the 2001 song "Eve's mouth." In the song, Olson, who describes herself as a "folk poet and progressive queer artist-activist," considers several different female icons such as Queen Victoria, Little Red Riding Hood, and Helen of Troy. She dedicates the opening stanza, however, to the first woman who, she says, would scoff at scholars' depiction of her as being simply half of someone else.[28] Olson refuses to accept the idea that Eve is an afterthought in the process of creation. Eve is, instead, an independent person who exists apart from her connection to the man Adam.

The opening credits of the hit TV series *Desperate Housewives*, which premiered in 2004, would seem to agree. The introduction to the show takes advantage of the notion that women should be subservient to men by turning it on its head. As energetic music plays in the background, viewers see an animated version of Lucas Cranach's painting titled "Adam and Eve" (1526). The two figures in the painting, modestly adorned with fig leaves, stand next to a fruit tree. A snake then appears, and Eve takes an apple from the reptile's mouth. As she does, another apple the size of a Volkswagen falls from the branches and crushes the hapless Adam. Clearly, though the women in the show are "desperate" in that they lead complex and often unfulfilling lives, they are nobody's "little helper."

You're Evil Like Eve

The *Desperate Housewives* sequence, by portraying Eve as responsible for the harm that befalls Adam, raises the ancient charge that Eve, and by extension, every woman, is responsible for the downfall of humanity. The third-century Christian theologian Tertullian, in his essay "On the Apparel of Women," excoriated his female audience, thundering, "And do you not know that you are each an Eve? The sentence of God on this sex of yours lives in this age: the guilt must of necessity live too. *You* are the devil's gateway."

Most of the portrayals of Eve as evil depend on the fact that in the biblical story, Eve both eats from the forbidden tree first and gives the fruit to her husband. The spare description of these acts in Genesis has been elaborated upon and embellished by commentators, artists, and poets in ways that perhaps tell us more about the interpreters than it does about the story itself. Even the apparently simple act of translation can reveal unconscious assumptions about what the text means. Compare, for example, these two versions of Genesis 3:6:

And the woman saw that the tree was good to eat, and fair to the eyes, and delightful to behold: and she took of the fruit thereof, and did eat, and gave to her husband who did eat (Douay-Rheims Bible).

So when the woman saw that the tree was good for food, and that it was a delight to the eyes, and that the tree was to be desired to make one wise, she took of its fruit and ate; and she also gave some to her husband, *who was with her*, and he ate (New Revised Standard Version, italics added).

The difference in these translations hinges on how one interprets the small Hebrew word *imah*. If one understands the word to mean "also," then it can be left out of the sentence without changing the meaning: Eve "gave to her husband [also], who did eat." One can imagine that Eve has been talking with the serpent, that Adam knows nothing of the conversation, and that, when offered the fruit by Eve, Adam does not realize where it came from. He can plausibly be said to have broken God's commandment by accident rather than by intent.

Countless artists have interpreted the scene in precisely this way. Hans Baldung Grien's 16th-century painting "Eve, the Serpent and Death" portrays Eve grasping the tail of the snake, and Death grasping Eve's wrist—and Adam nowhere in the picture. Adam also does not appear in Paul Gauguin's "Breton Eve," or "Eve Tahitienne," Henri Rousseau's "Eve and the Serpent," or William Blake's "Eve Tempted by the Serpent." Blake's "Temptation of Eve" does include Adam, but the man stands with his back turned as Eve caresses the reptile and takes the forbidden fruit from its mouth with her own. What all of these paintings do is to increase the woman's responsibility for Adam's disobedience.

This is the case despite the fact that, if one believes that the word *ha-adam* should be translated as "man" and that God created the man before the woman, then the woman was not even present when God issued the command not to eat the fruit. That command is given in 2:16–17, before Eve makes an appearance. The text does not record God saying anything at all to the woman. She clearly knows of the prohibition, but the text does not tell us how.

And yet, in John Huston's movie *The Bible . . . In the Beginning*, God directly orders both the man and the woman not to eat from the forbidden tree. The effect of this is not only to increase Eve's responsibility for her act but also to set up more of a dramatic tension in the story, as instead of hearing about the prohibition from an unknown source, Eve is expressly told by God not to eat from the tree. In the movie, as God issues the order, Eve stares with fascination at the succulent fruit. Adam, in contrast, hears God's command and dutifully turns away from the tree. Eve remains rooted in place, transfixed.

The movie also adds other non-biblical details in order to heighten the dramatic tension in the story as well as Eve's responsibility for the downfall of humanity. A scene or two after God has enjoined the couple not to eat the forbidden fruit, Eve is awakened in the night by a low voice beckoning her: "Eve! Eve!" She leaves the sleeping Adam behind and follows the serpent's call. Eventually she ends up standing before the tree once again, and once again she stares at it as if her very life depends upon her tasting its fruit. After a conversation with the serpent, she bites into the golden apple that hangs from a branch of the tree. When Adam finds her, she holds the fruit out to him and says, "Taste it, there's no harm." Adam resists: "It is disobedience." At Eve's urging, though, he too submits to temptation. Though little of this occurs in the biblical text itself, it does make for compelling drama.

As we have seen, not just movie-makers, but also painters have made it clear that in their view, Adam has no responsibility, or at least he is less culpable than Eve, for what he does. In Titian's "Adam and Eve" (1550), Adam is present but is using his left hand to push Eve away. He resists her sin. In a 15th-century manuscript illumination, Eve speaks with the serpent (who looks like a cross between a blonde girl and a salamander) while Adam is off to the side, apparently weeding the garden.[29] A painting done in 1975 by Evgenii Abezgauz makes the point even more clearly with the title, "Adam Ate and Ate of the Fruit that Eve Gave Him but Knew Nothing." Adam, in this view, is not to blame for what happened, and the responsibility lies solely with the woman Eve. One early rabbinic source speculated that Adam knew nothing about the conversation between Eve and the serpent because "He had engaged in his natural functions [that is, intercourse] and then fallen asleep."[30]

The idea that a woman is responsible for the downfall of the man and of humanity can be found in other stories as well. The ancient Greeks told the myth of Pandora, a beautiful maiden who because of her insatiable curiosity was responsible for all the sorrows in the world. According to the story, the gods presented a box to Pandora but cautioned her never to open it up. Unable to resist the temptation, Pandora lifted the lid, and out flew diseases and all manner of misfortunes. Pandora tried to shut the box to recapture the evils, but it was too late, and so the world is plagued by trouble and grief even to this day.[31] The16th-century artist Jean Cousin the Elder showed how easily the stories of Eve and Pandora could merge together in his painting entitled "Eva Prima Pandora," or "Eve, the First Pandora."[32] In the painting, a nearly nude woman reclines on the ground. She rests her right arm on a skull, and in her right hand she holds a small tree branch. Her other hand is placed casually on a decorated jar or vase, and a serpent encircles her left arm like a bracelet. Here the stories blur into one: forbidden tree, snake, forbidden box, skull—all of them portend death, and both stories seem to put the blame squarely on the woman.

But what if Eve was not the only one responsible? What if Adam bore as much blame for the suffering of humankind as his partner did? If one translates the Hebrew word *imah* not as "also" but rather as "beside her" or "with her" (as the New Revised Standard Version does), then quite a different picture emerges: "She also gave some to her husband, who was with her, and he ate."[33] Then Adam is not an innocent bystander but is present for the conversation between Eve and the serpent and is fully aware of the source of the fruit.

This version of the story, however, is not as sexy as the other. In this version there is no seductress, no siren song luring the unwary onto the rocks, no feminine wiles employed to bring down an innocent male. There are just two people presented with a choice and with the consequences of their choice.

The Lady Eve (1941)

If popular culture is any barometer, we seem to like our Eves to be evil, or at least a little shady. A comic portrayal of the evil Eve can be found in Preston Sturges's 1941 movie *The Lady Eve*, which stars Barbara Stanwyck and Henry Fonda. (The film was remade in 1956 with the title *The Birds and the Bees* and starred George Gobel and Mitzi Gaynor.) Fonda plays Charles Pike, a naive scientist whose interest is wholly taken up with various species of snake. Charles is set to become the heir to his family's lucrative brewery business and is thus the object of considerable interest from various eligible ladies, despite his bumbling, nerdy manner. Stanwyck plays Jean Harrington, a con artist who travels the world with her equally disreputable father in order to execute various scams. Jean and Charles meet on a cruise ship when Charles is returning from a scientific expedition to South America, and Jean and her father are trolling for easy marks. Jean first attracts Charles's attention by dropping an apple on his head from above-deck, an obvious allusion to the Genesis story.

At the start of their relationship, Jean wants only to play Charles for a sucker, as both she and her father are after the Pike family fortune. It does not take long, however, before she finds herself falling for the awkward zoologist, and he for her. In fact, he falls quite literally, tripping over the dainty foot that Jean has just happened to place in his path. One thing leads to another, and soon the happy couple becomes engaged. Just then disaster occurs, as the ship's security officer learns the real identities of Jean and her father, and he exposes the pair to Charles as crooks. Charles breaks off the engagement, and he and Jean part on bitter terms.

As fate would have it, though, Jean gets an unexpected opportunity to wreak revenge on Charles for the humiliation that he caused her. She teams up with another con artist, a confidence man who is posing as a British lord and who happens to live in the very same town where Charles resides. Jean pretends to be the man's niece who is visiting from England, and she disguises herself and adopts the name Lady Eve Sidwich. As the Lady Eve, Stanwyck again lures Charles to fall in love with her. Charles's manservant, "Muggsy" Murgatroyd, is suspicious of the newcomer: "You trying to tell me this ain't the same rib [as] was on the boat?" he demands. But Charles does not heed the warning, and he marries the Lady Eve. Eve/Jean then has the chance to enact revenge, telling stories to Charles on their wedding night about all of the various lovers she has had in the past. Charles is mortified and attempts to divorce her, but she refuses. Charles then seeks to flee back to the Amazon to be with the snakes he loves, and he books passage on a boat to South America. Eve/Jean, realizing that she truly loves Charles, follows after him and finally catches up with him on the ship. When Charles stumbles upon her, he takes her for Jean, and he realizes that he is still in love with her. He invites her to his cabin, still not knowing that she is not only Jean but also his wife Eve. As the door to the cabin closes behind them, Charles explains, "I have no right to be in your cabin. Because I'm married." To this Eve replies, "But so am I, darling. So am I."

The fact that the movie ends happily, with Charles falling in love with the woman who is his wife (what film theorist Stanley Cavell calls a "comedy of remarriage"[34]) does not entirely erase the unease that we feel with Jean/Eve. Yes, in the end, she herself succumbs to love. And yes, she is basically good-hearted and only schemes against Charles because she was hurt by his rejection. However, the fact remains that throughout the movie, she is a conniver; she plays Charles for a fool, and even at the end of the film, it is not clear that Charles will ever fully understand exactly what has transpired. When Eve tries to explain to him how she has come to be on the ship with him again, Charles interrupts: "I don't want to understand, I don't want to know. Whatever it is, keep it to yourself. All I know is I adore you." Charles has willed not to have his eyes opened by Eve. He remains in deliberate ignorance or, as one might put it, innocence.

A promotional poster for the 1941 release of *The Lady Eve* makes the distinction between the two characters quite clear: "Barbara Stanwyck has Henry Fonda Bewitched and Bewildered," it declares. The accompanying art shows Stanwyck/Eve with her arms wrapped around Fonda/Charles's neck. She looks composed and confident; he looks, as the poster says, bewitched and bewildered (or, as he describes himself in the film several times, "cockeyed").

The idea that Eves have the power to bewitch is nothing new. In the Middle Ages, a document used by the Inquisition to determine who was or was not a witch frequently referred to the first woman in order to bolster its claims that women were not to be trusted. The *Malleus Maleficarum*, or "Hammer Against Witches," explained, "[I]t should be noted that there was a defect in the formation of the first woman, since she was formed from a bent rib, that is, a rib of the breast, which is bent as it were in a contrary direction to a man. And since through this defect she is an imperfect animal, she always deceives."[35] The document goes on to say that the devil's power is most apparent in sexual acts and explains that "this is likely to be so, since those women are chiefly apt to be witches who are most disposed to such acts." In what can only be described as a deeply Freudian association, the text then cites Thomas Aquinas and makes a connection between sex and snakes:

> For he [Aquinas] says that, since the first corruption of sin by which man became the slave of the devil came to us through the act of generation, therefore greater power is allowed by God to the devil in this act than in all others. Also the power of witches is more apparent in serpents, as it is said, than in other animals, because through the means of a serpent the devil tempted woman.[36]

In many artistic depictions of the Genesis story, Eve is shown as being on intimate terms with the serpent, wrapping it around herself or, as in Blake's depiction, placing its mouth on hers. It thus might seem odd that in *The Lady Eve*, Charles is the one who is so at ease with reptiles. Charles is an ophiologist, or a scientist who specializes in snakes. He is immensely proud of the specimen that he has traveled to the Amazon to capture and which he is transporting back to the States. He has named the snake "Emma" and treats it with great affection. When he tries to show Emma to Jean, however, Jean screams and runs away and then goes so far as to make Charles check her cabin to make sure that the reptile has not climbed into her bed.

What does the snake signify in this film? On the one hand, snakes nearly always function as phallic symbols, and thus Jean's fear of Charles's snake might indicate a deep-seated fear of sexual intimacy. As Marian Keane observes in her commentary on the film, at one point Charles appears reading a book entitled *Are Snakes Necessary?* The title is an allusion to the classic book by James Thurber and E.B. White called *Is Sex Necessary?* which was first published in 1929.[37] Thus it is natural for viewers of the movie to associate the snake with sex. However, the fact that the snake is a female makes it an ambivalent phallic symbol at best and points us in another direction: toward the long history of portraying the snake in the Garden of Eden as a female. Look, for example, at Masolino's "Temptation of Adam and Eve" (c. 1425) or Hugo van der Goes's "Temptation" (c. 1470), or the Flemish Master of Lucretia's "Adam and Eve" (c. 1520), all of which feature distinctly female reptiles. Perhaps, then, we should think of Charles's Emma not so much as a sexual symbol but rather as a reminder of the downfall of our first mother, Eve. Jean is frightened of Emma, then, not because she fears sex with Charles but because the first snake in the first garden was able to persuade the first Eve to act in a way that brought disaster.

Charles, on the other hand, is immune to the danger represented by the snake. He is innocent of the complexities of human life and love and remains so throughout the movie. In the very first scene of *The Lady Eve*, Charles offers a farewell to his companions in the Amazon, telling them, "If I had my way, believe me, this is the way I'd like to spend all my time, in the company of men like yourselves in the pursuit of knowledge." Thus he is dedicated to scientific inquiry, but he knows next to nothing about relations between men and women; he is not enticed by the promise of knowing good and bad, as the biblical Eve was. Jean points out to him how limited his understanding of such matters is when she tells him, "You don't know very much about girls. The best ones aren't as good as you probably think they are, and the bad ones aren't as bad. Not nearly as bad." Charles displays an impenetrable naïveté about good girls and bad girls and the similarities and differences between them, and even in the very last scene, when he tells Jean/Eve, "I don't want to understand, I don't want to know," his ongoing ignorance/innocence is assured. He has not yet eaten from the forbidden fruit and, if he has his way, he never will.

All About Eve (1950)

The Lady Eve is one of the most famous screwball comedies of the 1940s, and in 1994 it won a place on the Library of Congress's National Film Registry.[38] It also influenced another highly regarded film, Joseph L. Mankiewicz's All About Eve (1950). The name of the main character in All About Eve, Eve Harrington, is a combination of the names of the two characters played by Barbara Stanwyck in The Lady Eve: Eve Sidwich and Jean Harrington.[39] Like The Lady Eve, Mankiewicz's All About Eve is considered a classic film and was named one of the top thirty movies of the past century by the American Film Institute.[40] It is not, however, a comedy. Though witty and filled with ironic banter, All About Eve presents a dim view of human life, or at least a dim view of life in the American theater. Unlike the Lady Eve Sidwich, Eve Harrington in All About Eve has no redeeming qualities, and viewers feel no remorse in despising her.

Consider director Mankiewicz's description of his title character: "Eves are predatory animals; they'll prefer a terrain best suited to their marauding techniques, hopefully abundant with the particular plunder they're after . . . Eve is essentially . . . the girl unceasingly, relentlessly on the make."[41] The plot of All About Eve is about just such a predator. It is the story of a seemingly mousy young woman who lies and deceives her way into the company of an aging Broadway star in order to destroy her and to take her place. Eve Harrington (played by Anne Baxter) claims to be a Midwestern girl whose husband was killed during military service. She professes adoration of the actress Margo Channing (Bette Davis) and says that she wants nothing more than a chance to meet her idol. Soon, however, Eve takes advantage of the goodwill that has been bestowed upon her by Margo, and she uses it to advance her own career. Eve will stop at nothing, it seems, to get what she wants. She even attempts to seduce Margo's boyfriend Bill, as well as the noted playwright Lloyd Richards, who is married to Margo's best friend Karen.

The movie contains no overt references to the biblical Eve. The closest it comes to making the connection explicitly is when Margo, realizing that she has been betrayed by the younger woman, describes her by saying, "Eve: evil. Little Miss Evil." However, the play on which the movie was based, Mary Orr's *The Wisdom of Eve*, makes frequent allusions to the Genesis story. Several times the drama associates Eve Harrington with her biblical predecessor. For example, when one character comments that he is uneasy with having Eve around, Margo dismisses his fears, saying, "It's probably her name. Men have been suspicious of girls called Eve since the first one listened to a snake." As the play progresses, Eve is twice identified with a serpent. Departing for a new life in Hollywood, she comments, "I feel I'm shedding my skin—like a snake." Then, after she has gone, Margo's maid calls the young actress a "bitch" and comments, "The snake is headed for the Garden of Eden."[42]

These references are omitted in the movie. One image in *All About Eve*, however, does evoke the Genesis story, or at least it evokes artists' renderings of the story. It occurs in the very first scene, though, since the movie's plot is told in flashback, the scene takes place after the events that it refers to have already taken place. As the movie opens, the film's narrator, Addison DeWitt (played by George Sanders), informs the audience via voice-over that we are at a banquet hosted by the Sarah Siddons Society, a venerable organization devoted to excellence in the theater. The Society is about to bestow its most prestigious award on the famous actress Eve Harrington. As DeWitt orients us to our surroundings and to the characters at the banquet, we see an aged and pompous thespian making a lengthy speech about the glories of the stage. After DeWitt has finished his introductions, we at last hear the voice of the elderly actor as he finishes his oration and makes ready to present the award—a small statuette—to Eve. What happens next is described in director Mankiewicz's script: "As she [Eve] nears her goal, the Aged Actor turns to her. He holds out the award. Her hand reaches out for it. At that precise moment—with the award just beyond her fingertips—THE PICTURE HOLDS, THE ACTION STOPS. THE SOUND STOPS."[43] We see Eve reaching for her prize, her arms and fingers outstretched, grasping for the statue. Eve Harrington evokes countless Eves reaching for the dangerous fruit in countless paintings: by Titian, Raphael, Rubens, and Michelangelo, among others. Eve is the greedy, rapacious female who, because of her insatiable hunger, will bring disaster upon herself and all her progeny.

And indeed she does have progeny, if only figuratively. The film ends by showing us that the cycle begun by Eve will continue. In the final scene, Eve returns to her hotel after having received the Sarah Siddons Society award. Arriving in her room, she finds an ingénue named Phoebe who has fallen asleep from waiting so long to meet her idol. Phoebe professes nothing but adoration for Eve, but the film makes it clear that what she really wants is to take her place. Eve's theatrical daughter will overthrow her in just the same way that Eve herself usurped Margo Channing. Eve has begotten evil.

The movie *All About Eve* itself has progeny, as references to it abound in culture. A 2008 installment of the cartoon series *The Simpsons*, for example, is entitled "All About Lisa" and is a parody of Mankiewicz's film. In the episode, young Lisa Simpson betrays local entertainer Krusty the Clown, takes over his show, and wins a prestigious award for her efforts. The episode begins, just as did *All About Eve*, at a banquet ceremony and, just as in its predecessor, the action in the cartoon freezes at just the moment when the award winner reaches for her prize.[44] In this version, though, Lisa repents of her ways and restores Krusty to his rightful place. As it turns out, Lisa does not have the heart to be an Eve.

Second Time Lucky (1984)

One of the clearest and most explicit connections between Eve and evil is made in the 1984 romantic comedy *Second Time Lucky*. The premise of the movie is that God and Satan have agreed to a wager to see if modern-day Adam and Eve will make the same choice to disobey God that their predecessors made the first time around. In order to test their subjects, God and Satan transport two college students (named, of course, Adam and Eve) back to the beginning of time. Adam is taken to the Garden of Eden by the angel Gabriel. Eve, on the other hand, is chosen by Satan himself. When Gabriel first catches sight of the nude Eve in the garden, he comments, "That Satan sure knows how to pick 'em." In other words, Satan has chosen the most beguiling woman he can find in order to tempt Adam into disobedience. Eve is literally the devil's instrument. She is Satan's tool for winning the cosmic wager.

For his part, Adam is utterly innocent and does not even know the difference between men and women. Gabriel has to watch him closely and give him stern warnings: "If you eat the apples, you succumb to Eve, God's bet is lost and the evil one will triumph. But the Good Lord in his infinite wisdom has provided you with a warning signal." That signal is Adam's ability to get an erection. When he finds himself sexually aroused, Gabriel says, Adam should remember God's warning and should refuse to succumb to Eve's wiles.

Of course, Adam does indeed succumb to Eve's invitation to eat the forbidden fruit; otherwise we would have no movie. It is a curious phenomenon that in order for a story to have a plot, the characters must change and grow—they must struggle and overcome. This is impossible if both characters remain in Edenic innocence. Therefore, it is necessary to the movie that Adam and Eve will be banished from God's garden, and it is necessary that they will spend the rest of the movie attempting to undo the damage that they have brought to themselves and to the cosmic order.

Most of *Second Time Lucky*, then, is a romp through history, with the two characters Adam and Eve morphing into, in succession, a soldier and an empress in the Roman empire; an English captain and a French nurse during World War I; a G-man and a gangster moll in a Chicago speakeasy; and a rock star and a beautiful seductress in a London music studio. In each case, Adam is an upright, decent man, and Eve is a treacherous, wicked woman. When, in her role as the Empress Devia, Eve tries to seduce the Roman centurion "Adameus," Gabriel warns Adam, "It's not just your body she's after. Your soul, Boy. Your immortal soul!" When the French nurse Eva is sentenced to be shot by a firing squad for collaborating with the Germans, a priest attempts to pray with her. She scorns him: "With my connections? You're joking, yes?" Her connections, obviously, are to Satan.

In the end, however, Eve manages to convince Adam that she has changed and that she truly cares for him: "Maybe I am trash. But I got a heart. And it beats. It could beat for you." Together, the couple manages to defeat Satan, who complains that they cheated: "You brought true love into it!" As the movie concludes, the college students Adam and Eve are restored to the present day and to the comfort of each other's arms. They retire to Adam's bedroom, but seconds later the door to the room opens up again. As if hanging a "Do Not Disturb" sign on the knob, a hand reaches out and places an apple with two bites taken out of it on the floor outside the bedroom. Thus we know that at long last Adam and Eve have not just fallen in love but have consummated their relationship sexually.

Eve as a woman on the make, as a temptress hungry for sex and power who is willing to bring down anyone who stands in her way, is a standard character in contemporary culture. For another example, see Elia Kazan's 1955 film *East of Eden* (based on the novel by John Steinbeck), in which an Eve resists the goodness of her husband and leaves both him and her newborn children in order to become proprietress of a whorehouse. Given the pervasiveness of this image, though, it is easy to forget that in the biblical story itself, there is no mention of Eve seducing her husband into eating the forbidden fruit, or of her tricking him. As we have seen, the text says simply that she took some of the fruit and ate, "and she also gave some to her husband [who was with her], and he ate."

Despite this fact, numerous writers have looked for ways to explain (if not to excuse) why Adam ate what Eve offered to him. These explanations tend to make the man seem less culpable than the woman. Augustine, for example, wrote that Adam ate Eve's offering because "he did not wish to make her unhappy, fearing she would waste away without his support, alienated from his affections, and that this dissension would be her death. He was not overcome by the concupiscence of the flesh . . . but by the sort of attachment and affection by which it often happens that we offend God while we try to keep the friendship of men."[45] Aquinas cited Augustine approvingly and, while acknowledging that both Adam and Eve sinned, and while stating that in one sense the man's sin was more grievous because he was more perfect than the woman, nonetheless offered three reasons to indict the woman; first, she was more puffed up by pride, as she wanted to be like God; second, she suggested sin to the man; and third, Adam only agreed to eat the fruit because he did not want to upset Eve.[46]

But what if Eve wasn't at fault at all? What if she has been the victim of libel all these years? A cartoon asks the same question. It shows Adam and Eve in the Garden of Eden, accompanied by another man writing something in a notebook. In answer to Eve's inquiring look, Adam nonchalantly hands her an apple and says, "That's just my publicist. I hired him to make sure the media get the story right."[47] The implication, of course, is that Eve ended up being blamed for something that Adam did. Perhaps all these years, the media *haven't* gotten the story right. Perhaps men have just had better publicists than women have had, and women have been paying for the sins of men without even realizing it. Maybe the connection between Eve and evil is simply the result of male, patriarchal propaganda.

Eve Was Framed

Such, in any case, is the position of theologian Mary Daly, whose book *Beyond God the Father* (1973) was something of a landmark in the development of feminist religious writing. The second chapter of Daly's book is entitled "Exorcising Evil from Eve: The Fall Into Freedom," and it argues both that the story of Adam and Eve has had devastating consequences for women and that the story, properly interpreted, can be a vehicle for women's liberation.

In Daly's view the Genesis story has caused untold harm to women. One effect of blaming women for "the Fall" has been what Daly terms "psychological paralysis," or "a general feeling of hopelessness, guilt, and anxiety over social disapproval."[48] This leads to other effects: "feminine antifeminism," or women's disapproval of any women who do not accept their inferior status; false humility, or "an internalization of masculine opinion"; and emotional dependence, in which women find their own self-worth solely by pleasing men.[49]

All of these effects are the result of what Daly calls the Scapegoat Syndrome, or humans' need to blame others in order to judge themselves to be good. If people are to think well of themselves, then they need to create an "Other" at whom they can point a finger and whom they can condemn as bad. Contends Daly, "Eve was such a production." Eve comes to stand for everything that "good" women are not. Good women are chaste and pure—Eve is a seductive harlot. Good women do what their men tell them to do—Eve ignores God and Adam's command. Good women are humble—Eve desires to be like God. Good women do not display their nakedness—Eve was naked and was unashamed. Good women stay at home and do not venture into public spaces—Eve goes off on her own and talks to strange serpents. Good women follow the rules—Eve does what she pleases. Eve, says Daly, is the creation of patriarchal society's need to blame someone for its own guilt.

This does not mean that Daly seeks to banish the story of Adam and Eve from women's consciousness. On the contrary, she sees the text as an important representation of how patriarchy (that is, male-dominated society) has projected its own sin onto its victim. The story itself enacts what it means. In other words, blaming women for the downfall of humanity *is itself* the downfall of humanity. The original sin is not Eve's eating of the forbidden fruit, but patriarchy's blaming women for evil. Writes Daly, "In a real sense the projection of guilt upon women *is* patriarchy's Fall, the primordial lie. Together with its offspring—the theology of 'original sin'—the myth reveals the 'Fall' of religion into the role of patriarchy's prostitute."[50] The way to overcome the sin of patriarchy, then, is for women to refuse to be characterized as evil, and to stop cooperating in their own self-destruction.

Thus, writes Daly, the real redemption of Eve will occur when women realize how they have assisted patriarchy by blaming themselves: "The movement beyond patriarchy's good and evil can be seen mythically as 'the Fall'—the dreaded Fall which is now finally beginning to occur, in which women are bringing ourselves and then the other half of the species to eat of the forbidden fruit—the knowledge refused by patriarchal society." This Fall is actually a rising up; it is "a Fall *into* the sacred and therefore into freedom."[51] Eating the fruit is not a sin but is an exercise in self-determination.

In one sense, Daly's approach to the Genesis story mirrors that of some of the ancient Gnostic thinkers who saw Eden's serpent as a kind of hero. The term "Gnosticism" is difficult to define and encompasses a wide diversity of worldviews that circulated in the Greco-Roman world in the first few centuries of the common era. Generally, however, Gnostics rejected the things of this earthly, material world (including sexual intercourse) in favor of a higher, spiritual realm. Their goal was to cultivate the spiritual sparks within themselves in order to free themselves from the chains of ignorance and bodily concerns that held them captive.[52] Gnosticism as a philosophical and theological movement cut across religious lines; often when one is reading ancient Gnostic texts, it is difficult to tell if writers thought of themselves as Jews, Christians, or members of one of the Greco-Roman mystery religions. What the writers held in common was an emphasis on *gnosis*, or knowledge, as the key to spiritual fulfillment.

When some of the Gnostic writers read Genesis, they saw God (that is, the Creator of the material world) as a contemptible deity to be spurned. God did not want to share his knowledge with the human beings, but the serpent was able to free Adam and Eve from God's tyranny. An ancient text called the *Hypostasis of the Archons* (written approximately third century C.E.) explains that the serpent revealed to the first humans the fact that God had lied to them: "And the snake, the instructor, said, 'With death you shall not die; for it was out of jealousy that he said this to you. Rather your eyes shall open and you shall come to be like gods, recognizing evil and good.'"[53] Thus, as in Mary Daly's twentieth-century reading, the eating of the forbidden fruit was not a fall into sin but was a liberation into wisdom and knowledge.

Sandra Stanton's 1996 oil painting "Eve, Mother of All Living" presents the first woman in precisely this moment of liberation. The painting portrays Eve as bursting forth from the shell of an egg, her nude body arched in ecstasy, her arms upraised, and her head thrown back in exultation. Eve holds a small figure of herself in one hand, and above her hovers a blue and red bird. Behind her appears the head of a serpent. Explaining the painting, Stanton writes, "Eve's title, 'Mother of All Living,' was a translation of 'Jaganmata,' Kali Ma's (Goddess of decay, death, and rejuvenation) title in India. Originally it was believed that Eve created all beings out of clay, some believing that she had the help of her serpent. The flying malachite kingfisher symbolizes the halcyon days of the Goddess before patriarchy."[54] The connections that Stanton makes between Eve and ancient goddesses are more likely associative than historical. That is, there is little evidence that worship of the Hindu goddess Kali actually had any influence on the development of the biblical figure of Eve. Moreover, the image of a female creator fashioning beings out of clay comes from an ancient Assyrian story rather than from a tradition about Eve herself.[55]

However, to say that there is an associative link rather than a historical one among these traditions is not at all to detract from the power of Stanton's imagery. Eggs connote both perfection and new life; in the ancient Orphic creation story, for example, the first god Phanes-Dionysus was born from a silver egg, and in some African stories, the "egg of God" gives birth to everything that exists. Likewise, the Indian god Prajapati emerged from an egg, as did the ancient Chinese deity P'an Ku.[56]

Moreover, birds symbolize freedom, whether it is the tragic freedom of Icarus, who flew too close to the sun, or the carefree joy of the "birds of the air" in the Christian New Testament's Gospel of Matthew who "neither sow nor reap nor gather into barns" but who are provided for by God (6:26).

Even the nakedness of Eve in Stanton's painting appeals as an arche-type. Genesis 2:25 tells us that in the Garden of Eden, the man and the woman "were both naked, and were not ashamed." The ancient Pelasgian (pre-Hellenistic Greek) creation story declared, "In the beginning, Eurynome, The Goddess of All Things, rose naked from Chaos."[57] Early Christians were baptized naked as a symbol of the purity of their new lives, and Orthodox Jewish women remove their clothing before entering the monthly ritual bath or *mikvah*. Initiation into the Afro-Cuban tradition called Santería involves having one's clothes ripped off and standing on them while taking a shower in order to purify oneself of the past.[58] Nakedness is primordial, and it reminds us of a time before we were burdened by the consequences of our decisions or by shame. In Stanton's painting, Eve revels in her nudity.

But what of the snake? Are snakes not symbols of evil? The presence of the serpent in this image seems to cast a pall over the rest of the painting.

It is true that, as we have already seen, serpents connote evil in con-temporary culture. They represent sin, poison, and Satan himself. And yet as we have also seen, the serpent can be interpreted as the hero of the Genesis story: the one who gives human beings knowledge. If we dig even more deeply into the history of the serpent symbol, we see still more al-ternatives for interpreting the snake in Stanton's work. In ancient India, for example, snakes represented fertility and new life.[59] It is not difficult to imagine why that is the case, as Sigmund Freud referred to the serpent as "the most important symbol for the male member."[60] Contemporary slang for male masturbation includes such euphemisms as "charming the snake" and "teasing the python."

Snakes have also served as symbols of health. In the Hellenistic world, the healer Asklepius, who was the son of Apollo and a mortal woman, carried a staff entwined with a serpent. In the Bible, Moses fashioned a serpent of bronze, "and whenever a serpent bit someone, that person would look at the serpent of bronze and live" (Numbers 21:9). Even to-day, the logo of the American Medical Association is a serpent wrapped around a pole, and the insignia for the Army Medical Corps is a *caduceus*, or two snakes wrapped around a staff or rod. Snakes also represent eter-nity, as they are able to shed their old skins, and it was thought by some in the ancient world that they thus live forever. The Egyptian symbol of the Ouroboros, which shows a serpent devouring its own tail, was an alchemical expression for the eternal oneness of all things.

In sum, we need not interpret the snake, either in Stanton's painting or in the Genesis story itself, as representing evil. It is true that for contemporary audiences, a determined act of will is required to overcome the long-standing association of serpents with sin. And yet, if we are able to make that leap, new insights into the story of Adam and Eve can arise.

For example, the connection between snakes and fertility reminds us that Eve, the woman who talked to the snake, was the first mother. Her name in Hebrew, *havah*, is related to the word for "life" and means, as the Bible says, "mother of all the living" (Genesis 3:20). Curiously, however, there are very few depictions of Eve with her children. One of only a handful of such representations appears in the *Nuremberg Chronicle*, a book originally published in Latin in 1493. The *Chronicle* recounts the history of the world as that history is told by the Bible, and it contains a woodcut entitled "The First Family" which shows Adam and Eve after they have been cast out of the Garden of Eden.[61] In the illustration, Adam wears a fur pelt and hacks away with a primitive scythe at the rocky ground beneath his bare feet. Eve, unshod like her husband, sits and offers her breast to a naked infant while a second infant looks on. The Bible tells us that these two children will come to a bad end; Cain will slay his younger brother Abel and be cast out from the presence of the Lord. Cain will go away and dwell in the land of Nod, "east of Eden" (Genesis 4:16). Rabbi Harold Kushner, author of *When Bad Things Happen to Good People*, points out that the first mention of "sin" in the Bible occurs not in connection with Adam and Eve's eating of the forbidden fruit, but rather in connection with this first human murder (Genesis 4:7).[62]

Despite the grief and suffering that mark the life of Eve, however, her tale is nonetheless the story of life itself. Her children, and her children's children, are the mythic ancestors (if not the biological predecessors) of all of us. Her womb is the wellspring of humanity. A work of art that emphasizes the importance of Eve as the source of life is Rita Denenberg's quilted artwork entitled "We Are All Connected to One Rib." The quilt celebrates Eve, whom Denenberg calls "the mother of all," as well as other groundbreaking women such as astronaut Sally Ride, the poet Maya Angelou, and the Native American Pocahontas. The artist explains, "This quilt is my tribute to women," and she notes that in the piece, "Each figure is connected to Eve or each other." In Denenberg's vision, the bonds among women, both across cultures and throughout history, are stitched together by our common ancestor, Eve.

The Franciscan Catholic painter Robert Lentz also captures this symbolic truth in his icon entitled "Eve, the Mother of All." The painting shows Eve as an old woman, gray-haired and wrinkled, presenting the viewer with a ripe red fruit. The fruit is not, however, the apple that we have come to associate with Eve. Explains the website that advertises the painting, "She [Eve] holds in her hands an opened pomegranate . . . The pomegranate is an ancient Middle Eastern symbol of the womb because of its red juice and its numerous seeds or offspring. . . . In this icon it represents all the descendants of Eve, the human race, and our debt to her and all our foremothers."[63]

It is worth noting that in mythology and iconography, the pomegranate symbolizes not just fertility, but also death and resurrection. In an ancient Homeric hymn, the young Persephone is held captive in the underworld by the fact that she has eaten a pomegranate seed. Her mother Demeter promises her, however, that "whenever the earth blossoms with all kinds of fragrant spring flowers, you will come back up again from the mist darkness, to the great astonishment of gods and mortal men."[64] In several Renaissance paintings, including Botticelli's "Madonna of the Pomegranate" and Leonardo da Vinci's "Dreyfus Madonna," the baby Jesus holds a pomegranate to indicate his future Passion and triumph over death. Thus the pomegranate captures the twin images of Eve as bringer of death and mother of life.

Where does all this diversity of interpretation leave us? What shall we conclude about the meaning of manhood and womanhood and how the sexes should think of one another? The story of Adam and Eve, like all great literature, provides more questions than answers, and these questions, as we have seen, continue to generate countless works of art, fiction, music, and cinema. The questions become even thornier and emotionally complex once we add sexual relations into the mix. The biblical tale speaks not just about sex and gender, but also about sexual attraction, sexual activity, and marriage. According to Genesis 2:23, when the first man became aware of the first woman, he exclaimed, "This at last is one bone of my bones and flesh of my flesh; this one shall be called Woman, for out of Man this one was taken." The narrator of the story then informs us, "Therefore a man leaves his father and his mother and clings to his wife, and they become one flesh." (2:24). How that plays out in life and in culture is the subject of the next chapter.

CHAPTER FOUR

Fig Leaves

The biblical story of Adam and Eve makes no connection between the couple's disobedience and sex. Eve eats the fruit of the forbidden tree not because she wants to experience sexual pleasure but because the tree was good for food, and it was a delight to the eyes, and it was to be desired to make one wise (Genesis 3:6). True, once they have eaten the fruit, the man and woman realize that they are naked and cover themselves with fig leaves; however, it is not clear that this gesture is meant to hide sexual shame.

In fact, according to some interpreters, the nakedness of the first couple had nothing at all to do with sex. Several early Jewish sources say that prior to their eating of the fruit, Adam and Eve had been covered with a scaly skin and a cloud of glory. Once the man and woman disobeyed God, their scales and the cloud dropped away, and thus the couple were "naked."[1] The implication is that the two people were ashamed not because of their sexuality but because there was now a visible sign of their disobedience.

Another interpretation says that Adam and Eve were "naked" in that they had been stripped of the beauty of the commandment that they had just broken.[2] Yet another notes that in the Bible, the word "naked" primarily conveys a sense of vulnerability.[3] In the book of Job, for example, Job reflects on his powerlessness before God by saying, "Naked I came from my mother's womb, and naked shall I return there" (1:21). In the case of Adam and Eve, then, nakedness meant that the man and woman were creatures of God whose every breath depended upon God's will. Prior to their forbidden eating, the couple was vulnerable but unaware of this fact. Once their eyes were opened, Adam and Eve saw precisely how precarious their existence was; "nakedness" meant not "sexual" but "exposed."

And yet, very early on, at least in Christian circles, the Genesis text came to be seen as primarily a story about sex. If one types "Adam and Eve" into an internet search engine, advertisements pop up for any number of online sex shops selling "adult" toys and videos. Indeed, there is even an "Adam and Eve" movie studio that produces erotic films with titles like *Dirty Little Devils*, *Bare Necessities*, and *Eden*, whose plot is summarized this way: "On a remote island a select few will experience dreams beyond their imagination!"

Goodness Has Nothing to Do With It:
Mae West on the *Chase & Sanborn Hour*

Why have Adam and Eve come to be seen as the first sexual swingers? The Christian Saint Augustine probably bears much of the responsibility for this. In his *City of God* he attributed the advent of lust in the world to the sin of our first human parents. Prior to their transgression, said Augustine, Adam and Eve would have had sexual intercourse, but they would have done so without lust. Adam's erection would have been completely under the control of his will, and the man and the woman would have copulated with the same dispassionate equanimity that they would have exhibited while sowing seeds in a field.[4] As things stand now, however, the descendants of Adam are both tormented by lust and unable to control their sexual arousal—or lack thereof. As Augustine noted, it happens to men that "sometimes this lust importunes them in spite of themselves, and sometimes fails them when they desire to feel it, so that though lust rages in the mind, it stirs not in the body."[5]

Augustine finds it self-evident that sexual lust is both the result of our first parents' transgression and a cause of shame in us. His evidence for the latter is that when we want to engage in sexual activities, we hide ourselves from sight: "What! Does not even conjugal intercourse, sanctioned as it is by law for the propagation of children, legitimate and honourable though it be, does it not seek retirement from every eye?" When a couple is married, everyone at the wedding knows that sexual relations will occur that night and yet, Augustine says, even when "this well-understood act is gone about for the procreation of children, not even the children themselves, who may already have been born to them, are suffered to be witnesses." For Augustine, all sexual activity, even when performed within the noble institution of marriage, is now "accompanied with a shame-begetting penalty of sin."[6]

It is important to emphasize that for Augustine, sex *in itself* is not sinful. That is, he thinks that Adam and Eve in the Garden would have engaged in non-sinful sexual activity, and in this opinion he has many followers. One of the sweetest descriptions of the sexual relations between Adam and Eve can be found in Milton's *Paradise Lost*. Milton describes the couple's conjugal bliss:

> Handed they went; and eas'd the putting off
> These troublesom disguises which wee wear,[7]
> Strait side by side were laid, nor turnd I weene
> *Adam* from his fair Spouse, nor *Eve* the Rites
> Mysterious of connubial Love refus'd.[8]

In a similar vein, John Huston's *The Bible . . . In the Beginning* indicates that Adam and Eve had sex in the Garden. In a scene that takes place before the couple are expelled for their disobedience, a naked Eve snuggles close to her naked man. As she does, the movie's narrator says, "And God blessed them and said unto them, 'Be fruitful and multiply.'"

On the other hand, however, numerous commentators have contended that Adam and Eve would not ever have had sex had they not been dismissed from the Garden. The fourth-century Christian writer John Chrysostom, for example, bade his readers to consider at what point Genesis says that Adam had intercourse with Eve: "After their disobedience, after their loss of the garden, then it was that the practice of intercourse had its beginning. You see, before their disobedience they followed a life like that of the angels, and there was no mention of intercourse. How could there be, when they were not subject to the needs of the body?" Chrysostom used the Genesis text as a way to urge his readers to esteem virginity over the married state.[9] Likewise, Gregory of Nyssa (fourth century) wrote that marriage was instituted as a compensation for Adam and Eve's having to die, and he encouraged his audience to leave the lure of marriage, and therefore sex, behind them as a step toward regaining Paradise: "Since the point of departure from the life in paradise was the married state, reason suggests to those returning to Christ that they, first, give this up as a kind of early stage of the journey."[10]

Surely it was the association between sex and sin that made blonde bombshell Mae West's radio depiction of Eve in 1937 so controversial. West appeared as a guest star on Edgar Bergen's *Chase & Sanborn Hour* in a nine-minute skit written by Arch Oboler.[11] The appearance caused such a furor that West was banned from the radio for decades; even mentioning her name on the air was forbidden. Looking at a transcript of the broadcast, it is difficult to see exactly what caused so much offense. As the *Washington Post* noted, "The Adam and Eve comedy was innocent enough when read the ordinary way."[12] The problem, then, seems to have stemmed from West's persona as well as from her inflection as she read.

In terms of her persona, she was larger than life, a dame who gave as good as she got and flaunted what she had. In the era of the Flapper, when slim boyish figures were all the rage, West dressed so as to call attention to her hips and breasts. In the movie *She Done Him Wrong* (1933), for example, she was outfitted by legendary designer Edith Head in dresses so tight that she wasn't even able to sit down between takes; the studio had to devise a tilting board with armrests so that she could at least lean against the wall. (For scenes in which she was seated, Head provided duplicate dresses with a little more room.)[13]

West had a history of offending public sensibilities. Ten years before the *Chase & Sanborn* incident, she had been arrested and found guilty of "giving an immoral performance" because of her role in the play *Sex*, which she had also coauthored. In that show, West took the role of Margy Lamont, a character whom one reviewer described as a lady "of the evening—and of, for that matter, the afternoon and morning too."[14] The judge in West's case sentenced her to spend ten days in a New York workhouse, and after paying her debt to society, West complained only that the "fuzzy" prison underwear was uncomfortable. In 1928, West again took on a controversial role, starring in *Diamond Lil*, a play about a character whom the *New York Times* described as a "scarlet woman." That same year, she was arrested once more and charged with indecency in connection with her play *Pleasure Man*, which a reviewer described as "a coarse, vulgar and objectionable specimen of its author's theatrical writings." In that case, the jury could not decide on a verdict, and so the case was dropped.[15]

When she moved from the stage to the cinema, West continued to play women who were unashamedly sexual. Her 1933 movie *I'm No Angel*, which also starred Cary Grant, featured the famous line, "Come up and see me sometime—any time!" In other films of the 1930s, West played a circus performer, a dance hall queen, and a gambler's mistress—not exactly the kind of wholesome characters of which Middle America might approve.

But it was more than her bawdy persona that infuriated some of the listeners to the *Chase & Sanborn Hour*; it was also her interpretation of the material. Much of West's fame came from the fact that she could say innocuous lines in such a way that they conveyed a double meaning. As Edgar Bergen once commented, "If she says 'I've got appendicitis,' it sounds like sex."[16] In large part, West's facility with veiled humor and double-entendres stemmed from the need to get material past her censors. The Motion Picture Production Code, which was first established in 1930 (though it was not uniformly enforced until 1934), imposed constraints on movies' ability to include lewd or sexually offensive dialogue, characters, or plot. Thus before the 1933 release of *She Done Him Wrong*, censors demanded that verses of West's song entitled "A Guy What Takes His Time" be cut because of their suggestive lyrics.[17] West also had to delete four and a half pages of the dialogue for *Belle of the Nineties* (1934), and Production Code authorities asked that that film include "compensating moral values" to make up for its overall questionable plot.[18] Frequently, then, the challenge for West was to take seemingly innocent lines, lines that had passed beneath the censors' radar, and turn them into something else altogether.

For example, in the 1932 movie *Night After Night*, West played the ex-girlfriend of the owner of a speakeasy. In one memorable scene, her character enters a club decked out in jewels. When a hat-check girl exclaims, "Goodness, what beautiful diamonds!" West replies, "Goodness had nothing to do with it, Dearie." (This line became so well-known that in 1959 West titled her autobiography *Goodness Had Nothing To Do With It*.) In *She Done Him Wrong*, West's character, a nightclub owner named Lady Lou, is praised as being "a fine woman." She agrees with this assessment, saying that she is "one of the finest women ever walked the streets." Indeed, the script for *She Done Him Wrong* is full of such witticisms spoken by Lady Lou, including "When women go wrong, men go right after them."

Even if the script of the "Adam and Eve" skit looked innocent enough, then, it caused an uproar when the lines were spoken by West. In one scene of the radio play, the snake attempted to wriggle through a picket fence that God had placed around the forbidden tree in order to keep Adam (played by Don Ameche) and Eve away. Finding the task difficult, the snake complained, "I'm, I'm stuck," to which Eve replied "Oh–shake your hips. There, there now, you're through. You're doing all right." It is hardly a stretch to think of the snake as a phallic symbol and of West's lines as a description of copulation.

The script also makes it clear that Eve is not happy in God's garden and that she prefers to "break the lease" that she and Adam have in Eden in order to go out and seek adventure. Eden is "too nice," she tells Adam: "A girl's gotta have a little fun once in a while. There's no future under a fig tree." When Adam asks why she wants to upset their nice arrangement and thus risk making trouble, she says, "If trouble means something that makes you catch your breath, if trouble means something that makes your blood run through your veins like seltzer water, mmmmm, Adam my man, give me trouble!" The implication is that Eve is willing to defy God in order to find sexual fulfillment. Several times, Eve says that Eden is "disgustin'" because in the garden she cannot develop her "personality"—which, when said in West's suggestive way, seems to imply her physical appetites. This impression is reinforced when she explains to the snake that she cannot get through the picket fence surrounding the tree because the spaces between the slats are too small for a woman of her "personality"—that is, her "womanly" figure.

It is implied by the script that Adam and Eve have not yet had sex. At one point Eve invites Adam to "C'mon over here." In the 1937 broadcast there was a meaningful pause at this point during which one can only imagine West vamping on the stage; in any case, at this point the audience, familiar with West's famous line "Come up and see me sometime," began to laugh. As Adam, however, Ameche acts oblivious. "What for?" he asks. "To hold hands?" Eve chuckles: "Oh, that old game? Can't ya think of somethin' new?"

In order to break free of Eden, Eve feeds Adam the forbidden fruit in the form of applesauce, and the couple is immediately "dispossessed." Eve is triumphant. When Adam asks, "Oh, Eve, what have you done?" she replies, "I've just made a little more history, that's all. I'm the first woman to have her own way, and a snake'll take the rap for it!" However, all is not lost. As a result of having eaten the applesauce, Adam is awakened to Eve's physical charms: "It's as if I see you for the first time," he says. "You're beautiful. Your eyes. Your lips. Come closer." The two then engage in what Eve calls the "Original Kiss," clearly connecting sexuality with the idea of "original sin."

The uproar caused by the *Chase & Sanborn* skit was immediate. Within a week, the Federal Communications Commission (FCC) ordered the National Broadcasting Company (NBC) to submit a copy of the skit's script for review, citing letters that it had received from listeners who described the sketch as profane, obscene, indecent, vulgar, filthy, dirty, insulting to the American public, and "sexy" (presumably in a bad way). The FCC ultimately sent a severe reprimand not only to NBC but also to the fifty-nine stations that had broadcast the program, calling the sketch "against all proprieties." For her part, West said that the FCC officials were not gentlemen; she complained that they were "letting a lady down." She also slyly blamed the controversy on the fact that boys at a Midwestern college had chosen to skip their evening prayer service in order to listen to the radio: "That started things popping," she said. "Not that I blame the minister for kicking. He thought I was going to be on the air every Sunday night and then where would his vespers [that is, evening prayers] have been?"[19]

One of the most striking aspects of the script is that it makes Eve the protagonist in the story. She initiates all of the action, and both Adam and the serpent merely respond to her. The author of the sketch, Arch Oboler, explained, "Instead of going on the premise that the snake tempted Eve, it occurred to me, since Miss West was such a dominant woman, to have Eve tempt the snake." In Oboler's vision, Eve is "a highly sophisticated, clever female who . . . induces the snake to do her bidding."[20] In fact, in the play, Eve convinces the snake (whom she calls "my palpitatin' python," another phallic allusion) to get her an apple by promising him that once she and Adam are evicted, the reptile will then have Paradise all to himself. The snake at first refuses: "But it's forbidden fruit." Eve taunts him, "Are you a snake or are you a mouse?" At that point the serpent agrees to do what she asks, but still he adds, "I shouldn't be doing this." Even he is reluctant to disobey God, and Eve must manipulate him into doing her bidding.

There are at least two ways to understand this presentation of Eve. The first is that she is a confident, mature woman who is in touch with her needs and is not shy about expressing and fulfilling them. The other is that she is a brazen hussy with no regard for the word of God or the teachings of religion. The FCC sided with the latter. And yet, there is evidence that the hullabaloo over the sketch may have been initiated and sustained mostly by a vocal minority. A Gallup poll taken two months after the incident found that when asked, "During the past year have you heard any broadcast that has offended you by its vulgarity?" only 15 percent answered yes. [21] Moreover, one source puts the number of initial complaints to the FCC at only four hundred, and makes the case that the letters sent to the FCC were not spontaneous outpourings of indignation but rather the orchestrated, preplanned response of the Legion of Decency, a reform group with largely Catholic roots. [22]

Therefore a Man Clings to His Wife

In the *Chase & Sanborn* skit, Adam and Eve are married. We know this because Eve at one point complains, "A couple of months of peace and security, and a woman's bored all the way down to the bottom of her marriage certificate." We also know it because when the serpent shows up, he offers salutations to "Mrs. Eve." This is true despite the fact that the biblical text itself never mentions a wedding, nor is it entirely clear that the first couple should be assumed to be married. Genesis 2:25 tells us, "And the man and his wife were both naked, and were not ashamed," and yet, the word that is translated as "wife" also means simply "woman." Biblical scholar Robert Alter translates the same passage this way: "And the two of them were naked, the human and his woman, and they were not ashamed."[23]

If the biblical text does not make it clear that the first man and woman were married, however, virtually every commentary since then has assumed that they were. Augustine asserted of marriage that "God instituted it from the beginning before man sinned, when He created them male and female."[24] The medieval Muslim text *The Tales of the Prophets* says that Adam only accepted Eve as his companion on the condition that God perform a wedding ceremony for the two of them: "And so Adam was married to Eve before entering Paradise."[25] A Jewish tradition likewise holds that God performed the first marriage ceremony in blessing the union of Adam and Eve, and that the angels Michael and Gabriel acted as Adam's best men.[26]

Fig Leaves (1926)

Indeed, many early mass-media presentations of the Genesis story also focused on marriage as a key component in the relationship between our first parents. Howard Hawks's 1926 movie *Fig Leaves* (which was notable not only for its use of the Genesis story but also because it included an early experiment with color) is a comedy about domestic life. The film begins in the Garden of Eden, where Adam wakes up to an alarm clock that triggers a coconut to fall on his head. Adam then reads the morning stone tablet at the breakfast table, and Eve muses about a sale on fig leaves. After Adam has gone off to work via brontosaurus, a friendly serpent visits Eve and explains to her that "men don't realize women must have pretty things." Then the scene shifts to modern New York; Adam is a plumber, Eve is again complaining that she does not have enough money to buy the clothes that she wants, and the serpent has been transformed into a lovely blonde who lives across the hall from the couple. Eve serendipitously meets a clothing designer named Josef André and, without Adam s permission, becomes a fashion model. She is so attracted to the revealing costumes she wears on the job that Adam complains, "A fig leaf would be an overcoat to you."[27] Indeed, the fashions in the movie are so risqué that *Variety* compared their effect to "the sex kick of a night club show." The newspaper hastily added, though, that "the undraped girls never offend, probably because the whole scene and its background, as well as the models who take part, are of breath-taking beauty." The scene in which Eve and her fellow models exhibit the latest clothing styles is shot in color; *Variety* described this portion of the movie as "the most elaborate (and most beautiful) fashion show the screen has shown this long time—if it has ever been equaled before is a question." According to the studio that released the picture, Eve's wardrobe cost $50,000, a figure that *Variety* did not dispute.[28]

In *Fig Leaves*, the original sin is associated primarily with consumer appetites and only secondarily with sex. At one point Adam says to Eve, "Ever since you ate that apple, you've had the gimmes—first twin beds and now clothes." What Eve longs for is not carnal pleasure but the acquisition of things. However, in the movie, as often occurs in life, money is inseparable from sex; it is also inseparable from power. As Jeanne Thomas Allen observes, the movie's comedy "is based on gender stereotypes and the threat of role reversal . . . female greed exceeding patriarchal loyalty."[29] When Eve takes a job outside of her home, she threatens

Adam's economic superiority, and by displaying her sexuality outside of the marital bedroom, she threatens her husband's control of her body. After he sees his wife modeling skimpy negligees, Adam complains to Eve that "every man's right is to respect his wife and not have her parade around half naked. You cared more for clothes than you did for me."[30] He is threatened both by the thought that she is not dependent on him for money and by the thought that she might offer herself sexually to another man. Indeed, much of the couple's marital strife stems from the fact that André is interested in Eve (though it is exacerbated by the fact that the blonde neighbor has her sights set on Adam). In the end, however, both Adam and Eve renounce their respective temptations, and at the conclusion of the film they are together again, though Eve is still complaining that she has nothing to wear.

One critic has described *Fig Leaves* as contemptuous of women for its portrayal of Eve as obsessed with clothing and fashion. The movie, says Vito Russo, author of *The Celluloid Closet*, is "typical of the kind of male celebration that saw women as mothers or mattresses and took great care to deny any feminine implication in the closeness of comrades." Though it plays with gender roles by portraying André as foppish and effeminate, it nonetheless affirms that men are to act masculine. As one of the male characters says of women, "Treat 'em rough, but don't kill 'em, you might need 'em fer something."[31] In 1926, the disturbing implications of this viewpoint did not seem to trouble reviewers; the *Washington Post* described Adam simply as "a stingy but otherwise lovable husband," and Eve as "a pretty wife who loves her husband and pretty things, too."[32] *Variety* described the movie as a "winner."

The Garden of Eden (1928)

In some ways, a film released two years later entitled *The Garden of Eden* had much in common with *Fig Leaves*. Both movies lured viewers with the promise of nudity and sexual license, and both delivered on their promise, at least to the extent that social mores of the time allowed. Both also affirmed that despite the temptations that modern life affords, women should satisfy their sexual appetites only in the marriage bed. The films differ significantly, though, in how they present the relationship between being married and being tempted by illicit sexual desire.

The Garden of Eden (1928) tells the story of a young Viennese singer named Toni who leaves home in order to seek fame and fortune in Budapest.[33] Instead of finding a job at an opera house, as she had dreamed she would, Toni ends up at a sleazy nightclub run by a masculine-looking woman named Madame Bauer who gazes at Toni's legs with frank sexual interest. Madame Bauer orders Toni to wear a revealing outfit ("Be sure to put her in the *Seemore* costume" she tells the cabaret's seamstress, a kindly old woman named Rosa), but Toni refuses to go out onto the stage in such scanty attire. Madame Bauer then tricks Toni into wearing a Puritan costume which, when lit from beneath, proves to be see-through. Humiliated by the ogling of the audience, Toni runs away with her only friend, the seamstress Rosa, who turns out to be a baroness in disguise. Rosa takes Toni to Monte Carlo, and there the two women check in to the Hotel Eden, a beautiful establishment with a lush garden on the grounds. In the hotel, Toni meets the man of her dreams, is wed in a Christian ceremony, and, presumably, lives happily ever after.

The movie offers an unusual perspective on the connection between Eden and sexuality. Toni is sexually naive when she first arrives in Budapest, and she is horrified by the sordid nightclub where she is expected to put her body on display. The Hotel Eden in Monte Carlo offers a stark contrast to such lewdness; Eden is a place of grace and refinement where Toni is able to meet a proper suitor, to get married, and only then to engage in sexual relations, which are symbolized by the "Do Not Disturb" sign hanging on the newlyweds' door. Paradise is imagined as true love that is sanctioned by society and religious authority and that expresses itself sexually only within those boundaries. The title of the movie, "The Garden of Eden," titillates viewers with the implication that they will see bare skin and sexual freedom portrayed on the big screen, and indeed, like *Fig Leaves*, the movie does not disappoint. Where it differs from its predecessor, however, is that it portrays marriage as the solution to the problem of unlawful sexual desire rather than its premise. In *Fig Leaves*, Adam and Eve face temptation despite their marital state. The serpent (that is, the blonde neighbor) crawls into the garden and there disrupts the couple's relationship. In *The Garden of Eden*, by contrast, the serpent (that is, the debauchery of the cabaret) threatens Toni before she enters Eden, and once she is safe within the walls of the Garden, she is no longer troubled by illicit sexual desires.

The Garden of Eden was made before the Motion Picture Production Code went into effect, and thus it was not subject to the kind of censorship that later movies would face. It includes scenes of scantily clad women dancing onstage, and it implies that the manager of the club not only is sexually attracted to her dancers but also acts as a procurer for the men who come to ogle them. At one point Madame Bauer describes Toni as "specially selected young Vienna squab—country style," and she locks the girl in a room with an interested customer. The only thing that saves Toni from the man's assault is the determination of Rosa, who breaks into the room and, in the confusion that ensues, manages to take Toni's place in the customer's arms. When he realizes that he has kissed the wrong woman, the would-be Lothario complains to Madame Bauer, "You promised me squab, but they served me seagull."

It is worth noting that *Fig Leaves* and *The Garden of Eden* are only two of many silent films about Adam and Eve. As early as 1912, a pair of movies was released with titles that evoked the Genesis story: *The Tree of Knowledge* and *Adam and Eve*. Three years later, *Children of Eve*, *The New Adam and Eve*, and *Forbidden Fruit* premiered. In 1916 two more films came out: *The Return of Eve* and *The Gates of Eden*. These were followed by *The Secret of Eve* and *The Garden of Knowledge* (which promoted eugenics), *The Sin Woman* (which traced both witches and vampires back to the sin of Eve), *The Curse of Eve*, and *The Warfare of the Flesh* (a morality tale which featured characters named Sinn and Goode) in 1917. That same year saw the release of a series of films called *The Seven Deadly Sins* which followed the moral missteps of two characters named Eve Leslie and Adam Moore. The films were titled *Passion*, *Sloth*, *Greed*, *Wrath*, *Pride*, *Envy*, and *The Seventh Sin*; apparently calling the last one "Gluttony" was considered too offensive.

The year 1918 was something of a banner year for films that made reference to Adam and Eve, with no fewer than seventeen films being released during that period. These included *Woman*, which looked at the changing position of women in history, *The Birth of a Race* (featuring a quick frontal shot of a nude Adam),[34] *Caino*, *Eve's Daughter*, and twelve short comedies all starring Eileen Molyneux, including *Eve Assists the Censor* and *Eve and the Nervous Curate*.[35] The following year saw the release of *A Daughter of Eve* and *The Woman Thou Gavest Me*. In 1920, William C. de Mille, older brother of the famous Cecil B. DeMille (C.B. slightly changed the spelling of the family name) directed *The Tree of Knowledge*; that same year, *Young Eve and Old Adam* premiered. The following year, *Ever Since Eve* and *Forbidden Fruit* were released, as well as a movie called *Eve's Leaves* that depicted the history of women's fashion.[36]

During the next few years there was a slowdown in films about the biblical text. A ten-part movie called *The Bible* was imported from Italy in 1922 which included "flashes of an undraped Adam and Eve that," opined *Variety*, "may give the censors a good deal of study."[37] In 1923 a version of *The Blue Lagoon* was released, as well as movies titled *Adam's Rib* and *Adam and Eva*. These were followed by *Eve's Secret* in 1925, all of which brings us back to 1926 and *Fig Leaves*.

Temptations

As we have seen, both *Fig Leaves* and *The Garden of Eden* portray sexual relations as the prerogative of married heterosexual couples. Other films, however, have used the Genesis story to explore less conventional arrangements.

. . . And God Created Woman (1956)

For example, in 1956, Brigitte Bardot created quite a stir with her portrayal of a promiscuous teenager on the beaches of St. Tropez in Roger Vadim's film . . . *And God Created Woman*. Indeed, the movie was so controversial that the Legion of Decency challenged its exhibition in every city in which it was released, and the city of Philadelphia forbade theaters to show the film.[38] In the movie, Bardot stars as Juliete, an orphaned teenager with the sensual seductiveness of a grown woman. The film opens with Juliete sunbathing nude in a backyard. An older man gets out of a car, approaches her, and says, "I brought the apple." When she asks, "Which apple?" he replies, "The forbidden fruit." This sets the tone for the complicated sexual pairings that shape the rest of the movie. Juliete, in order to avoid being sent back to an orphanage, must find a man to marry. She does marry, but she then also has sex with her husband's brother.

Throughout the film, Juliete is portrayed as consumed by her sexual hungers. The trailer for the movie promised viewers an eyeful: "Set in the pagan paradise of the French Riviera swirls the fast-moving, fascinating story of a demon-driven temptress who thought the future was invented only to spoil the present!" At various points Juliete is shown eating a banana and eating a carrot (both obvious references to fellatio) and playing with an umbrella that she holds between her legs. Director Vadim later described Bardot as suffering from none of the inhibitions that might have been expected of a girl who had been raised in a religious household (or what he called "the Judeo-Christian mishmash attached to the notion of pleasure"). Continued Vadim, "She was an Eve before God lost his temper in the Garden. She was an Eve particularly talented at making love, who seemed to know everything about it without ever having had to learn."[39]

. . . *And God Created Woman* was remade by Vadim in 1988 in a version starring Rebecca De Mornay as Robin, a prison inmate who marries a construction worker whom she barely knows in order to qualify for early parole. The movie has little in common with its predecessor, though it does feature a remarkable scene in which Robin has sex with the construction worker in the prison while wearing only tube socks. The only reference the 1988 version makes to the story of Adam and Eve can be found on the movie's promotional art. The advertisement for the film features De Mornay clad in a white dress and lying on what appears to be a white sofa. In a pose similar to that of Adam in Michelangelo's Sistine Chapel, De Mornay lazily lifts one hand up towards the sky, where her finger almost touches the finger of God. The tagline says, ". . . and on the Seventh Day, He got creative."

Forbidden Fruit (2002)

Other uses of the Adam and Eve story also explore nonmarital sexual relationships. For example, the Canadian movie *Adam & Eve*, released in the United States as *Forbidden Fruit*, centers on a young woman named Eve who seduces a Roman Catholic priest named Adam. Eve is a college student who sings in the local church choir. In the opening scene of the movie, the choir performs the hymn "Immaculate Mary," which sets up a contrast between the sinless Virgin Mary and the sinfully seductive Eve. Soon afterward, Eve acts on her budding attraction to Father Adam by kissing him. The priest protests, and Eve dares him to stop her. He says, "But I can't," and she replies, "I know you can't. You want me." Eventually the pair engages in sexual intercourse, but Adam remains ambivalent: "Our relationship cannot continue," he says, "I can't live with this sin." By the end of the film, however, Adam has changed his mind. He tells Eve, "I love you. I'm yours. If you want me," and he tells his bishop that he is resigning from the priesthood. In the last scene, Adam tells Eve that he is in love with her, and the two walk off hand in hand.

Forbidden Fruit also includes a third character, a young gay dancer named Jason. At times Jason appears to be Eve's friend, and at times he appears to work against her, as in a scene in which he attempts to sexually seduce Father Adam himself. Jason is, it seems, the serpent in the story, though his role and his motives remain unclear. What is clear, however, is that the story of Adam and Eve as it is presented in popular culture nearly always includes a third character who shakes up the couple's relationship and introduces new, sometimes frightening, possibilities into it. Often, that character is some version of the malevolent figure found in ancient Jewish literature called Lilith.

Three's a Crowd: Lilith

Connecting Adam and Eve's transgression with sexuality is a theological move that occurs almost exclusively in Christian thought. It should be noted that Judaism has by and large taken a very different approach and has refused to equate sex with sin. Early rabbinic thinking stressed that both marriage and sexuality were goods that belonged to the original creation rather than being concessions devised by God as a result of human sinfulness.[40] They are part of God's plan for how humans ought to live.

This is made clear in the Jewish practice of celebrating the Shabbat (Sabbath) by having sexual intercourse with one's spouse. Writes contemporary Orthodox rabbi Irving Greenberg, "It is a special Shabbat mitzvah [commandment/good deed] to make love on Friday night."[41] The Jewish Sabbath recalls the seventh day of creation, the day on which God rested after having made human beings and telling them to go forth and multiply. The world that God created was, God said, "very good," and making love on the Sabbath is seen by many as a celebration of that goodness.

And yet at the same time, in Jewish commentaries on Genesis, the sexual relationship between Adam and Eve is often complicated by a character referred to as Lilith. Lilith takes many forms. The Bible suggests that she is a demon who inhabits abandoned wastelands (see Isaiah 34:14). In the Talmud, she appears as a demon with long hair, a woman's face, and wings (see, for example, Tractate Niddah 24b). In some legends, Lilith is a demon who seduces Adam and then gives birth to male and female demons.

In the Middle Ages, a version of Lilith's story appeared in a Jewish text called the *Alphabet of Ben Sira*. The *Alphabet* says that Lilith was created by God just as Adam was. When God brought her to Adam, Adam told her, "You shall lie below"—that is, when the two of them had sex, she would have to lie beneath him. Lilith refused this proposition, arguing, "You shall lie below, for we are equal and both of us were [created] from earth." Lilith then flew off in a fury, and Adam complained to God. God sent three angels after the woman and told them to bring her back by force if necessary. The angels followed these directions and caught hold of Lilith in the Red Sea. There she said to them, "Darlings, I know myself that God created me only to afflict babies with fatal disease when they are eight days old." She refused to return with God's envoys, but after further arguing, she finally agreed that she would leave newborns alone if they were wearing amulets inscribed with the names of the three angels.[42] The custom of providing babies with protective amulets to ward off the malevolence of Lilith was already widespread by the time the *Alphabet* was written, and it continued well into the eighteenth century.[43]

The horror movie *Sinful* (2006) picks up on the image of Lilith as an evil woman obsessed with babies. The plot features a young woman named Lilith who is unable to conceive a child. Sinking into madness, she befriends her pregnant next-door neighbor and contrives to steal the woman's infant. The fact that the cover-art features a drawing of a girl holding a sharp knife, and the fact that the movie was released by "Shock-O-Rama Cinema" tells you all that you need to know about what happens next.

Portrayals of Lilith as an evil monster abound. The 2007 movie *Succubus: Hell-Bent* tells the story of Adam, a college student who travels to Mexico for spring break and has a one-night stand with a beautiful woman named Lilith. ("I prefer to be on top," Lilith tells Adam, a line that recurs throughout the movie.) Little does Adam know that Lilith is actually a demon; when he rejects her the next day, Lilith decides to wreak revenge. She follows Adam back to Los Angeles and embarks on a series of grisly murders and implicates him in the process.

In a similar vein, the *Witchouse* trilogy (1999, 2000, 2001) features a witch named Lilith who was burned at the stake in the seventeenth century and who returns from the grave to get revenge on the descendants of the Puritans who killed her. The long-running British science fiction series *Dr. Who* also invoked the Jewish legend in a 2007 episode in which

Lilith was the leader of a group called the Carrionite Witches (carrion, of course, means the decaying flesh of a dead body) who were attempting to invade the Earth. In the director's commentary on the avant-garde short film *Inauguration of the Pleasure Dome* (1954), Kenneth Anger describes Lilith as a "female demon of discontent."[44]

Often Lilith is portrayed less as a demon and more as a sexual temptress. She is the "other woman" who threatens the domestic bliss of Adam and Eve. For example, Martha Graham's ballet titled "Embattled Garden" features four characters: Adam, Eve, a serpent-like character named The Stranger, and Lilith. As the dance begins, Lilith sits at the base of a tree in which lounges The Stranger. Eve combs her own hair as Adam watches. Then:

> As Adam surveys the scene, The Stranger slides down the tree with a back roll across the floor, approaches Paradise, kisses Eve. She is retrieved by Adam, but he is overcome by The Stranger and collapses, seemingly inept, befuddled, very young. Lilith circles Paradise, enters it, goes first to Eve and then kisses Adam who is awakened. The Stranger then dances a brilliant demonic solo of exultation that seems to be a forecast of events to come.[45]

During the course of the ballet, the innocence of Adam and Eve is taken from them by the ministrations of Lilith and The Stranger. The Stranger dances with Eve, and Lilith plaits Eve's free-flowing tresses, an action which symbolizes the loss of Eve's girlhood and virginity. Adam and Eve quarrel, and Adam drags Eve across the stage by her newly bound hair. As one reviewer explains, "By the end, we know considerable damage has been done. Adam and Eve will never be the same after this encounter."[46] Once Lilith intervenes, sex loses its innocence.

The Private Lives of Adam and Eve (1960)

Much the same dynamic occurs in the 1960 movie *The Private Lives of Adam and Eve*. Directed by Mickey Rooney, the movie was severely criticized by various watchdog agencies even before it was released. To be fair, any movie about Adam and Eve would have faced an uphill battle. As early as 1920, a movie version of the Bible was excoriated by the Vatican because it showed Adam and Eve naked. According to one report, Pope Benedict XV was so shocked at what he saw at a special Vatican screening of *The Holy Bible* that he tried to have the film destroyed. In the end, he had to settle for issuing a proclamation forbidding Catholics from seeing the picture.[47] Prior to Rooney's project, the Production Code Administration (PCA) had already rejected several proposed films because of the nudity inherent in the Genesis story. When the PCA saw the first cut of *Private Lives*, it objected to the character Lilith's costume because it showed her navel. Then the National Legion of Decency weighed in, protesting that certain shots of Eve made it appear as if she were naked. The Legion gave the movie a "Condemned" rating because, it said, it was "blasphemous and sacrilegious in its presentation of man's sex life as the invention of the devil, rather than the handiwork of God."[48]

In response to this hail of criticism, Producer Albert Zugsmith edited the movie, though in the process he ended up with what *Variety* described as a work "less morally objectionable than artistically chaotic."[49] Zugsmith took care to emphasize via a new prologue that the movie was no more than "a pipe dream, a fantasy, a fable" that took place "once upon a time, not too many years from now." That way he could distance himself from critics who felt that he was taking too many liberties with sacred scripture.

Despite the movie's numerous failings, which include corny costuming and scenery, the movie actually contains a remarkable theological perspective. The plot is fairly simple. It begins on a bus to Reno that stops in the dusty little town of Paradise. There the bus picks up several passengers, including two couples: a gambler named Nick and his wife Lil, and a young woman named Evie and her husband, a strapping fellow named Ad. Apparently there has been trouble in Paradise, as both couples are on their way to Reno to get divorced. Lil has been seen making out with Ad, and Nick has been making moves on Evie.

As the bus heads toward Reno, a storm blows up and wipes out a bridge. The bus driver and his passengers are forced to take refuge in a nearby church where they argue about theology as the storm rages outside. Eventually they all succumb to weariness, and Ad and Evie fall asleep. As soon as they nod off, scenes of the creation of the world explode on the screen: collisions between planets, great gaseous eruptions, and balls of fire streaking across the sky. A deep male voice intones, "God created the heaven and the earth. He created man. He created woman to place alongside of man. And what the Almighty did was good. And God created love, and sex, and these were the work of his hands." The voice continues, "The devil in hell saw what God had wrought, and he tempted man."

Then God's new human creation appears. Adam (played by Martin Milner, who also plays Ad) wears a loincloth and lies in a fetal position in a garden. Gradually he uncurls himself and laughs. He tastes his fingers, feels his limbs, and takes his first faltering steps. He is an infant in Paradise, delighted with everything he sees and smells. He goes about the garden naming all the animals in alphabetical order: Alligator, Ant, Anteater, Bear. However, Satan (played by Rooney himself, who also plays the gambler Nick) wants to disrupt God's plans. He sends Lilith (who is dressed in a short-sleeved leotard and is played by the same actress who plays Nick's wife Lil) to tempt Adam. Lilith tries to get Adam to eat from the forbidden tree in the garden by telling him that it "helps you learn all about evil and how good it is." She is unsuccessful in her seduction, however.

Seeing the danger that Lilith poses to Adam, God provides the man with a more fitting companion: Eve (played of course by the actress who plays Evie). Adam instructs Eve not to eat from the apple tree, but Eve is lonely and resents Adam's closeness with God. Thus, when Satan shows up, Eve is eager for his company. Satan advises Eve to eat the forbidden apples, and she complies; at that instant, thunder and lightning crash through the sky. Adam runs to Eve and embraces her, and when Eve hands him an apple, he eats as well. The two are then expelled from the garden.

The story does not end there, however. Satan and Lilith are still working hard to break the couple up through various temptations. Lilith shows off her bikini-clad body to Adam as she showers in a nearby waterfall, and she caresses Adam's chest as she listens to his woes. Meanwhile, Satan hints to Eve that Adam is returning Lilith's affections. When Eve investigates for herself and finds her husband at Lilith's abode, she throws fruit at him and storms off.

What follows is a remarkable scene in which Eve speaks to God of her despair: "If only you'd have spoken to me!" she sobs. "I'm sorry I lost the garden for him. I'm sorry I spoiled your plan. I know there's nothing I can do, but I am sorry. Please forgive me. Can you forgive me? Oh, why don't you speak to me?" The scene is distinctive in its attempt to present Eve sympathetically as a woman who seeks the same intimacy with God that her husband has. Her eating the fruit, we come to see, is the result not of sexual desire or even pride, but of her longing for God. God's answer to Eve is a clap of thunder that causes Eve to clutch at her belly. She has just conceived her first child. God has heard her prayer and has given her a baby as compensation.

At that moment the dream ends. Ad gently shakes Evie awake in order to tell her that the storm is over. When Evie begins to describe her dream, he indicates that he had the same experience—and so, we understand, it was not merely a dream at all. As the movie ends, Ad and Evie are reunited in their love for each other, and they will now share that love with a child. Evie's pregnancy is confirmed when she voices a sudden craving for "some strawberries or ice cream or, how 'bout a great big dill pickle?"

For his part, Nick/Satan will have to look elsewhere in his search for followers. Speaking the final line of the movie, he looks up at the church where the group had spent the night and says, "I oughta have known the odds'd be all with the house." Meanwhile, Lil/Lilith walks arm in arm with another passenger from the bus—a lingerie salesman—saying to him, "C'mon, Sweetie, let's go." Having failed in her seduction of Ad/Adam, she is moving on to more promising prospects.

In popular culture, there is a long history of giving the name of Lilith, Lil, or Lola to women of questionable virtue.[50] We have already noted that Mae West's title character in *Diamond Lil* (1928) was deemed a "scarlet woman" by the critics. In 1932, Jean Harlow starred as a black-mailer named Lil in *Red-Headed Woman*; that film was considered to be so indecent that the head of the Hollywood PCA pulled it from circulation in 1934 and ordered that the studio never re-release it.[51] In *Satan's Cradle* (1949) Lil is a swindler; in the 1958 movie *Damn Yankees*, Lola is an employee of the devil (who in a nod to the Genesis story is named Mr. Applegate), and she sings a song entitled "Whatever Lola Wants, Lola Gets"; in *Gaily, Gaily* (1969) Queen Lil runs a brothel; in *Darling Lili* (1970), the title character is a music hall singer who is also a German spy. In *Islands in the Stream* (1977) Lil is a hooker; in *Johnny Dangerously* (1984) she is a torch singer; in *Coyote Ugly* (2000) she owns a bar. The children's cartoon *Rugrats* (1991–2004) featured a character named Lil DeVille who ate worms and drank from a toilet—though to be fair, her twin brother Phil did the same thing. Perhaps the most notorious use of the name occurred in the 1963 nudie film *The Orgy At Lil's Place*. Promotional posters invited viewers to "See the wild, wild parties of 'Sex Sophisticates'!"; to "See beautiful girls wrestling!"; to "See the strip dice game!"; and to "See passions run riot!" The movie promised to be "Like nothing—but nothing you've seen before—*EVER!*"

Of course not every Lil is shady, but frequently the name is used to signal that we should be wary of a character. The TV show *Frasier*, for example, portrayed radio personality Frasier Crane as perpetually cowed by his brainy and severe ex-wife Lilith Sternin. Lilith, a psychiatrist like her former husband, always wore her dark hair pulled back into a tight bun, and she spoke in a monotone. In one episode of the show, she introduced herself to a fellow passenger on an airplane. Hearing her name, the man said, "Ah, the demon goddess!" and asked if she were anything like her menacing predecessor. To this Lilith replied, "I make her look like a vacillating cream puff."[52]

Lilith (1964)

The 1964 movie *Lilith* pulls together many of these themes surrounding the myth of Adam's first wife. The film stars Warren Beatty as a returning soldier named Vincent who takes a job at an upscale mental institution. There he meets Lilith (Jean Seberg), a young woman who has been diagnosed with schizophrenia. Vincent falls in love with his patient, but the relationship between them has disastrous consequences; nothing good, after all, can come from a woman named Lilith.

First, Lilith is a sexual temptress who ignores all boundaries and proprieties. She is attracted to Vincent, but she also has sex with one of the women in the institution, and she kisses and fondles a little boy with what looks like sexual hunger.

Second, the movie depicts Lilith not just as sexually ravenous but also as dangerous. At several points she is compared to a spider. For example, the opening credits appear against a background showing a butterfly caught in a spider's web. Later, the doctor who runs the institution gives a lecture to his staff and explains that schizophrenia can actually be induced in some animals, including dogs and spiders; the affected spiders, he says, weave webs with "fantastic, asymmetrical, and rather nightmarish designs." Shortly after the lecture, Lilith is shown sitting at a loom and weaving her own hair into a blanket for Vincent.

Lilith is a schemer and seducer who destroys anyone who wanders into her web. During one scene she looks at her own reflection in the surface of a stream and says, "She wants to be like me. She's lovely. My kisses kill her. She's like all of them. It destroys them to be loved." Later Lilith tells Vincent that before she entered the institution, she had tried to seduce her brother, and that he had died as a result: "I didn't kill my brother," she says. "He jumped. Jumped because he didn't dare to love me. I wanted him to. I wanted him to."

However, for all of her dangerous qualities, the Lilith of this movie also has an otherworldly quality that attracts and fascinates. Like the Lilith of legend, she seems to have supernatural powers. She speaks and writes a language that is all her own, and she compares herself to God. Looking at Vincent, she notes that as a soldier, he has killed with his hands: "You must love your god a great deal to kill for him and still go on loving him. I'd never ask that of a lover. I'd only ask his joy." The movie suggests that perhaps Lilith has had a more intimate experience of God than the rest of us; the doctor who runs the hospital explains that schizophrenics are like "fine crystal which has been shattered by the shock of some intoler-able revelation." He continues, "They have been close to some extreme. To something absolute and been blasted by it." The doctor concludes, "Regarded in this way, they are the heroes of the universe."

"The Coming of Lilith" (1979)

It is this aspect of Lilith, her bravery and independence in the face of what society and religion consider "normal," that has been the focus of much contemporary feminist scholarship. One of the most provocative articulations of Lilith-as-hero was published in 1979 by Jewish theologian Judith Plaskow. Titled "The Coming of Lilith: Toward a Feminist Theol-ogy," Plaskow's essay reimagines the Genesis story. In Plaskow's version, Adam is a chauvinist who orders Lilith about by telling her to fetch his figs for him and to do all of his daily chores. When Lilith decides that she has had enough of Adam's bullying and she leaves, Adam complains to God, "'Well now, Lord, that uppity woman you sent me has gone and deserted me.'" God tries to get Lilith to return but is unsuccessful, and so instead God creates Eve to be Adam's companion. Eve is more or less satisfied with being Adam's wife and helper, but she resents the closeness between Adam and God. She observes that "Adam and God just seemed to have more in common, both being men, and Adam came to identify with God more and more." One day Eve decides to climb an apple tree whose branches extend over the garden wall, and from her perch, she spies Lilith. At first she is afraid because Adam has told her horror stories about his first wife—how she was a demon who wanted to kill children. Soon, however, Eve realizes that she has nothing to fear from the strong and beautiful Lilith, and the two women become friends. They share their stories and they teach each other skills. Then, concludes Plaskow, "God and Adam were expectant and afraid the day Eve and Lilith returned to the garden, bursting with possibilities, ready to rebuild it together."[53]

The idea that God would be afraid of women's power might seem shocking. Plaskow's point is that religion has for too long created God in the image of man. That is, male-dominated religions have portrayed both God and men as having "superior" qualities, and they have denigrated the characteristics that society often associates with women. Reflecting on her version of the Garden of Eden story, Plaskow explains "Lilith is not a demon; rather she is a woman named a demon by a tradition that does not know what to do with strong women."[54]

Celebrating the strength and creativity of women was the point of singer-songwriter Sarah McLachlan's founding of the "Lilith Fair." This music festival ran during the summers of 1997–1999 and featured women artists such as Shawn Colvin, Queen Latifah, Emmylou Harris, and the Indigo Girls. The title "Lilith Fair" was chosen because, as the fair's spokesperson explained, Lilith was a woman who sought equality and independence.[55] The name did raise some eyebrows, however. When the Lilith Fairs began, the editor of Christian fundamentalist Jerry Falwell's newspaper opined that the fair's title was "having a negative impact when it's linking itself to a demon culture." Lilith, said the editor, "mated with demons and had a demonic brood of children, according to her legend. That is dangerous, and parents need to know that."[56]

Adam and Steve

All of the cultural expressions of the Genesis story that we have examined thus far focus on relations between men and women, whether married or unmarried. In American society, however, the biblical text is also at the center of discussions of homosexual relationships. For some, the creation story is a clear indictment of such unions. One can buy T-shirts, mugs, and even baby clothes that bear the slogan "God made Adam and Eve, not Adam and Steve." By way of reply, one can also purchase merchandise that says, "Actually, God did make Adam & Steve . . . And everybody else, too" as well as "Adam and Steve" cake toppers for gay weddings.

Big Eden (2000)

Only a few movies have taken on the theme of lesbian and gay relationships in the context of Adam and Eve. *Big Eden* is a romantic comedy that won audience awards at the Los Angeles Gay and Lesbian Film Festival, the San Francisco International Lesbian and Gay Film Festival, the Seattle Lesbian and Gay Film Festival, and the Toronto Inside Out Lesbian and Gay Film and Video Festival. When it premiered commercially, however, the movie was shown in only eight theaters nationwide, and since its release in 2000 it has grossed only a little more than half a million dollars. It is not, then, a "mainstream" film, though it is widely available on DVD.[57]

Big Eden tells the story of Henry Hart, a successful artist who lives in New York. When his grandfather in Montana has a stroke, Henry returns to the town of Big Eden to care for the old man. There Henry reunites with a cast of quirky characters that includes his best friend from high school, who is named Dean. Henry has been in love with Dean since the two of them were teenagers; unfortunately, however, Dean does not reciprocate the sexual aspect of the attraction. Though he loves Henry, after the two share a passionate kiss, Dean concludes simply, "I can't."

Henry has never told his grandfather, a crusty character named Sam, of his sexual orientation, though it is clear that Sam is aware of it. In one conversation with Henry, Sam tries to get his grandson to talk about his plans for the future. Where does Henry want to make a home for himself? Will he go back to New York or stay in Big Eden? When Henry attempts to divert the conversation, Sam does not relent. He muses that he will be dying soon and that he hopes to be reunited with Henry's grandmother in heaven. There, he says, he wants to be able to look his wife in the eye and tell her that he did his best to give Henry a sense of how loved he is:

> I feel like maybe we taught you something wrong because—you won't tell me . . . who you are. Did we teach you shame? Did I teach you that? Because it would break my heart if I had. Can't you see what a good job God did here? Can't you see how beautiful he made you?

Sam's speech is a clear, if not explicit, refutation of the idea that "God did not make Adam and Steve." In Sam's view, God made Henry just as he is, and Sam is dismayed that Henry cannot see how much God and the people of Big Eden love him. Even with so open an invitation to speak, however, Henry cannot bring himself to tell his grandfather that he is gay.

In the movie, Henry's sexual attraction to Dean is not consummated. As it happens, however, love is waiting in the wings for Henry in the form of Pike Dexter, a Native American who owns the local general store. Pike has fallen in love with Henry, but he is so shy that the only way he feels comfortable expressing his affection is by cooking food for Henry's grandfather. For his part, Henry is determined to return to New York where some of his paintings have recently been purchased by the Whitney Museum of American Art. It takes the good-natured conspiring of practically the entire town of Big Eden to get Pike and Henry together at last.

Big Eden is a fantasy of what life would be like if everyone were accepting of love and sexual attraction between same-sex couples. In this sense it is perhaps not a realistic portrayal of American society. As Roger Ebert observes, the movie takes place in Montana, "the same Montana that's next door to Wyoming, where a gay man named Matthew Shepard was murdered not long ago." Reflecting on the locals who hang around Big Eden's general store and who connive to bring Pike and Henry together, Ebert writes, "I doubt that in the real world all six of these bewhiskered, pipe-puffing, jeans-wearing, cowboy-hatted old cowboys would be cheerleaders for a gay romance."[58] No such doubts trouble *Big Eden*, however. Even the local minister preaches only "God's single message of love," adding that "there are no limits or boundaries or constraints on our ability to spread his love."

Adam & Steve (2005)

In contrast to *Big Eden*, the 2005 romantic comedy *Adam & Steve* contains much more evidence of public disapproval of gay relationships. The plot concerns two men named, not surprisingly, Adam and Steve. At the beginning of the film, the two meet at a 1980s nightclub and share some cocaine. They then head home for a night of hot sex, but the evening is spoiled when the cocaine causes the contents of the men's stomachs to erupt in ways better left undescribed. Seventeen years later, Adam and Steve run into one another once again and begin dating but do not realize that they had met before.

Throughout the film, the characters encounter frequent and some-times violent expressions of disapproval of their love and sexual attrac-tion for each other. One neighbor in particular is quite vocal with his opinions, yelling, "God made Adam and Eve, not Adam and Steve!" Toward the end of the movie, after the two lovers have gone through the same ups and downs in their relationship that make up the plot of any romantic comedy (boy meets boy, boy loses boy, boy gets boy), Steve finally confronts the neighbor who has been taunting him throughout the film. After beating him up, he forces the man to say that God did, in fact, make Adam and Steve: "Because here we are." In the end, Adam and Steve marry one another in a wedding attended by their family, friends, and the formerly hostile neighbor.

Like *Big Eden*, *Adam & Steve* did not make much money. It premiered on only seventeen screens and grossed less than a third of a million dollars during its run. Those numbers stand in stark contrast to the box-office earnings of the 2005 blockbuster *Brokeback Mountain*, which portrayed two Wyoming cowboys whose love for each other ends in heartbreak and death. *Brokeback* opened on 683 screens and at one point was showing in over two thousand theaters. Worldwide, it grossed over $178 million. Though of course one cannot conclude too much from these numbers, one might suspect that America is comfortable with cinematic gay ro-mances only if the couple in question does not live happily ever after.

This disinclination to sanction same-sex relationships often has re-ligious roots. Though many Christian groups, including some United Church of Christ, Episcopal, Unitarian Universalist, and Presbyterian churches, as well as some Reform and Conservative Jewish congregations, bless same-sex unions, many other religious communities do not. Nota-bly, the Roman Catholic Church remains opposed to any homosexual activity.

In order to understand the Catholic Church's position, it is first nec-essary to distinguish between "homosexuality" and homosexual activity. In 2003 the American Catholic Bishops' Committee on Marriage and Family issued a statement called *Always Our Children: A Pastoral Message to Parents of Homosexual Children and Suggestions for Pastoral Ministers*. The document describes sexual orientation as "a deep-seated dimension of one's personality" and defines homosexual orientation as "a stronger emotional and sexual attraction toward individuals of the same sex, rather than toward those of the opposite sex." It continues, "Generally, homosexual orientation is experienced as a given, not as something freely chosen. By itself, therefore, a homosexual orientation cannot be considered sinful, for morality presumes the freedom to choose."[59] *Always Our Children* then explains why the Catholic Church considers homosexual activity (as opposed to homosexual orientation, or homosexuality) to be sinful: "First, it is God's plan that sexual intercourse occur only within marriage between a man and a woman. Second, every act of intercourse must be open to the possible creation of human life."[60]

The 2003 *Catechism of the Catholic Church* likewise describes homosexual acts as "contrary to the natural law" because they "close the sexual act to the gift of life" and "do not proceed from a genuine affective and sexual complementarity." The importance of this complementarity is inferred from Genesis 1:27, which says that God created human beings "male and female."[61]

It is important to point out that in the *Catechism*'s view, homosexual acts are far from the only sexual activities that are contrary to natural law. The *Catechism* also designates as "morally disordered" any sexual pleasure that is "sought for itself, isolated from its procreative and unitive purposes," and it thus calls masturbation "an intrinsically and gravely disordered action." Nonmarital sexual activity such as fornication (that is, sex between an unmarried man and an unmarried woman) is described as "gravely contrary to the dignity of persons and of human sexuality"; pornography is "a grave offense," as is prostitution.[62] The use of artificial methods of birth control is prohibited, and "techniques that entail the dissociation of husband and wife, by the intrusion of a person other than the couple (donation of sperm or ovum, surrogate uterus), are gravely immoral."[63] Thus homosexual acts are part of a long list of sexual activities that the Church sees as sinful.

It is also important to point how much of the *Catechism*'s objection to homosexual activity rests not on biblical interpretation but rather on an interpretation of the workings of nature. When the *Catechism* describes homosexual acts as "contrary to the natural law," it is invoking not biblical revelation but a sense that what is "right" can be determined by observing the natural world. This is a very old tradition in Catholic thinking. In the thirteenth century, for example, Thomas Aquinas considered the question of whether or not "generation by coition" would have existed in the Garden of Eden. He answers that it would have, because "generation by coition is natural to man by reason of his animal life, which he possessed even before sin."[64] In other words, animals reproduce by sexual means, and so Adam and Eve, just like other creatures, would have done likewise.

Much of the argument about the morality of homosexual acts, then, rests on the question of whether or not those acts are in accordance with God's will as it has been revealed in nature. Both *Big Eden* and *Adam & Steve* make the case that for some people, being gay is precisely what God intended. When in *Big Eden* Sam asks Henry, "Can't you see what a good job God did here? Can't you see how beautiful he made you?" he is making an appeal to natural law; because Sam believes that Henry is naturally gay (that is, God made him that way), being homosexual is, in his view, as good as is being heterosexual.

At this point, readers may be wondering what the point of all of these different portrayals of Adam and Eve is. What difference does it make? After all, it's all just speculation, right? But in fact, it makes a tremendous difference how we interpret the story. Whether we believe that Genesis describes what really happened a long time ago, or that it is a myth expressing a religious worldview, the story and our interpretations of it tell us how we think life "ought" to be. Is sex a good and blessed thing, or is it merely a consolation prize to ease our fears of death? Is erotic passion a gift or a curse? Should we express our sexuality only with partners of a different sex, and only within the bonds of marriage? Or are sexual relations a valid way of expressing love outside of those limits? How do we view our bodies and their needs and their functions—as a burden or as a delight, or both?

CHAPTER FIVE

The Curse of Adam

In popular culture, possibly the only topic more interesting than sex is death. We are curious about mortality even as we fear it, and this fact helps explain the enduring appeal of murder-mystery novels, hospital TV shows, violent video games, and horror films. It may also explain in part the hold that the Genesis story has on the popular imagination. The dramatic tension in that tale, after all, comes from God's prediction (or is it a threat?) that on the day that Adam eats of the forbidden fruit, the man will die.

Theologians differ quite a bit in their opinions about the relation between Adam's disobedience and death. Some hold that our first parents would have died even if they had remained in the Garden—that death is simply a natural part of being human and thus should not be thought of as a punishment. Others insist that Adam and Eve would have been immortal if they had only listened to their creator and not eaten that fruit. For these thinkers, death can be described as "the curse of Adam."

In this chapter we will look at death to see how religious traditions regarding this "curse" have shaped contemporary pop culture. Before we begin to look at the consequences of Adam's disobedience, though, we should pause to consider the word "curse." In the Bible, the word means primarily "an utterance intended to harm."[1] To pronounce someone to be "cursed," therefore, is not merely to describe him or her. Instead, a curse is performative; it enacts a change in the one who is cursed, or at the very least it enacts a change in the relationship between the one who curses and the one who is cursed.

Thus, for example, in the Genesis story, when God finds out what the serpent has done, God says that the reptile is more cursed than all of the cattle and all of the beasts of the field (3:14). This cursing involves a pun; previously, the serpent had been described as more crafty (*arum*) than the other animals, and now he is more cursed (*arur*) than the others. Thus, as biblical scholar Phyllis Trible observes, "A wordplay has transformed cunning into curse."[2] God's curse actually causes a change in the serpent; as a result of its actions and God's anger, the snake must now crawl on its belly.

It is interesting to note that this description of the serpent's newly imposed means of transportation has led numerous interpreters to wonder how the serpent traveled previous to its transgression. One Muslim tradition says that the serpent originally walked upright and was shaped like a camel, with a multicolored tail and a mane of pearl.[3] In Christian paintings, the serpent is sometimes portrayed as a salamander with the head of a woman or girl. In the Middle Ages, salamanders were thought to poison the wells and the fruit trees in which they lived, so it would have made sense to place a salamander in the forbidden tree of Eden.[4]

Whatever the serpent may have looked like when it talked with Adam and Eve, the story says that it would henceforth crawl on its belly till the end of its days. Significantly, the serpent is the only one of the trio, though, that God curses directly. True, the man is cursed indirectly; God says to him, "Cursed is the ground because of you." However, God never says, "Cursed are you, Adam." And when speaking to the woman, God does not use the word "curse" at all. Nevertheless, tradition and popular culture have handed on the idea that death is the curse of Adam.

Death

When God learns that Adam has listened to the voice of the woman and has eaten of the forbidden tree, God says to him, "By the sweat of your face you shall eat bread until you return to the ground, for out of it you were taken; you are dust, and to dust you shall return" (Genesis 3:19). There is something puzzling about this text. Earlier, God had told the man that he must not eat from the forbidden tree, "for in the day that you eat of it you shall die" (2:17). It would seem, then, that God had been predicting an immediate demise for the man should he disobey. And yet, once Adam does eat, God simply tells him that he will have to work hard for his bread *until* he dies. Moreover, that death turns out to be a long way off, as the Bible says that Adam lived to the age of 930 years (Genesis 5:5). What accounts for this apparent change of plan?

There are several ways of interpreting what seems like a contradiction in the text, and below we will explore four of them. Though they will be listed separately, at times the interpretations overlap, and one might find two or more of them within the same work. In each case, we will begin by examining theological texts and then move to see how each interpretation manifests itself in movies, novels, and television shows.

Interpretation #1: God Did Not Speak the Truth

According to the Genesis story, the serpent asks Eve if God had ordered her and the man not to eat from any tree in the garden. She answers that they were permitted to eat from all of the trees except the one in the center, and that from that one they were forbidden lest they die. (She also adds that she and the man may not even touch the tree, a detail not contained in God's original statement.) Hearing this response, the serpent corrects her. He contends, "You will not die; for God knows that when you eat of it your eyes will be opened, and you will be like God, knowing good and evil" (3:4–5).

At least part of what the serpent predicts comes true. When they eat the fruit, Adam and Eve do find that their eyes are opened (3:7). Given that the serpent was right about that fact, perhaps he was right about death as well—perhaps God was mistaken about what would occur. Or, perhaps God was exaggerating the threat in order to protect the man, the way that one might tell a child to keep away from a stove even when it is not turned on. Or, perhaps God simply lied.[5]

This last possibility was, as we saw in chapter 3, the opinion of some early Christians known as Gnostics. Given their emphasis on attaining wisdom, it makes sense that for at least some Gnostics, the serpent was the hero of the Genesis story. The serpent, after all, was the one who offered knowledge to the first humans. God, on the other hand, was understood by the Gnostics to be an inferior and jealous being:

But of what sort is this God? First [he] maliciously refused Adam from eating of the tree of knowledge. And secondly he said, "Adam, where are you?" God does not have foreknowledge; (otherwise), would he not know from the beginning? [And] afterwards he said, "Let us cast him [out] of this place, lest he eat of the tree of life and live for ever." Surely he has shown himself to be a malicious grudger. And what kind of a God is this?[6]

As this excerpt from *The Testimony of Truth* shows, for some ancient Gnostic thinkers, the creator God was not to be trusted.

In this respect, the writings of the ancient Gnostics had much in common with the contemporary fantasy trilogy by Philip Pullman entitled *His Dark Materials*. Pullman's complex story focuses on a young girl named Lyra who is destined, as some of the characters explain, to become a second Eve. Lyra lives in a world that Pullman describes as "like ours, but different."[7] For example, in Lyra's world people's souls are called dæmons and appear in physical form in the shapes of animals.

Like her foremother Eve, Lyra will be faced with a decision, the outcome of which will affect the very constitution of the universe. In the eyes of the religious authorities of her world (whom the novels call "the Magisterium" or "the Church"), Lyra must be prevented from making the same choice that Eve did—she must be prevented from choosing knowledge over ignorance. In their effort to head off what they see as a second Fall of humanity, the leaders of the Magisterium dispatch a priest to kill Lyra.

At issue for both the Church and for Lyra is the existence of a substance called "Dust" which the Church sees as the physical evidence of original sin.[8] In Lyra's world, Dust does not cling to children until they reach puberty. The Church reasons that if they can separate children from their dæmons before adolescence, they can prevent original sin from affecting the youth. Therefore the Church develops a process called "intercision" to remove children's dæmons. As one character explains to Lyra,

All that happens is a little cut, and then everything's peaceful. Forever! You see, your dæmon's a wonderful friend and companion when you're young, but at the age we call puberty, the age you're coming to very soon, darling, dæmons bring all sort of troublesome thoughts and feelings, and that's what lets Dust in. A quick little operation before that, and you're never troubled again.[9]

The problem is that once people are separated from their souls, they can live only a semi-human existence. True, they are spared the difficulties that come with freedom, but the price they pay for their "happiness" is the capacity to make adult moral decisions. Without their souls, people have neither imagination nor free will.[10]

Thus, as Lyra comes to realize, Dust is not really an evil but is rather something "to be sought and welcomed and cherished."[11] Therefore, Lyra concludes, the Magisterium has not told her the truth, and it is not to be trusted. The Church, she realizes, wants people to be humble and submit to its power rather than to learn to be wiser and stronger.[12] Moreover, the God whom the Magisterium serves, who is known variously as The Authority, the Creator, Yahweh, El, Adonai, and the Almighty, is apparently uninterested in the welfare of human beings. This "God," as Lyra learns, is not really a god at all. He is simply an angel who in his younger days thirsted for power and therefore did everything he could to keep people ignorant. By the time Lyra discovers him, the angel has grown old and is merely a helpless and demented creature who cries like a baby and cowers in a corner when he is confronted.[13]

Nonetheless, the Church that worships this "God" uses every means at its disposal to keep people from seeing the truth. In particular, its leaders fight desperately to keep Lyra and her (significantly named) young friend Will from acquiring wisdom. Ultimately, the Church is defeated, as Lyra "falls" just as Eve did. In one of the final scenes of Pullman's trilogy, Lyra and Will go on a picnic and take with them a bundle filled with bread and cheese and "sweet, thirst-quenching red fruits." Stopping to rest by a stream, the children unpack their food and eat: "Then Lyra took one of those little red fruits. With a fast-beating heart, she turned to him and said, 'Will. . .' And she lifted the fruit gently to his mouth."[14] Once again, Eve feeds knowledge to her Adam, and humanity is, in the eyes of the novel at least, the better for it.

Concerning the Adam-and-Eve imagery that permeates his three books, Philip Pullman explains that in his view, the "fall" of human beings into freedom is not something to be feared or regretted: "The Fall is something that happens to all of us when we move from childhood through adolescence to adulthood and I wanted to find a way of presenting it as something natural and good, and to be welcomed, and, you know—celebrated, rather than deplored."[15] When asked his views about God, Pullman describes the deity as "a character in fiction, and a very interesting one too: one of the greatest and most complex villains of all—savage, petty, boastful and jealous, and yet capable of moments of tenderness and extremes of arbitrary affection."[16] His words sound very much like *The Testimony of Truth*'s description of God as a "malicious grudger."

Regarding death, Pullman's novels make the point that it is nothing to be feared. The novels say that during the time when God the Authority reigned, the dead were consigned to a shadowy underworld in which neither memory nor joy could live. Lyra and Will, however, are able to free the dead from this world, and by the end of the trilogy the dead are no longer condemned to an eternity of soulless existence. Instead, they (or at least the particles by which they had been constituted) are able to rejoin the world they left: "All the atoms that were them, they've gone into the air and the wind and the trees and the earth and all the living things. They'll never vanish. They're just part of everything," explains one character.[17] This is the happy fate that the Authority and the Magisterium had tried to prevent people from discovering. Through bullying and lies, God and Church had tried to stop people from acquiring true knowledge. Lyra and Will, however, fell into wisdom and thereby saved the world.

It is worth pointing out that though Pullman's theological vision has much in common with that of the Gnostics, it differs in an important way as well. Specifically, Pullman rejects the Gnostics' emphasis on the "spiritual" world as opposed to the world of the senses. *His Dark Materials* several times makes the point that bodies, as well as their needs and desires, are good and should be cherished. In the final book of the trilogy, for example, a character named Mary who had once been a nun explains that she left the Church because of its disapproval of sensual pleasures. Mary describes how, while she was still a member of her religious order, she accompanied friends to a party one evening where she drank wine and ate marzipan and flirted with a man. At that point, she says, she realized that she could no longer accept the Church's description of such pleasures as "temptations," and so she left both her religious order and the Church.[18] While the Gnostics would have decried Mary's weakness, Pullman presents her "fall" into sensuality as an awakening to the beauties and wonders of the world. Again, though God and the Magisterium conspired to prevent her from awakening, Mary was able to defeat their lies and to realize the truth.

Interpretation #2: God Has a Change of Heart

A second way to deal with the apparent discrepancy between what God says will happen and what actually happens is to say that the text is simply inconsistent. This may be because, as some interpreters argue, the Adam and Eve narrative is actually composed of several traditions which were subsequently pasted together.[19] Perhaps in one version of the story God did strike the first people dead, and then this earlier version was grafted onto another in which God deemed a lesser punishment more fitting.

Or, perhaps in the story God undergoes a change of heart. As German biblical scholar Gerhard von Rad asserts, "[O]ne of the narrator's concerns may have been to show that God did not make good his terrible threat but had allowed grace to prevail."[20] Perhaps, rather than keep to his word, God opted for mercy instead.

This method of explaining why Adam remains alive despite God's prediction that the man would die from eating the fruit has few representations in popular culture. Perhaps the reason is that many people would judge it inconceivable that God would change God's mind. After all, why would God need to change? Was God's initial statement incorrect? Or, could God not have foreseen that Adam would eventually disobey? Is God not all-knowing? Is God not perfect? If God changes, then perhaps there is no rock to which we can cling in this constantly changing world. As the old Anglican hymn prays, "Change and decay in all around I see;/ O Thou who changest not, abide with me!"[21]

And yet there is at least one popular presentation of the idea that God did indeed undergo a change of heart and took pity on Adam and Eve. It occurs in Mickey Rooney's *The Private Lives of Adam and Eve*, which we have already examined in terms of its presentation of Lilith. Rooney's film understands the penalty threatened by God to be death: literal bodily death. When Adam and Eve eat the fruit, Satan exults, "You eat from that tree and you're dead, man, you're dead. That was the rule!" However, the movie also says that this penalty was canceled by divine fiat. The narrator explains, "But they didn't die. They had broken God's law. They had committed the sin of disobedience. But God, in his mercy, spared them." This is one of very few instances in which popular culture allows that God might not be immutable after all.

Interpretation #3: The Humans Do Not
Die but Become Subject to Death

In this third interpretation, what God meant in Genesis 2:17 ("in the day that you eat . . . you shall die") was simply that if Adam and Eve ate the fruit, they would become mortal and thus subject to *eventual* death. This idea has a long history in Christian thought. Augustine, for example, opined that we members of the human race would not now have to die if the first two humans had not sinned: "[F]or by them so great a sin was committed, that by it the human nature was altered for the worse, and was transmitted also to their posterity, liable to sin and subject to death."[22] In other words, Adam and Eve's transgression brought about a sort of internal mutation that the first people then passed on to all of their descendants. The penalty of death was not administered from the outside; instead, it became a deformity that they carried in their very beings and that made them subject to death. In the beginning, says Augustine, "God had not made man like the angels, in such a condition that, even though they had sinned, they could none the more die." Rather, "He had so made them, that if they discharged the obligations of obedience, an angelic im-mortality and a blessed eternity might ensue, without the intervention of death."[23] However, our parents did not listen to the voice of their Maker, and so all of us now carry the flaw of mortality. The recent *Catechism of the Catholic Church* (2003) agrees. While affirming that "man's nature is mortal," the *Catechism* nonetheless asserts that "God had destined him not to die. Death was therefore contrary to the plans of God the Creator and entered the world as a consequence of sin."[24]

For most Christians, the idea that death is the penalty for Adam's sin is central because it paves the way for the claim that resurrection is the reward for those who follow Christ. In his letter to the followers of Jesus living in Corinth, the first-century thinker Paul wrote, "For since death came through a human being, the resurrection of the dead has also come through a human being; for as all die in Adam, so all will be made alive in Christ" (1 Corinthians 15:21–22). Jesus, in other words, is the New Adam who undoes the harm that Adam brought into the world. Medieval art makes this point again and again. Numerous paintings show Jesus's cross planted on the precise spot where Adam was buried; from the death of Adam springs the life brought by Christ.[25] A medieval Christian legend says that the cross on which Jesus was executed was made from the very tree that had stood in Eden. According to the story, when Adam was dying, he sent his son Seth to the gates of Paradise to beg for healing oil. The angel who guarded the gate refused to grant Adam's request but instead gave Seth a shoot from the tree under which Adam had commit-ted his sin. When Adam died, Seth planted the tree on his father's grave. After many further adventures (including being cut down by Solomon to be used in the Jewish Temple, and forming part of a bridge over which the Queen of Sheba passed on her way to Jerusalem), the wood from Adam's tree was finally used to form Jesus's cross.[26]

Yet another Christian tradition holds that during the hours between his death and his resurrection, Jesus descended into the underworld (variously named Hell, Hades, or Limbo) in order to free the waiting dead. Who were the first people whom he called forth? Adam and Eve, of course. Several paintings depict this event which, it should be pointed out, has no basis in the Bible. The paintings typically show Jesus breaking open coffins and helping our first parents out of their graves. A famous Christian homily depicts Jesus arriving in the underworld and assuring Adam, "I slept on the cross and a sword pierced my side for you who slept in paradise and brought forth Eve from your side. My side has healed the pain in yours."[27]

For some Christians (most notably the ancient thinker Pelagius), as well as for many Jews, Adam's transgression was the source of his *own* death but not of anyone else's. One Jewish tradition holds that in his last days, Adam became concerned about the kind of reputation that he was leaving behind him. He told God that he did not mind being blamed for the deaths of the wicked, but he did not want pious people to hold him responsible for their mortality. God agreed that Adam made a good point, and so now when people die, God demands from them an accounting of their deeds and assures them that they are dying for their own actions rather than for Adam's. If anyone does try to turn Adam into a scapegoat, Adam will retort, "I committed but one trespass. Is there any among you, and be he the most pious, who has not been guilty of more than one?"[28]

The association between the first couple and human mortality finds expression in several contemporary movies. One of the most disturbing of these is Mike Figgis's *The Loss of Sexual Innocence* (1999). The movie does not contain a conventional plot; rather, it proceeds more as a series of short stories (many based on episodes from the director's own life) intercut with scenes of the story of Adam and Eve.[29] As the film's title suggests, the flow of events moves from innocence to culpability. The opening shots of the movie show a small white boy, aged five, wandering around an African village. The boy approaches a bungalow and peers into a window. There he sees an elderly white Englishman sitting in a chair as a mixed-race African girl, dressed in bra, panties, stockings, and heels, all of which are much too big for her, reads aloud from the Bible's erotic love poem known as the "Song of Songs." The girl's lipstick is applied inexpertly and is smeared across her cheek. The script for the movie explains that the boy "is intrigued" by what he sees. "Although it is not explicitly sexual he knows it means something strange."[30]

Two scenes later, we see that the boy, Nicolas, has become a young man. Nic is now at a funeral in the north of England comforting his girlfriend whose father has just died. Later, at the reception following the funeral, he stumbles upon the girl, who is very drunk, lying on a bed with her skirt around her hips and another man fondling her thighs. Death and sex become joined in the plot and will remain so throughout the film.

Immediately after this episode in the bedroom, Figgis inserts the first of several of what are called "Scenes from Nature." As soft piano music plays in the background, a shimmering lake appears, and slowly a naked African man emerges from the water. The man looks around and sees a white horse and a tree. Shortly after, another "scene from nature" shows a pale, red-haired young woman emerge from the same lake. She opens her eyes and observes the landscape around her. Adam and Eve have just entered the world. (In his "director's notes," Figgis writes that "Adam had to be black, Eve had not just to be white but Nordic white." Unfortunately, he does not explain the reason for this casting decision.)[31] In subsequent short takes, Adam and Eve will hold hands, enter the lake in order to catch fish, and laughingly explore each other's genitals. All of this is performed with the curious interest and innocence of children. The man and woman are not alone in their wilderness, however. As they splash delightedly in the water, a serpent looks on.

Meanwhile, various events take place in Nic's life. We see him walk into the bathroom of a service station only to discover that someone has ripped apart a pornographic magazine and stuffed the toilet with it. We see him prepare to take a film crew to Tunisia to make a documentary about the ecological impact of global warming. We see that all is not well between Nic and his wife, and we sense trouble when we learn that one member of the film crew that will accompany Nic to Tunisia is a beautiful Italian woman. We also see various flashbacks. One shows the child Nic's first encounter with a dead body: a worker who had been killed in an industrial accident. As Nic looks on, police carry the worker's body from the factory and pull a sheet over the dead man's face. Another flashback shows Nic as a pudgy adolescent who, because he has forgotten his equipment for gym class, is forced to run, wearing only his undershorts, through a gauntlet of boys who savagely beat him with their shoes. All of these vignettes build a picture of life as difficult, filled with pain, and, at times, sordid and cruel.

As the details of Nic's life emerge, Adam and Eve begin their descent from innocence. Apparently tired of eating grass and weeds, Eve strikes out on her own. She enters a ruined garden and sees an old rusted car and a large crucifix as well as the tree in which lounges the snake. She picks fruit from the tree and eats it, and the fruit's juice runs down her mouth like blood. A few scenes later, Adam joins her in eating; both stuff the fruit into their mouths as if they cannot get enough. They then both begin to retch even while continuing to eat. Doubled over in pain and nausea, the couple enters a small house in the garden. Eve's naked body is smeared with juice, and her hand covers her groin. Adam looks at her with lust, and the two copulate with brutal intensity.

Intercut with these scenes are short takes of Nic and his film crew out in the Tunisian desert. Nic earnestly explains to the others that he wants to alert the world to the dangers of global warming, and he is very conscious of respecting native customs and of not trampling the desert's ecosystem during their filming. He has only the best of intentions, but events quickly begin to spiral downward. One of the men in the film crew is furiously jealous because Nic has slept with the Italian beauty whom he himself had been eyeing. An argument breaks out in the car in which the group is traveling, and as a result, the driver takes his eyes from the road and accidentally strikes a young Bedouin child. Before the movie ends, a member of the film crew will be killed savagely. Once again, sex and death join together in an ugly union.

Meanwhile, Adam and Eve have brought fear and shame into the world. After their copulation, they look at each other with sadness. Suddenly, fascist police invade the garden with spotlights and dogs. Adam and Eve are terrified and begin to run through the densely wooded garden, but they are no match for the men and their German shepherds. The naked man and woman are driven outside the garden gates and emerge onto a crowded street in Rome, suddenly surrounded by more spotlights and by paparazzi with cameras. From the chaotic swirl of flashbulbs and jeering onlookers, someone tosses clothes at them, and Eve and her mate manage to cover themselves and flee. The world has now become harsh and menacing, and the innocence of the man and the woman from the garden is gone forever. With the loss of sexual innocence has come violence and discord and, inevitably, the ugliness of death.

Eve's Bayou (1997)

Of course, with human mortality comes the possibility of new life. Curiously, death is intimately related to sexual reproduction in several ways. Virtually all organisms are programmed by nature to pass on their genetic material to offspring, and in many cases, once that task is accomplished, death comes swiftly. Think, for example, of Pacific salmon swimming upstream to spawn, only to die soon after, or of male praying mantises who continue to copulate even as they are being cannibalized by their female partners. In some species of spiders, the male actually jumps onto its partner's fangs in order to mate, a procedure that quickly results in his demise.[32]

On yet another level, sex and death are related from a historical point of view. According to evolutionary biologists, the first living organisms consisted of only one cell and reproduced asexually simply by splitting. These organisms did not "die"—they simply reconstituted themselves as a new pair of offspring. As multicellular organisms developed, however, reproduction became sexual. Two members of a species could come together and contribute their genetic material in order to create a third. Though the genes, or what biologists call "germ lines" of the pair lived on, the nonreproductive parts of their bodies, or their "soma" did not. Explains English biologist Tom Kirkwood, "The result was that the soma became disposable, and with that came aging."[33] In other words, sexual beings get old and die because their bodies spend the largest part of their energy ensuring that their genes can be passed on. They simply do not have the resources to prevent their nonreproducing cells from deteriorating. Thus, though single-celled organisms can be immortal, because we are sexual animals, we die.

However, because we are sexual animals, we also produce life. This is one of the paradoxes at the heart of the Adam and Eve story. Yes, the first two people bring disaster upon themselves and, perhaps, depending upon one's interpretation of the text, upon all others as well. And yet they are also the origin of humankind. After they have been dismissed from the Garden, Adam gives the woman the name Eve (Hebrew, *Havah*) because she is mother of all the living (3:20). From death, or at least along with death, comes life.

A sensitive depiction of this duality emerges in Kasi Lemmons's 1997 film *Eve's Bayou*. The movie opens with a voice-over in which a woman reflects, "Memory is a selection of images, some elusive, others printed indelibly on the brain. The summer I killed my father, I was 10 years old." The voice then tells the story of the origins of the narrator's family. The Batiste clan began, she says, when an African slave named Eve nursed her French master through a bout of cholera. In gratitude for her kindness to him, the man freed Eve, and she then bore him sixteen children. The descendants of that pairing now populate the bayou of the movie's title. Eve Batiste gave life to multitudes. Explains the narrator, "I was named for her."

When the movie begins, the narrator Eve is a young girl living in Louisiana in 1962. At first, nothing seems to mar Eve's happy life as part of the Batiste family. Her father (played with rakish charm by Samuel L. Jackson) is a handsome physician. Her mother is an attractive woman whose perfectly coiffed hair and beautiful clothes are as meticulously cared for as is her home. Inevitably, however, Eve's life takes a tragic turn. Her father, she learns, is a Lothario who is romancing another man's wife; much worse, he has also (at least as Eve understands the matter) tried to molest Eve's older sister. In retaliation, Eve determines to kill the father whom she adores. She consults a local voodoo practitioner (Diahann Carroll) and pays her twenty dollars to conjure her father's death.

The fact that Eve's name is meant to evoke the Eve of the Bible is made apparent at two points in the story. In one scene, Eve and her younger brother are playing at the edge of the bayou when they encounter what they think is a dead snake. When the snake rears up, the children scream and run. Ever the mischievous older sister, Eve later takes a toy snake and places it on the pillow of her sleeping little brother. When the child wakes up and commences screaming, Eve pretends innocence.

The movie also includes another visual reminder of the Genesis story in a scene that takes place in the town marketplace where local vendors have gathered to sell their produce. There Eve strolls among the various stalls until she spies one selling apples. Approaching the booth, she eyes the fruit. At that moment, she hears the voice of the man whose wife is having an affair with her father. In the conversation that follows, Eve cunningly hints to the man that he is being cuckolded by her father. This sets in motion the course of events that will lead to the death of Dr. Batiste. Director Kasi Lemmons notes that numerous viewers have asked her if the use of the snake and the apples was deliberate and if she is intending to make a statement with them. "Of course I am," she says. When Eve is in the marketplace longing for the apples, explains Lemmons, "She's about to commit a sin, in a sense."[34] Once again, sin, sex, and death intertwine in this film in such complex ways that it is not easy to separate the strands from each other. And though the ancestor for whom she is named was the mother of all the Batiste clan, young Eve herself brings about the death of her own father.

Interpretation #4: The Humans Undergo a Moral or Spiritual Death

Not everyone agrees that the disobedience of Adam and Eve resulted in their being subject to mortality. For example, Julian of Eclanum, a fifth-century Christian bishop and a learned scholar, thought that Augustine was wrong to say that human death could be attributed to the actions of our first parents. Julian argued instead that Adam's mortality stemmed from the simple fact that he had been made from clay. Referring to Genesis 3:19, where God says, "By the sweat of your face you shall eat bread until you return to the ground, for out of it you were taken; you are dust, and to dust you shall return," Julian writes:

> Our mortality is not the result of sin, but of nature! Why does Genesis not say, "because you sinned and transgressed my precepts"? This should have been said, if bodily dissolution were connected with a crime. But recall, what does it say? "Because you are earth." Surely this is the reason why one returns to earth, "because you were taken out of it." If this, then, is the reason God gives, that one was from earth, I think it can be assumed that one cannot blame sin. Without doubt it is not because of sin, but because of our mortal nature . . . that the body dissolves back into the elements.[35]

For Julian, mortality was a natural and hence God-given component of human existence, and what God had made could not be evil. However, Julian lost that theological argument, at least as far as orthodox Christian teaching is concerned. For most of its history Christianity has taught that Adam and Eve's sin did not affect just themselves but also brought mortality to all of us.

Moreover, that sin brought something else with it as well: spiritual or moral death. As Augustine wrote, at the moment of Adam and Eve's disobedience, "divine grace forsook them."[36] Augustine taught that the very bodies and souls of our first parents became corrupted when Adam and Eve sinned, and that that corruption was passed on to us. We became afflicted, he believed, with what is known as "original sin." As the old *Baltimore Catechism* (a compendium of the faith that millions of Catholic schoolchildren up to the middle of the 20th century were made to memorize) instructs, "The chief punishments of Adam which we inherit through original sin are: death, suffering, ignorance, and a strong inclination to sin."[37] Though the sacrament of baptism washes away original sin itself, according to Catholic teaching the effects of the sin remain, and so we are still subject to death, our intellects remain darkened, we still experience pain, and we remain attracted to sin. We are, in other words, morally corrupted.

Not everyone agreed with Augustine. The fifth-century Christian thinker Pelagius, for example, taught that sinfulness is not inherited and that all of us are responsible for our own transgressions. A *Calvin and Hobbes* cartoon seems to agree. The strip portrays the boy Calvin talking to his tiger-friend Hobbes about human nature (see fig. 5.1). "Do you think babies are born sinful? That they come into the world as sinners?" asks Calvin. To this, Hobbes replies, "No, I think they're just quick studies." Calvin concludes to himself, "Whenever you discuss certain things with animals, you get insulted."[38]

Nonetheless, orthodox Christian thought has sided with Augustine and has held that human beings are born into the sinfulness that they inherited from Adam and Eve.

Young Adam (2003)
The effects of this sinfulness are spelled out in the 2003 film *Young Adam*, which stars Ewan McGregor and Tilda Swinton. McGregor plays Joe

Figure 5.1

Calvin and Hobbes cartoon.

Taylor, a young Scottish drifter who, when we first meet him, is working on a barge named the "Atlantic Eve." The boat is owned by a woman named Ella (Swinton) and her husband Les. As the movie opens, Joe and Les come upon the half-naked body of a young woman floating in the water. They pull the body onto the boat and call the police, and it would seem that that is the end of the matter: two disinterested bystanders happened to find a corpse and notified the proper authorities.

As the story develops, however, we discover that Joe actually knew the young woman, whom we learn was named Cathie, quite intimately. In a series of flashbacks, we see that the two of them had lived together and that Cathie had become pregnant with Joe's child. During an argument between them on a dockside, Cathie had slipped and fallen into the water, and Joe, frightened or perhaps merely relieved, had failed to report the matter.

Meanwhile, Joe has begun sleeping with Les's wife Ella. He seems to have no compunction about this. At one point Joe and Ella lie in bed together in the bowels of the barge, and as they engage in a postcoital smoke, they hear Les's boots pacing back and forth on the deck above; neither hurries to cover up their infidelity. Later, Joe also has sex with Ella's sister in an alleyway, as well as with a married woman who rents him a room.

As the inquiry into Cathie's death continues, Joe does not come forward to tell the investigators what he knows. The police discover that Cathie had been having an affair with a married man, and they indict the man for what they believe to have been a murder. Since the movie takes place before the era of DNA analysis, there is no thought of doing a paternity test on Cathie's unborn baby, and her married lover is assumed to have been the father. A trial ensues, which Joe follows closely by attending the proceedings as if he were simply another gawker in the gallery.

When Cathie's married lover is sentenced to death, the central dilemma of the movie reaches its climax. Will Joe come forward to explain what really happened? If he does not, he is essentially guilty of murdering an innocent man. If he does, however, he risks being found guilty himself. As film critic Roger Ebert comments, Joe "is not a murderer but a man unwilling to intervene, a man so detached, so cold, so willing to sacrifice others to his own convenience, that perhaps in his mind it occurs that he would feel better about the young woman's death if he had actually, actively, killed her. Then at least he would know what he had done and would not find such emptiness when he looks inside himself."[39]

The challenge for Joe to look inside himself is a key theme in the movie. Cathie, we learn, had at one point given Joe a gift: a small mirror. Inscribed on it was an injunction to think of her whenever he looked at himself. As the movie draws to a close, however, Joe throws the mirror into the river and walks away. This young Adam has not died physically, but he is a mere shell of a man who cannot stand to see the barrenness of his own soul.

Overcoming Death

As we have seen, movie-makers and novelists come to different conclusions about the meaning of "the curse of Adam." They are nearly univocal, however, in the opinion that humans should not try to overcome death. Over and over again, popular culture warns against the quest for immortality.

At the end of the Genesis story, after God has expelled the first two humans, God says, "See, the man has become like one of us, knowing good and evil; and now, he might reach out his hand and take also from the tree of life, and eat, and live forever." In order to prevent this, God "placed the cherubim, and a sword flaming and turning to guard the way to the tree of life" (3:22, 24). But what if a person could sneak past that flaming sword and get another chance at that tree? For centuries, if not since the beginning of human consciousness, people have sought to overcome death. Whether it manifests itself as a quest for the fountain of youth or as an alchemical attempt to achieve immortality, the desire to "put a stopper in death" (as Professor Snape says in the 2001 movie *Harry Potter and the Sorcerer's Stone*) holds a powerful allure. At least in popular culture, however, the attempt to cheat the Grim Reaper invariably ends badly.

Death Becomes Her (1992)

In the 1992 comedy *Death Becomes Her*, for example, an aging actress named Madeline (Meryl Streep) reverses the process of aging by taking a potion that promises "the gift of life and youth forever!" The potion is given to her by a beauty named Lisle (Isabella Rossellini) who claims to be in her seventies but whose flawless skin and body look decades younger. The primary reference to Genesis in the story occurs when we see that Lisle's mansion features a stained glass reproduction of

Michelangelo's "Creation of Adam." The window is of course an allusion to the eternal life that the first couple might have enjoyed had they not disobeyed God.

In *Death Becomes Her*, though, eternal life is at least as much curse as blessing. During the course of the movie, the now-immortal Madeline sustains a number of injuries that maim and twist her body into comically grotesque shapes. When she falls down a set of stairs and breaks her neck, for example, Madeline must seek medical attention to get her head turned around and facing forward again. Yes, she will live forever, but her body will require constant maintenance to repair damage from accidents that would kill a normal person. Madeline's husband Ernest (Bruce Willis) is so repulsed at the idea of living forever that he chooses not to drink the potion when it is offered to him. In fact, during the course of the movie he accidentally falls through the stained glass window, an event that serves as a symbol of his rejection of immortality. *Death Becomes Her* is a comedy, but underlying its humor is a serious grappling with contemporary society's obsessive pursuit of youth.

The Island (2005)

The science fiction film *The Island*, a thriller set in the year 2019, also tries to imagine what would happen if the Tree of Life did not remain off-limits to us. The premise of *The Island* (2005) is that a scientist named Dr. Merrick has figured out a way to clone human beings. He develops these clones for wealthy clients as "insurance policies" so that if a client ever needs a transplant, or just wants younger-looking skin, his or her clone can provide spare parts. Those who pay Merrick's fee are assured by his Institute that their clones will be simply "vegetative matter" rather than true humans.

The Institute's product is easy to sell. After all, who would not want to have an extra set of lungs or kidneys, or a spare heart or liver, in case something goes wrong? The problem, however, is that Dr. Merrick and his scientists are lying. The clones, who are being grown in an underground bunker near Tucson, are living, breathing, thinking people who have no idea that they came into being artificially. The clones have been given false memories so that they believe that they once had normal lives. They come to believe that prior to a catastrophic accident that caused the earth to become contaminated, they had had normal childhoods, and they had grown up to acquire jobs and families. They also believe that they were lucky to survive the catastrophe and that if they ever leave their underground world, they will die instantly.

In their bunker, the clones are very well cared for. Their diet and sleep are monitored, and their moods are carefully noted down. Doctors are available at all times to tend to them at the first sign of trouble. Dr. Merrick describes his Institute as "a Garden of Eden" and explains that the clones are protected from the problems that ordinary people face: "To avoid obvious complications, they aren't imprinted with an awareness of sex. We find it simpler to eliminate the drive altogether. In a very real sense, they're like children." At several points in the movie, Merrick is compared by other characters to God. He is, after all, the creator of the clones, and as he says of himself, "I give life."

As in every Garden of Eden, though, there is a tempter who hints at forbidden knowledge. In this case, the tempter is an insect that happens to flutter past one of the clones, a young man named Lincoln 6 Echo (played by Ewan McGregor). Lincoln is astonished to see the bug, as he has been told repeatedly that nothing can live outside of the bunker. He follows the insect and in doing so stumbles upon the secret of the Institute: that the scientists are killing the clones and harvesting their organs. Once his eyes have been opened, he searches out his beautiful friend Jordan 2 Delta (Scarlett Johansson), and the two of them manage to escape to the outside world. There they receive an explanation of why they were created: "The whole reason you exist is 'cause everyone wants to live forever. It's the new American dream."

Meanwhile, the Institute has begun a frantic search to find and recover its lost "product." What troubles Dr. Merrick is not simply the fact that Lincoln and Jordan have escaped. What seems to worry him even more is that the two clones have somehow managed to develop a defect: human curiosity. Lincoln is, says Merrick, merely "the first one to question his environment, his whole existence here." Eventually, Merrick fears, all of the others will do likewise. And so as a precaution, the director begins the systematic slaughter of the remaining clones.

The Island uses its allusions to Adam and Eve (which also include an encounter with a snake and a reference to an apple) to raise several issues. First, what does it mean to be a person? Is curiosity a defect or an indispensable part of being human? Would it be better to remain innocent, or is it better to become aware of the complexities of life that include sex and death?

Second, what are the risks of venturing back into the Garden in search of immortality? Is death something to be avoided at all cost, or should humans simply accept our finitude?

And finally, if human curiosity brings with it the possibility of disobedience to our Creator, is it better to remain in ignorance? After Merrick realizes that Lincoln has defied him, he threatens, "I brought you into this world. And I can take you out of it." Are we better off developing our intellects, or should we listen to the one who gave us life and who can bring us death? The movie, like many other works of popular culture, ends up praising human curiosity and ingenuity even when those traits lead to disobedience of authority. At the same time, though, it cautions against trying to reverse the course of human mortality. We are free, the movie seems to say, to question God. We are not free, however, to become like God.

The Fountain (2006)

A more lyrical exploration of the same themes occurs in Darren Aronofsky's 2006 film *The Fountain*. The movie opens with a description of the expulsion of Adam and Eve: "Therefore, the Lord God banished Adam and Eve from the Garden of Eden and placed a flaming sword to protect the tree of life." The entire work is a meditation on the themes in the Genesis story. Explains Aronofsky, "It's asking the same questions that all people have been asking since the beginning of time, which is why are we here, what is life, what is death, what happens when you die, can you love, what is love, can you love forever?"[40]

The movie is an interweaving of three stories. The main story takes place in the present and depicts the relationship between a scientist named Tommy Creo (Hugh Jackman) and his wife Izzi (Rachel Weisz), a writer who is completing a novel about 16th-century Spain. Izzi is dying of cancer, and Tommy is using all of his time and energy to search for a cure for her disease. When Izzi visits his laboratory to ask him to accompany her on a walk to celebrate the first snowfall of the season, Tommy refuses by saying that he has too much work to do. The desire for a cure so consumes him that he cannot take his eyes from that goal long enough to gaze at his dying wife.

Izzi's novel, which is titled *The Fountain*, takes us into the movie's second story. When Tommy happens to pick up Izzi's unfinished manuscript and begins to read it, viewers are transported back to the court of Queen

Isabella. There the queen (played by Weisz) commissions a conquistador named Tomás (Jackman) to sail to the New World and to search for the Tree of Life, which according to Mayan legend will confer immortality upon anyone who eats from it. The tree is, the queen believes, the same one that God hid from Adam and Eve when he expelled them from Eden. As a token of her love, the queen gives Tomás her ring: "You shall wear it when you find Eden. And when you return, I shall be your Eve."

The Mayans in the movie adhere to a different account of the tree's origins, however. According to their mythology, the tree sprouted when their ancestor, named First Father, sacrificed himself to make the world. Thus, the Mayans believe that out of death grows new life; "Death is the road to awe," they say. Out of First Father's body grew roots that became the earth, and his soul became the sky. His head was then thrown into space by his children, and it became the nebula Xibalba, the place where the dead go to be reborn.

Izzi's story reflects her fascination with the Mayan mythology, and she herself finds comfort in the myth's understanding of death as an act of creation. She remembers having once met a Mayan tour guide who told her that when his father died, the guide planted a seed on his father's grave. The seed, using the father's body as nourishment, became a tree, and when a bird ate the fruit of the tree, the guide's father flew with the bird. Death was, again, the road to awe.

Izzi herself is not afraid to die and tries to communicate the peace that she feels to Tommy. He, though, refuses to surrender to mortality: "Death is a disease," he says fiercely. "It's like any other. And there's a cure. A cure. And I will find it." He is so consumed with his work that he leaves his beloved wife to suffer alone in her hospital bed. Izzi's only visitor in her sickbed is Tommy's supervisor, a scientist named Lillian who, like Izzi, sees death not as an enemy but rather as a natural part of the cycle of life. The supervisor's name is perhaps significant. Lillian is a Lilith who bonds with Izzi/Eve and who, like her, possesses a wisdom that eludes Tommy/Adam.

When Izzi realizes that she does not have much longer to live, she asks Tommy to complete the manuscript that she has been writing. She hopes that by doing so he will come to accept the fact of her death. The final chapter that he writes forms the third narrative that runs throughout the movie. The chapter depicts an astronaut (Jackman again) floating through space in a glass bubble, at the center of which is a gnarled tree.

The tree is dying, and the astronaut is taking it to Xibalba, the nebula of Mayan myth, so that it can be born anew. What he discovers there is that death is not, as he feared, the end of life, but is part of an eternal process. Death is a creative act that brings regeneration.

At the end of the movie Tommy visits Izzi's grave, and there he hears his wife's voice asking "Is everything all right?" Having finally come to some peace with her death, he answers, "Yes, everything is all right." The words echo those of the medieval mystic Julian of Norwich who, while seriously ill, had a series of visions. In one of her revelations, she found herself wondering why God had not prevented the beginning of sin: "For then, thought I, all would have been well." Jesus answers her by saying, "'Sin was necessary—but it is all going to be all right; it is all going to be all right; everything is going to be all right."⁴¹ By placing these words in the mouth of Tommy, the movie makes the point that death is not a curse to be overcome but a transformation to be welcomed.

The Fountain is not a philosophical treatise, and it explores the themes of life and death and love poetically rather than systematically. Aronofsky recognizes that the movie does not provide all of the answers to humans' deepest questions: "There are no answers, there are just ideas that we think about and we talk about and that's what *The Fountain* is for me."⁴² The movie relies heavily on allusion; for example, the name Tommy evokes the "doubting Thomas" in the New Testament who refused to believe that Jesus had risen from the dead. And yet Tommy's last name is Creo, which is a Spanish word that means "I believe." Taken together, the two names might remind viewers of the man in the Gospel of Mark whose child was ill and who asked Jesus for help. When Jesus said to the man, "All things can be done for the one who believes," the father responded, "I believe; help my unbelief!" (9:23–24). At the end of Aronofsky's movie we may find ourselves similarly torn: wanting to see death as a friend rather than an enemy, but still faced with the cold starkness of the grave.

As we have seen, movies, like religious traditions themselves, differ quite a bit in how they understand the meaning of death. They also differ in how they present another of the apparent consequences of Adam and Eve's disobedience, the "curse of Eve."

CHAPTER SIX

The Curse of Eve

If death is the curse of Adam, what then is the curse of Eve? The answer to that question goes by many different names: "that time of the
month," "a visit from Aunt Flo," "being on the rag," "my friend," and
other euphemisms too numerous to list. "The curse of Eve" is another
term for menstruation. Because Eve sinned (advertisements, movies, and
television shows inform us) a woman must endure monthly mood swings,
bloating, cramps, and, worst of all, the potential humiliation of having a
male discover a tampon in her purse.

In 1981, *Time* magazine published an article about menstruation entitled "Coping with Eve's Curse." The article quoted a family practitioner
as saying, "Many physicians act as if [menstrual] pain is women's due and
getting rid of it is almost sacrilegious."[1] Significantly, the Bible itself does
not mention menstruation as one of Eve's burdens. What God says to the
woman in Genesis 3:16 is, "I will greatly increase your pangs in childbearing; in pain you shall bring forth children." Or, "I will multiply thy sorrows, and thy conceptions: in sorrow shalt thou bring forth children"; or
again, "I shall give you great labour in childbearing; with labour you will
bear children."[2] Depending on one's interpretation, God imposes difficult
labors, a number of conceptions, and/or sorrow on the woman. Nowhere,
though, does God mention menstruation.

And yet, both religious authority and popular culture have combined
to make the association commonplace. In one ancient Jewish rendering

of the Genesis text, God tells Eve, "I will greatly increase your pains and your periods."[3] The Babylonian Talmud says that God imposed ten curses on Eve, including the blood of a virgin's first sexual intercourse and the blood of menstruation ('Erubin 100b). (Of course, many women do not bleed when they have intercourse for the first time.) In Muslim tradition, although the Quran does not say that the first woman began to menstruate because she disobeyed God, the ninth-century scholar al-Tabari wrote, "If it were not for the misfortune which befell Eve, women on Earth would not menstruate and they would be good-natured and would have easy pregnancies and births."[4]

In Christian tradition, the medieval mystic Hildegard of Bingen wrote that God had appeared to her and had stated that a man should not have sex with his wife during her menses lest the flow of her blood carry his seed away and thus prevent it from being planted in the womb. God explained to Hildegard that during her menstrual period, "the woman is in pain and in prison, suffering a small portion of the pain of childbirth." God continued, "I do not remit this time of pain for women, because I gave it to Eve when she conceived sin in the taste of the fruit." Significantly, however, God then added that "therefore the woman should be cherished in this time with a great and healing tenderness."[5]

Despite the widespread association of menstruation with Eve in religious traditions, it is not clear exactly how the English word "curse" came to refer to women's periods. According to the Oxford English Dictionary, the first use of "curse" as a euphemism for menstruation did not appear until 1930.[6] It is possible that the association in English results in part from the similarity between the words "curse" and "courses," the latter of which was one of the most common term for menstruation in seventeenth-century England.[7] In any case, as we will see, in contemporary culture the connection between Eve's actions and menstrual periods has been firmly established.

One of the clearest examples of this can be found in the blockbuster horror film Carrie, directed by Brian De Palma (1976). The movie stars Sissy Spacek as a shy and awkward teenager whose social development has been thwarted by her fervently religious mother. In the opening scenes of the film, Carrie White showers in the girls' locker room of Bates High School. As nude and partially dressed young women frolic and laugh in the background, Carrie stands in the stall and soaps herself. A close-up of the water cascading off of her thighs shows, though, that something is terribly wrong; blood is pouring from Carrie's body. (This scene is reminiscent of Alfred Hitchcock's 1960 movie *Psycho*, in which a woman is murdered while taking a shower, and her blood mingles with water as it swirls down the bathtub's drain. The similarity is surely no coincidence, as the name of Carrie's high school is the same as that of the troubled stalker, Norman Bates, in Hitchcock's film.) When she becomes aware of the blood coursing down her legs, Carrie begins to scream hysterically and rushes naked into the crowd of girls nearby who are getting dressed. With bloody hands she reaches out to them begging for help, but the other girls begin to laugh and taunt her. Far more worldly than she, they realize what has happened—Carrie has just started her period. The mocking girls chant "Plug it up!" as they toss tampons and pads at the weeping Carrie. Only when a sympathetic gym teacher intervenes is Carrie rescued from the adolescent mob.

When she arrives home after her ordeal, Carrie does not find the warm maternal reassurance that one might expect. Carrie's mother, it seems, is a deeply religious woman who distributes pamphlets with titles like "The Teenager's Path to Salvation Through the Cross of Jesus" to her neighbors. Mrs. White is more than just a pious Christian, however; she is a zealot who sees all sex, even that between husband and wife, as the work of Satan. She also blames menstruation on the Fall of the first woman and on the sins of every woman since Eve. When Carrie asks her mother why she never told her about normal female reproductive cycles, Mrs. White responds by hitting the girl across the head with a thick religious tome. Opening the book to a page entitled "The Sins of Women," Mrs. White reads: "And God made Eve from the rib of Adam. And it was weak and loosed the raven on the world. And the raven was called 'sin.'" Repeatedly commanding Carrie to repeat her words, she continues, "The first sin was intercourse. And the Lord visited Eve with a curse. And the curse was a Curse of Blood!" While Carrie desperately pleads her innocence, Mrs. White prays to God, "Show her that if she had remained sinless, the Curse of Blood would never have come on her!" Mrs. White then proceeds to drag her daughter to a closet to lock her in with a gruesome statue of Saint Sebastian, a Christian martyr. There Carrie is to meditate on her sins.

Of course, this depiction of a Christian attitude towards menstruation is exaggerated and is intended to shock. Virtually no Christians actually hold that an individual girl could prevent menstruation if only she could refrain from sinning. Nonetheless, the idea that menstruation is a curse is prevalent in culture. The TV sitcom *The Golden Girls* was perhaps one of the first to deal openly with this concept. In an episode from 1986 entitled "End of the Curse," the southern belle named Blanche believes that she is pregnant because she has stopped menstruating. A visit to her doctor, though, reveals that she is not going to have a baby; instead, she is going through menopause. At this news, Blanche is devastated. She describes menopause as "the end of my life," and she wails that she is "not a real woman anymore." Gradually, Blanche comes to accept menopause as simply another stage in her life.

In one of the cheesecake-and-gossip sessions that she and her housemates indulged in throughout the series's seven-year run, Blanche remembers when she first started her period. She recalls that throughout her childhood, she had been told that when she turned thirteen she would be visited by "the curse." Blanche says, "Oh, I was absolutely terrified. The year of my thirteenth birthday, I slept with the lights on all year. Oh, I was sure there was a witch behind every wisteria." A few years went by, and Blanche did not receive "the curse." Finally her mother took her to the family doctor to see if she was developing normally. Blanche describes what happened: "[The doctor] said, 'Blanche, do you mean to tell me you still don't have your period?' And I said, 'Well of course I have my period, you fool, I'm not a child. I've had my period almost two years. It's "the curse" I don't have!'"[8]

The episode vacillates between depicting menstruation as a good and natural part of life and depicting it as a negative aspect of women's biology. On the one hand, the women on the show describe the discomforts associated with periods: mood swings, binge eating, and cramps. On the other hand, when Blanche's periods stop, she feels that she has lost something precious. What others describe as a curse she treasures as a sign of her womanhood.

This same ambivalence marks an episode from *The Cosby Show* from 1990. The episode is called "The Infantry Has Landed"—a phrase that is, apparently, yet another euphemism for menstruation. In the episode, twelve-year-old Rudy Huxtable gets her period for the first time. She and her middle-school friends discuss all of the "facts" that they have heard about menstruation: that, for example, a woman should not attend a circus during "that time of the month" because her presence will upset the animals; or, that she should not swim in the ocean lest she attract sharks. Rudy is extremely uncomfortable with her newfound womanhood, and she squirms away when her mother Clair wants to discuss the matter. Clair wants to make sure that Rudy does not receive the same negative messages about menstruation that she herself did as a girl, and so she proposes that the two of them celebrate this new stage of Rudy's life by declaring a holiday: "Woman's Day." Rudy, she says, may choose any activity she wishes—a carriage ride in Central Park, a movie, dinner at a favorite restaurant—"The city is yours," says Mrs. Huxtable.

In the end, Rudy chooses to celebrate Woman's Day simply by watching *Gone With the Wind* with her mother. The two Huxtable women snuggle in their pajamas on the couch in the family living room with a bowl of popcorn at the ready. Shyly, Rudy explains that she didn't want her mother to make a big deal out of the onset of menstruation because, as she says, she did not see why they should celebrate "the most humiliating day of my life." Responds Clair, "That's why they call it the curse." Clair expresses great sympathy for her daughter and explains, "It's been going on since the beginning of time." Though she says that menstruation brings painful and embarrassing moments, Mrs. Huxtable points out that it also means that Rudy is now able to give birth: "See, some day you'll be able to have children of your own," she notes.

The same ambiguity characterizes a 1999 episode of the satirical cartoon series *King of the Hill,* in which the Hill family's young neighbor, a girl named Connie, gets her period for the first time. Because she is staying with the Hills while her parents are out of town, when she realizes that she is menstruating, Connie has no one to turn to for help except the hapless Hank Hill. Hank realizes that in order to get the supplies that Connie needs, he must make a trip to the drugstore's dreaded Aisle 8A ("Feminine Hygiene Products") to buy tampons and pads. Meanwhile, Hank's son Bobby, who considers Connie his girlfriend, has to cope with the changes that Connie is going through: "She's got the curse, and I think I caused it. All my hormones bein' too close to her hormones." A friend of Bobby's tries to explain to him how girls become different when they begin menstruating: "It's all over, Bobby. I heard that when girls get the curse, they only go out with hairy high school guys with cars." Poor Bobby can only respond, "I've got peach fuzz and a bike!"

Reversing the Curse: Eve Versus Mary

In 2008 the makers of Midol, a pain reliever designed for women with menstrual discomfort, introduced the advertising slogan "Reverse the Curse." The idea behind the ad seemed to be that through pharmaceutical intervention, one could overcome the affliction to which women had been sentenced at the start of time. The ad did not seem to consider the origin of the so-called curse; after all, if one really believes that menstruation is the result of God's punishment of Eve and her daughters, one might hesitate before trying to reverse it with a few grams of acetaminophen.

Responses to the ad, though, at least the responses that appeared in the blogosphere, were not upset that Midol was explicitly attempting to counteract what tradition holds to be God's word. Instead, those who saw the advertisement were upset because they felt that Midol was perpetuating negative views about menstruation. For example, one blogger wrote, "'Reverse the curse'?! . . . I cannot believe that Midol just said that out loud on their TV commercial . . . ?! Curse?! This is how people should refer to female biology?"[9] An editorial in the *Indiana Daily Student* newspaper urged, "It's time to reverse the curse. No, Midol commercials, I don't mean ending my period. I mean reversing the curse you have conjured up against periods."[10] Likewise, a progressive organization called the Feminist Peace Network urged its members to "Reverse the Curse: Don't Buy Midol."[11] Many people at this point are loathe, it seems, to accept the time-honored teaching that menstruation is the result of Eve's sin.

And yet, as we have seen, that teaching has roots that run deep. Equally old is the Catholic teaching that there has already been a woman who was able to reverse the curse of Eve: the Virgin Mary. Eve, according to Genesis, suffered in bringing forth children, desired her husband, and was subject to death. Catholic tradition says that Mary, in contrast, did not suffer in giving birth to Jesus, remained ever-virgin, and did not die. Mary thus points the way out of the fallen state into which Adam and Eve brought the rest of us.

Medieval theologians made much of the fact that the name Eva is the Latin word *Ave* (as in "*Ave Maria*," English: "Hail Mary") spelled backwards. Peter Damian, for example, offered this prayer to the Virgin: "That angel who greets you with 'Ave'/ Reverses sinful Eva's name./ Lead us back, O holy Virgin/ Whence the falling sinner came."[12] The notorious *Malleus Maleficarum*, the Inquisitor's manual for identifying women who were witches, noted that "the whole sin of Eve [is] taken away by

the benediction of Mary."[13] Painters made the same point by contrasting the two biblical women visually. One fifteenth-century illustration
called "The Tree of Death and Life" shows a naked Eve taking fruit from
a serpent who is wrapped around a tree, and then giving it to her demonic
children. At the same time, Mary, clothed in a blue robe, plucks com-
munion wafers from the tree and gives them to the Christians who kneel
at her feet. The contrast is clear: Eve is the sexual sinner who brought
death into the world, while Mary is the pure virgin who gave birth to the
savior Jesus.

Often the difference between Eve and Mary is made by showing the
contrasting relations between the two women and the snake. In Genesis
3:15, God says to the serpent, "I will put enmity between you and the
woman, and between your offspring and hers; he will strike your head,
and you will strike his heel." However, an early Latin translation of the
Bible called the Vulgate rendered the text this way: "She shall crush thy
head, and thou shalt lie in wait for her heel." In other words, the woman,
rather than her offspring, would conquer the snake. On the face of it,
this translation did not make sense, since Eve had yielded to the serpent
instead of crushing it. Interpretations solved this problem by concluding
that the text must refer not to Mary but to Eve. Mary would be the one
to crush sin.

Eve Versus Mary: Original Sin

Thus in virtually any Catholic gift shop one can find sculptures and
paintings of the Virgin Mary standing placidly on top of a defeated reptile. Often the title of these images is "The Immaculate Conception."
The Catholic teaching about the Immaculate Conception was declared
to be infallible teaching in 1854 by Pope Pius IX. It says that "the most
Blessed Virgin Mary, in the first instance of her conception, by a singular
grace and privilege granted by Almighty God, in view of the merits of
Jesus Christ, the Savior of the human race, was preserved free from all
stain of original sin."[14] In other words, unlike all of the other descendants
of Adam and Eve, Mary was not infected by the corruption that occurred
when our first parents ate the forbidden fruit.

Depictions of the Immaculate Conception frequently portray Mary as
overcoming original sin by crushing a serpent. For example, Giovanni
Battista Tiepolo's painting from the 18th century shows Mary standing
atop a globe of the earth. Splayed across the earth underneath her bare

feet is a dragon-like snake with an apple in its mouth. Mary, however, is unconcerned about the creature. She is surrounded by cherubs, and above her head is a dove which symbolizes the Holy Spirit. She has conquered Eve's sin through her very conception, and she now reigns in the heavens.

In popular culture, the doctrine that Mary was spared original sin is almost always confused with the Christian assertion that Mary conceived Jesus without having had sex. The Immaculate Conception, in other words, becomes confused with the Virgin Birth.

The dogma concerning the Immaculate Conception holds that Mary was conceived in the usual way: her parents had sex and her mother became pregnant with her. However, at that moment, at the moment when Mary's mother became pregnant, God intervened and spared the newly conceived baby Mary from original sin. The teaching concerning the Virgin Birth, on the other hand, says that Mary herself became pregnant without having had sex.

It is difficult to explain why this misunderstanding about the meaning of Catholic teaching about Mary is so widespread. Perhaps the answer is that, post-Augustine, Christians (and cultures that have been influenced by Christianity) have come to think of sex as tainted by sin. If sex is "dirty," then not having sex would be "immaculate." This may explain why when people hear "immaculate conception," what they hear is, "conception without sex." In any case, the mistake appears again and again in mass culture.

Consider a few examples: In a 2001 episode of *CSI: Crime Scene Investigation*, two detectives investigate the murder of a young woman named Erin.

> Detective #1: You really think Erin knew she was pregnant? I mean, six weeks?"
> Detective #2: Twenty-year-old girl, living at home? She would have taken a test if she was five seconds late—panic city.
> Detective #1: Yeah . . . Brass talked to her parents. There was no guy in her life.
> Detective #2: Well, it's not the immaculate conception. If the guy was Mr. Right she would have told her folks. Which means he was Mr. Wrong. Maybe Mr. Married.[15]

Clearly the detectives have confused the idea of the Immaculate Conception with the idea that the young girl became pregnant without having had sex.

The same mistake occurs in an episode of the medical drama *House M. D.* when a physician informs a patient that she has miscarried. The woman protests that she has not had sex recently and therefore could not have been pregnant:

> Dr. Gregory House: Fine. Have it your way. Immaculate conception.
> Patient: Um, what do I do?
> Dr. Gregory House: Well, it's obvious—start a religion.[16]

Other examples can be found in the Showtime series *Californication*, in an episode of Fox's *Prison Break*, and in the Cartoon Network's *Aqua Teen Hunger Force*.[17]

Eve Versus Mary: Pain in Childbirth

The Genesis story says that Eve would experience pain in bearing children. Did Mary suffer during the birth of Jesus? Catholic tradition says no. As the *New Catholic Encyclopedia* explains, "Mary . . . as the new Eve, blessed among women (Luke 1.28) in contrast with the malediction of the first Eve, is seen by the Fathers [that is, early Church authorities] as free from the punishments of Genesis 3.16, which include the pangs of childbirth."[18] A second-century noncanonical text called the Infancy Gospel of James illustrates this point. According to the text (which is not included in the Bible), as Jesus was being born, Joseph and a midwife stood in the cave where Mary lay. The cave was shrouded by a cloud, "And immediately the cloud withdrew from the cave, and a great light appeared in the cave so that their eyes could not bear it. After a while the light withdrew, until the baby appeared." The gospel emphasizes that Mary remained a virgin even during the birth of Jesus. According to the story, an attendant who refused to believe that such a thing was possible decided to examine Mary's hymen herself. Immediately, however, the hand that she stretched out towards Mary's body withered as if it were on fire. The attendant was later healed miraculously when she picked up the baby Jesus.[19]

A medieval hymn made the same point by proclaiming, "The Virgin rose and stood erect against a column that was there. But Joseph remained seated . . . taking some hay from the manger, placed it at the Lady's feet and turned away. Then the Son of the eternal God came out of the womb of the mother without a murmur or lesion, in a moment."[20] So important was Mary's virginity to the medieval mind that Catholics claimed not only that Mary conceived Jesus without having had sex, but also that Jesus's passage down the birth canal did not violate the intactness of Mary's body.

Movies about the nativity of Jesus are mixed on this subject. Two blockbuster films from the 1960s skirted the issue of whether or not Mary experienced labor pains by not including scenes of Jesus's actual birth. In *King of Kings* (1961) Mary appears on screen shortly before the parturition looking calm and unruffled, and she has no obvious belly despite her husband's prediction that she will have her baby later that night. Likewise, *The Greatest Story Ever Told* (1965) does not show Mary during the delivery, and when the Virgin appears after her baby is born, she looks fresh and rumple-free.

On the other hand, *Jesus of Nazareth* (1977) and *The Nativity Story* (2006) both include labor scenes during which Mary cries out in pain. These movies, it seems, sought a more natural presentation of Jesus's birth. *The Nativity Story* was directed by Catherine Hardwicke, who had previously directed *Thirteen* (2003), a coming-of-age story about a young girl who becomes involved in drug use and sex. Hardwicke had also directed *Lords of Dogtown* (2005), a movie about teens from the wrong side of the tracks who learn to skateboard. Perhaps because of her earlier work portraying less-than-perfect young people, Hardwicke wanted to give a more realistic edge to the story of Mary.

Eve Versus Mary: Perpetual Virginity

Catholic tradition holds not just that Mary conceived Jesus without having had sex, but also that Mary remained a virgin throughout the rest of her life. As the first edition of the *New Catholic Encyclopedia* explained, "The significance of Mary's virginity after the birth of Jesus consists in the reverence due to Mary as the sanctuary of God's presence on earth through her role in the Incarnation and also through her role as the new Eve, totally dedicated to the service of God as the handmaid of the Lord."[21] The first Eve had sex and became mother of all the living. Mary did not have sex and, says Catholic teaching, became mother of the savior who restored eternal life to the children of Eve.

Hail Mary (1985)

The idea that virginal faith can redeem sinful sexuality is developed in several movies, including Jean-Luc Godard's controversial *Hail Mary*

(1985).[22] The movie at several points contrasts two female characters: Mary, who is the daughter of a gas-station attendant and who refuses to have sex with her boyfriend, and Eva, a young student of science and philosophy who is having an affair with her married professor.

Mary is a virgin. She declares to her taxi-driving boyfriend Joseph, "I sleep with no one." When Joseph tries to kiss her, she turns her head away. She even eschews wearing lipstick, as doing so is apparently too worldly. And yet, somehow, miraculously, Mary becomes pregnant. In a strange encounter at the gas station, she is told by a small girl and the girl's seedy-looking Uncle Gabriel that she is going to give birth.

Joseph, understandably, is skeptical about Mary's claim that she has not slept with another man. Eventually Gabriel convinces him that Mary is telling the truth, and Joseph and Mary come to a kind of agreement about what kind of physical relationship they will share. There is a long scene in which Joseph learns from Mary how to tell her that he loves her. At first he does this wrongly, reaching out to touch her belly while declaring his love. Eventually, however, he learns that he must withdraw his hand rather than reaching it out to her. In order to say "I love you," he must pull away from her body rather than approaching it. Mary tells Joseph, "The hand of God is upon me, and you can't interfere."

Meanwhile, Eva is pursuing an affair with her philosophy teacher. The professor is convinced that, contrary to what some scientists think, "The astonishing truth is that life was willed, desired, anticipated, organized, programmed by a determined intelligence." Humans did not emerge from an amino-acid soup, he says. Rather, our ancestors, in the form of primitive bacteria, came from space: "We wonder what an extraterrestrial looks like. Go to a mirror and look at yourself."

The professor is married, but his wife and son are back in Czechoslovakia, and so he is sleeping with Eva, whom he insists on calling Eve. There can be no doubt about the significance of Eva's name; when she and her lover go away together for a vacation, it is to a place called the Paradise Villa that they head. There Eva/Eve toys with an apple until she finally picks it up and slowly, delicately, bites into it.

The affair between teacher and student ends badly. The professor decides to return home to his family and Eva is left in despair. She sobs, "The world's too sad" and asks "Don't I count for you?" As the professor picks up his suitcase and walks towards the train that will take him back to his wife and son, Eva tells him, "You really are a nothing."[23]

In contrast, Mary and Joseph are learning how to express their love in nonphysical ways. Mary consistently portrays the soul as more important than the body. When she asks her doctor, "Does the soul have a body?" he answers, "The body has a soul." Replies Mary, "I thought it was the opposite." Later, she declares, "Let the soul be body. Then no one can say that the body is soul, since the soul shall be body." The central element of personhood is, for Godard's version of Mary, the soul. The soul may temporarily become body, but it remains soul nonetheless, and it is the constant marker of identity.

At the end of *Hail Mary*, a kind of resolution is suggested between the twin images of Eve and Mary: between sexual fallenness and virginal purity. The very last scene of the movie shows Mary, now a married woman and the mother of a young son, approaching her car. Standing nearby is Gabriel. He calls to her: "Madam! Hey, Madam!" She asks, "What is it?" Responds Gabriel, "Nothing. Hail, Mary!" At that moment, church bells ring out, and Mary turns her face up to look at the sun. She gets into her car and lights a cigarette, smiling a little. Then she takes up a tube of lipstick. She pulls the tube straight toward her mouth, an image that suggests fellatio or sexual intercourse. At first, she does not allow the tube to touch her lips. She hesitates several times. Then, at last, she applies the lipstick. The last shot is of Mary's open, reddened mouth.

It is difficult to know how to interpret this scene. Perhaps the gesture means that Mary has finally resolved the conflict between her body and her soul. She is both the chosen one of God and a modern, sexual woman.[24] On the other hand, perhaps the ending of the film merely reinforces the dichotomy that it had set up earlier. Perhaps what it says is that once Mary had fulfilled the task that God gave her, she reverted to the "fallen" ways of every other woman. If the latter, then the movie's failure to reconcile the purity of virginity with the sinfulness of sexuality puts most women in an untenable position. Apart from Mary, it is impossible for women who are virgins to give birth. As historian Marina Warner observes, "Accepting the Virgin as the ideal of purity implicitly demands rejecting the ordinary female condition as impure."[25]

Polish Wedding (1998)

This seems to be the point that the movie *Polish Wedding* (1998) wishes to make. The film tells the story of a Polish-American family living in Detroit. Bolek (played by Gabriel Byrne) is the titular head of the Pzoniak clan, but it is his wife Jadzia (Lena Olin) who wields the most power in the family. Jadzia is having an affair with another man, and her baker-husband has all but resigned himself to his status as a cuckold. When the couple's teenaged daughter Hala (Claire Danes) becomes pregnant, however, Bolek and Jadzia are forced to examine their views of love and sexuality more deeply.

Hala is an unwed high school dropout who sneaks out of her parents' house at night to run barefoot through the streets and alleys of her moon-lit neighborhood. The father of Hala's unborn baby is a young police officer with whom the girl has had sex only once. Hala's pregnancy com-plicates her life for several reasons, but most of all because it threatens her ability to participate in an upcoming parish festival. As it happens, Hala has been chosen to place a wreath of flowers on a statue of the Vir-gin Mary during the church's annual procession in honor of Our Lady of Czestochowa, patroness of Poland. The honor is significant; as the local priest explains, "To lead the Virgin's procession is a high and solemn privilege reserved for one who embodies all that we prize in womanly virtue: innocence, chastity, and purity." Hala's pregnancy would seem to indicate that she is not the best representative of those virtues.

Or is she? Why, the movie asks, does sexual activity make one less innocent or less pure? Why is chastity privileged above the very activity that makes life possible: making love? At one point in the film, Bolek is frustrated with his wife's unfaithfulness, and he asks her, "Don't you believe in anything more important than yourself? Your religion? God?" Jadzia, pointing to the child of one of her sons, a baby grandson whom she is holding in her arms, replies, "Nothing on earth is more sacred to me than this. Making life and love. That's my religion." Though eventually Jadzia abandons her extramarital affair and returns to her husband's bed, she never surrenders her conviction that it is her sexual and generative powers that matter most.

This conviction is solidified in one of the movie's final scenes, in which Hala marches in the procession to honor the Virgin. Surrounded by the parishioners, the priest prays to Mary, "You are blessed and full of grace. You are the tender giver of life. The innocent bearer of holy fruit." At this point Hala approaches Mary's statue in order to crown it with flowers, but several people in the crowd begin to murmur. Someone shouts "Sinner!" and a young man in the crowd asks loudly how it is possible for a virgin to be pregnant. Standing in front of the statue as the crowd's taunting grows louder, Hala prays to Mary for help. Suddenly, she turns and places the crown of blossoms on her own head, yelling to the crowd, "Put this in your pipe and smoke it!" The parish priest at this point realizes that Hala is not the "good girl" that he thought she was, and he threatens to strike her with an upraised hand. Before he can reach her, however, Hala's mother comes to her rescue. Then Jadzia, wearing a tight-fitting red dress, walks the pregnant Hala, dressed in white and still wearing the wreath on her head, through the assembly. The crowd suddenly becomes quiet. Men, women, and children kneel in awe and bless themselves with the sign of the cross as they watch Hala and her mother proceed through their midst with dignity and honor. The movie's point becomes clear. Life is sacred, the film asserts, and women should be cherished for their sexuality instead of condemned because of it.

At several points in the movie a contrast is set up between Mary, on the one hand, and the Roman goddess Venus (Greek: Aphrodite) on the other. Bolek describes Hala to a friend as "a Venus," and in one shot we see Hala standing with her blonde tresses blowing out to the side, just as the goddess's hair does in Botticelli's fifteenth-century painting "The Birth of Venus." However, there are also hints that Hala is not just Venus but also Eve. This blurring of roles makes sense in terms of iconography and visual imagination. After all, one of the most famous stories from Greek mythology tells how Paris was asked to choose among three goddesses: Athena, Hera, and Aphrodite. He chose Aphrodite and signaled his choice by awarding her a golden apple. Thus Aphrodite/Venus is often shown reaching for or holding that fruit.

In *Polish Wedding*, there are two allusions to Eve, one implicit and the other explicit. At one point Jadzia serves the family soup made of ducks' blood, which only she and Hala will eat. None of the men at the table will touch the stuff, but the two women "lap it up like milk." Given the association between Eve and menstruation, this seems to be a reference to the supposed curse of our first mother, which in fact makes pregnancy and thus new life possible. The second and more overt reference occurs when Hala goes to her father's bakery to tell him about her pregnancy. As she tries to explain her problem, Bolek takes a lump of dough and says, "In the beginning, there was a lump of dough. You and I. Dough. Until the Master Breadmaker himself, with his own two hands, gave us shape. First he made man, and out of man's body, woman." Bolek's account of creation makes no sense to Hala: "How could a woman come out of a man?

It had to be the other way around. In the beginning there was a woman." Hala here identifies herself with Eve, who, in her thinking, had to have been created before Adam. She and Eve are both givers of life, something no man could ever hope to be.

Eve Versus Mary: Menstruation

Before concluding this discussion of Eve's curse, we must consider one other aspect of Mary as the New Eve. If Eve was the bringer of menstruation, then was Mary spared this monthly trouble? The question is not merely academic. In 2005, the cable television network Comedy Central caused worldwide protests when it aired an episode of the satirical cartoon *South Park* entitled "Bloody Mary." In the episode, a statue of the Virgin begins to exude menstrual blood, but the cartoon pope declares that the event is not a miracle: "A chick bleeding out her vagina is no miracle. Chicks bleed out their vaginas all the time," he concludes. A conservative organization called the Catholic League protested the episode, and as a result, Comedy Central agreed not to rerun it.[26]

Some medieval theologians held that the Virgin Mary did not in fact menstruate because as the New Eve she was exempt from the curse. Others, though, contended that Mary must have menstruated. Medieval biology held that breast milk was a transmuted form of menstrual fluid, and since innumerable paintings showed Mary breast-feeding her son, it was thought that she must have menstruated as well.[27] Though there is no dogmatic position on this issue, some Christians continue to hold that Mary did not in fact menstruate.[28]

In sum, the Adam and Eve story, for all of its apparent simplicity, actually preserves a deeply profound insight. Once our original parents were cast out of Eden, they both were subject to death and they reproduced sexually. A few short verses recapitulate an evolutionary process that took millions of years.

If, that is, you believe in evolution.

CHAPTER SEVEN

Monkeyshines

In January of 2008, *Mad* magazine published a list of "The Dumbest People, Events and Things of 2007!" Included on the roster was the opening of the Creation Museum in Kentucky, which *Mad* described as "proof positive that man's intelligence has not evolved in eons." The magazine opined that the museum's exhibits "don't merely challenge science, they ignore it completely!" and featured an accompanying cartoon entitled "Charles Darwin's Night at the Creation Museum" that shows Eve holding aloft a bright red apple for Adam to admire, Moses riding atop a Tyrannosaurus rex, and Darwin pulling out his hair, screaming in horror, and fleeing the museum's hallowed halls.[1] The article and cartoon capture both the intensity and the acrimony that mark debates about the origins of human life: were we created as the Bible tells us in Genesis 2–3, or did we evolve in the way described by Darwin?

One of the most famous and most important confrontations in the long-running argument about whether or not Adam and Eve were literally the ancestors of all people was the court battle known as the Scopes Monkey Trial. And yet, when John T. Scopes agreed to contest the Tennessee law that forbade the teaching of evolution in public schools, he had no idea what he was getting himself into. The football coach and substitute biology teacher later admitted that he was not even sure that he had ever actually taught Darwin to his students.[2] Still, the 1925 Scopes Monkey Trial became a turning point in American history. On the one hand, it provided a staging area for many of the cultural skirmishes that had been taking place for decades. On the other, it provided fuel for conflicts that would last all the way into the twenty-first century.

Today, the debate between creationists (that is, those who hold to a literal interpretation of the Genesis creation account) and evolutionists (who find Darwin's explanation for the development of humans more plausible) continues.[3] A survey done in 2007 asked American adults if they agreed or disagreed with this statement: "Human beings, as we know them, developed from earlier species of animals." The results showed a split, as 40 percent said that they agreed and 39 percent disagreed (while 21 percent said that they were not sure). Other studies have shown that Americans are among those least likely to believe in evolution. In Iceland, Denmark, Sweden, and France, for example, at least 80 percent of people agree that humans evolved from other species.[4]

The split in American opinion is reflected in popular culture as well, though most expressions in the media tend to favor Darwin. Critical presentations of creationism appear in Bill Maher's documentary *Religulous* (2008) and on at least two episodes of *The Simpsons*, and they routinely show up in Comedy Central's mock news program *The Colbert Report*. The powerful 1960 film *Inherit the Wind*, as well as its 1999 small-screen remake, both use the Scopes Trial as a setting in which to ridicule creationism and to preach the primacy of the human intellect instead. The Smithsonian National Museum of Natural History, which is visited by six million people per year, stands squarely on the side of evolution. Its website explains, "Evolutionary theory provides a logical framework for making sense of the great diversity of organisms on earth—for understanding both differences and similarities among them."[5]

However, creationism does have its place in popular culture. The Creation Museum in Petersburg, Kentucky, which was founded to defend a literal interpretation of Genesis, attracted more than four hundred thousand visitors in its first year and was endorsed by Christian media giant Jerry Falwell Ministries.[6] A radio program that features the museum's founder, entitled "*Answers. . . with Ken Ham*," is heard on more than nine hundred radio stations worldwide,[7] and the museum itself was featured in the HBO documentary *Friends of God* (2007). Creationist views also appear in the 2006 documentary *Jesus Camp*.

That the evolutionist/creationism debate should find its way into popular culture is not surprising. The same thing, after all, has been happening for almost a century.

The Scopes Trial

In January of 1925, the Tennessee House of Representatives passed a bill concerning the teaching of evolution. "Be it enacted by the general assembly of the state of Tennessee," declared House Bill 185, "that it shall be unlawful for any teacher in any of the universities, normals and all other public schools of the state which are supported in whole or in part by the public school funds of the state, to teach any theory that denies the story of the divine creation of man as taught in the Bible, and to teach instead that man has descended from a lower order of animals."[8] The Tennessee Senate soon followed suit, and in March of that year, the Butler Bill (named for the representative who had introduced it on the House floor) became state law. Apparently when Tennessee Governor Austin Peay signed the bill, he was primarily interested in appeasing some of his constituents and did not think that the legislation would actually affect what was taught in Tennessee's classrooms: "Nobody believes that it is going to be an active statute," he explained.[9]

Nonetheless, the newly launched American Civil Liberties Union (ACLU) in New York was not about to let the law go unchallenged. The organization published advertisements in Tennessee newspapers seeking someone willing to challenge the statute, and it got a response from a group of citizens in the small town of Dayton. Looking to bring some publicity (and some business) to its area, the group persuaded high school coach Scopes to act as plaintiff in challenging the Butler Act, and Scopes agreed. Legal legend Clarence Darrow acted as lawyer for the defense, and the famous populist William Jennings Bryan represented the prosecution. At the end of the famous trial, Scopes was found guilty of violating Tennessee law, and he was fined one hundred dollars. The fine was never paid, and two years later the conviction was overturned. The Butler Act itself was repealed in 1967.[10]

Background of the Scopes Trial

The Scopes trial brought to a boil many of the cultural conflicts that had been brewing in the opening decades of the twentieth century. One of these conflicts pitted small-town life against the allure of the big city. In the years following World War I, soldiers returning from Europe were often reluctant to go back to the homes they had left behind. The 1918 song "How 'Ya Gonna Keep 'Em Down on the Farm (After They've Seen Paree)?" captured the anxiety that Americans felt as they saw their young men abandoning country life and moving to the cities. In fact, the post-war years saw a significant demographic shift; the 1920 census revealed that for the first time, more Americans lived in urban districts than in rural areas.[11]

A shift in cultural mores occurred as well. The Jazz Age encouraged women to bob their hair and shorten their hems, and to use tobacco and alcohol as much as their male counterparts did. In 1920, the 19th Amendment to the U.S. Constitution gave women the right to vote. Meanwhile, new inventions like telephones, radios, phonographs, auto-mobiles, airplanes, and motion picture cameras gave Americans in even the smallest hamlets unprecedented access to the wider world. Along with this access came exposure to new and sometimes threatening ideas, including those of Charles Darwin, who in 1859 had published *On the Origin of Species by Means of Natural Selection*. In his work Darwin sought to account for the astonishing diversity of the earth's biological life. After its publication, Darwin's theory began to receive wider and wider accep-tance, and it gradually began to influence school curricula.

Darwin was not the first to discuss evolution or the idea that species changed over time. In fact, there had been a number of evolutionary theories circulating in the 19th century. What then set Darwin apart? According to naturalist Stephen Jay Gould, three things. First, in Dar-win's theory, evolution has no "purpose"; it relies on chance rather than on a foreordained design. Second, evolution has no direction; it does not lead inevitably from "lower" species to "higher" ones. In fact, in the first edition of his book, Darwin did not use the word "evolution" at all because the term seemed to imply progress. Instead, he simply used the neutral phrase "descent with modification" to explain how, as local envi-ronments change, organisms become either more or less well-adapted to their surroundings. As Gould puts the matter, "[I]f an amoeba is as well adapted to its environment as we are to ours, who is to say that we are higher creatures?" Finally, Darwin's theory was philosophically material-istic. Summarizing Darwin's position, Gould writes, "Matter is the ground of all existence; mind, spirit, and God as well, are just words that express the wondrous results of neuronal complexity."[12]

It is easy to see why Darwin's theories posed a threat to much of Chris-tian teaching. If Darwin were correct, then human beings were not the pinnacle of God's creation, as Genesis seemed to imply. Instead, we were mercly the result of random genetic mutations that happened to have made us well-adapted to our environment.

The theory of evolution was not the only idea circulating that seemed to challenge Christian teachings. Eleven years before Darwin had published his seminal work, Karl Marx had set forth his *Communist Manifesto*, and in 1882, Friedrich Nietzsche had written *The Joyful Wisdom*, in which he declared that God was dead. In 1906, physician and theologian Albert Schweitzer authored *The Quest of the Historical Jesus* which called into question the relation between the Jesus of history and the Jesus of Christian dogma. In 1913 Sigmund Freud published *Totem and Taboo*, which proposed a psychological theory for the origins of religion, and in 1916 Albert Einstein turned the world upside-down with his general theory of relativity.

All of this took place at the same time that reforms were beginning to make education mandatory for America's children. In the late nineteenth century, fewer than two hundred thousand young people attended high school—less than 5 percent of those eligible. By 1920, the number was ten times that.[13] Fierce debates broke out concerning what books these students would read and to what ideas they would be exposed. The very future of the United States seemed to hinge on the decisions that were made concerning school curricula.

Sideshows

The Monkey Trial was as much theater as it was legal battle. Media flocked to the small town of Dayton to witness the Scopes spectacle, and many journalists were forced to sleep in a downtown hardware store because all of the local hotels were full.[14] Special telephone and telegraph wires were installed so that reporters could transmit their stories, and a radio network was set up so that listeners around the nation could follow the court's proceedings. The Scopes affair was in fact the first time in American history that a trial was broadcast in real time.[15]

Near the Dayton courthouse, vendors sold stuffed monkeys while musicians performed songs written specially for the occasion, including one titled "You Can't Make a Monkey Out of Me." The owner of a drug store in Dayton dressed a chimp in a three-piece suit complete with polka-dotted bow tie, fedora, and white spats, and had him sip sodas along with the human customers. Other chimps were dressed in specially tailored soldiers' costumes and marched in formation carrying toy rifles, or they performed on piano and banjo while amused crowds looked on.[16]

Meanwhile, comedians and satirists took full advantage of the occasion. A cartoon in the *Nashville Tennessean* showed two monkeys reading a newspaper filled with headlines about cruelty to animals, auto accidents, child labor, murder, alcohol abuse, and short skirts for women. The monkeys in the cartoon worried that their reputation would be sullied by Darwin's associating them with human beings. In New Jersey, members of a local Rotary Club staged a mock version of the trial complete with a judge who presided while using a monkey wrench for a gavel; the hearing broke up when a man dressed as an ape appeared in the courtroom and leapt from table to table. In London, a newspaper held a contest to see who could write the best limerick about the trial. The ten-dollar prize was awarded to a poem that questioned the intelligence of people in Tennessee by speculating that perhaps monkeys were evolved from humans, rather than the other way around.[17]

The Scopes Trial and Hollywood: *Inherit the Wind*

The actual proceedings of the Scopes Trial have been practically eclipsed by Hollywood's portrayal of the famous conflict. The most influential of these portrayals has been the 1960 movie *Inherit the Wind*, which was based on a play written by Jerome Lawrence and Robert E. Lee. The movie, with its version set in the fictional town of Hillsboro, has for all practical purposes replaced the story of what actually happened in the Scopes trial.

Inherit the Wind opens with vocalist Leslie Uggams singing the hymn "Gimme That Old Time Religion." As the clock on the Hillsboro courthouse strikes eight, a determined group of town officials marches to the local schoolhouse where young biology teacher Bertram T. Cates is delivering a lecture on the evolution of human beings. Though startled by the arrival of the grim-faced men in his classroom, Cates nonetheless continues his lesson until he is arrested and thrown into jail. There he is visited by his fiancée Rachel, who is the daughter of a local fundamentalist minister. Rachel tries to get Bert to retract his teachings but he refuses, asking incredulously, "Tell them if they let my body out of jail I'd lock up my mind?"

Already, the movie diverges significantly from Scopes's actual history. As we saw above, the young teacher was not an ardent evolutionist.

Because he had occasionally acted as a substitute for the regular biology teacher, and because the state-approved biology textbook used by Dayton's high school at that time included a version of evolutionary teaching, Scopes agreed to stand for trial.[18] He never spent any time in jail, however, nor was he ever threatened with lynching, as Bert Cates is in the film. In fact, Scopes later recalled that during the trial, the people of Dayton did not treat him any differently than they had before: "I could detect neither suspicion nor fulsome praise for my part in making the town the scene of action."[19] Scopes also did not have a girlfriend, much less a fiancée, at the time of the trial. Rachel and her fire-and-brimstone father are fictional creations.

The authors of the play on which the movie was based were clear when they published the drama that they were not presenting history. In their introduction, Lawrence and Lee stated, "*Inherit the Wind* does not pretend to be journalism. It is theatre. It is not 1925. The stage directions set the time as 'Not too long ago.' It might have been yesterday. It could be tomorrow."[20] In fact, the authors were not really writing about the Scopes Trial at all. They had quite another issue in mind when they penned the play: McCarthyism. In the 1950s, Senator Joseph McCarthy had zealously attempted to identify and punish Communists and those who sympathized with Communist ideas. The result in Hollywood was that a number of screenwriters, actors, and directors were blacklisted and forced out of their jobs. Lawrence and Lee were concerned about this development and used the Scopes Trial as a setting in which to protest what they saw as government's encroaching on freedom of thought and speech.[21]

The director of the 1960 film, Stanley Kramer, had similar concerns. When the movie was released he issued a statement in which he explained, "The spirit of the trial lives on, because the real issues of that trial were man's right to think and man's right to teach. These are issues for which the never-ending struggle continues and they constitute the real theme of *Inherit the Wind*."[22] Years later, Kramer reiterated his position: "To me at least, the whole story is about freedom of expression, its importance in our society, and the challenges to it."[23]

Seen as a vehicle to promote the sacredness of human inquiry, *Inherit the Wind* is spectacularly successful. As the burly agnostic lawyer Henry Drummond (the movie's counterpart to Darrow), actor Spencer Tracy is powerful and compelling. During the trial Drummond argues that there is nothing holier than the human mind and that "an idea is a greater monument than a cathedral." Questioning Matthew Harrison Brady (the film's version of Bryan) on the witness stand, he demands, "Why do you deny the one faculty of man that raises him above the other creatures of the earth: the power of his brain to reason!" When Brady counters that the Bible should be trusted because God "spake" it, Drummond retorts, "How do you know that God didn't spake to Charles Darwin?"

For his part, Brady (played by Fredric March) appears as a pompous old fool who craves the adoration of the crowds outside the courtroom but lacks the intellectual force of his courtroom opponent. Though physically nearly identical to the real-life William Jennings Bryan, in personality Brady bears only a passing resemblance to the great populist and orator. The Bryan of history was a reformer who was in many ways, though not in all, well ahead of his time. Bryan endorsed women's right to vote as early as 1910 and frequently represented the interests of farmers and wage-earners against the domination of corporations. He supported the establishment of a nationalized railway system, pushed for government subsidies for crops, and believed in laws that would guarantee workers a living wage. He also, however, endorsed segregation and felt that the "Caucasian race" was superior to all others.[24]

When it came to Darwinism, one of Bryan's primary objections was that it seemed to undercut the basis for morality. If people were taught that they were nothing better than animals, he reasoned, then they would act no better than do animals. Specifically, they would have no reason to care for the old or for the weak and helpless—those who could not contribute to the perpetuation of the species. Another of Bryan's objections had to do with a form of social Darwinism that sought to prevent "inferior" people from reproducing. Eugenics was at that point gaining popularity in the United States, and Bryan saw it as a dangerous force.[25]

Inherit the Wind offers only hints of these issues that so consumed the real-life Bryan. At one point in the movie, in response to people who praise the virtues of science, Brady says, "I have been to their cities and I have seen the altars upon which they sacrifice the futures of their children to the gods of science. And what are their rewards? Confusion and self-destruction. New ways to kill each other in wars." This statement reflects Bryan's concerns about the effect of Darwinism on morality. For the most part, however, the fictional Brady seems concerned with defending a literal interpretation of the Bible for its own sake rather than out of concern for the world's downtrodden.

The movie also features another quasihistorical character named E. K. Hornbeck (played by Gene Kelly), a cinematic counterpoint to the real-life journalist H. L. Mencken. Mencken was a columnist for the *Baltimore Sun* and editor of the *American Mercury*, and during the trial he turned his caustic wit squarely against Bryan and the people of Dayton. At the end of the court proceedings, Mencken wrote that the judge in the case had "postured before the yokels like a clown in a ten-cent show." He opined that "almost every word he has uttered has been an undisguised appeal to their prejudices and superstitions." Mencken described Bryan as "old, disappointed and embittered" and as suffering from "religious hallucinations."[26] The people of Dayton he cast as morons and hillbillies, which caused some of the local citizenry to become so enraged that they threatened to take Mencken into an alley and beat him up.[27] In the film, E. K. Hornbeck is similarly contemptuous of the townsfolk of Hillsboro. When a woman offers him a room to rent, asking him, "Are you looking for a nice, clean place to stay?" he answers, "I had a clean place to stay, Madame, and I left it to come here."

The movie's first glimpse of Hornbeck comes when the journalist arrives at the Hillsboro jail to offer his services to Bert. He appears in the foreground wearing a suit, bow tie, and white straw hat, and biting into an apple. He offers the fruit to Bert's girlfriend Rachel, and when she refuses to take it, he laughs, "Oh, don't worry, I'm not the serpent, little Eva. This isn't from the Tree of Knowledge. Oh, no. You won't find one growing in Heavenly Hillsboro. A few Ignorance Bushes, perhaps, but no Tree of Knowledge." Gesturing toward Bert, he adds, "Ask Adam." In several places the journalist is referred to in devilish terms. A woman calls him "the Stranger," and his very name, "Horn-beck," suggests a connection with Satan. If he is fiendish, however, it is primarily because he and his newspaper have paid for the services of lawyer Henry Drummond, whom Hornbeck welcomes to Hillsboro by saying, "Hello, Devil. Welcome to Hell."

Throughout the movie, Hornbeck never surrenders his cynical demeanor. Drummond, however, comes across as both the defender of human reason and an admirer of his opponent, Brady. This is shown at the very end of the trial, when Brady dies suddenly. (It should be noted that while in the movie Brady dies in the courtroom itself as the proceedings are wrapping up, in real life Bryan died while taking a nap several days after the end of the case.) Hearing the news of Brady's passing, Hornbeck continues to ridicule the lawyer as a closed-minded bigot and as a "Bible-beating bunko artist." Drummond, however, turns on Hornbeck: "You have no meaning. You're like a ghost pointing an empty sleeve and smirking at everything that people feel or want or struggle for. I pity you."

In the very last scene of the film, as he is gathering his belongings together in order to leave, Drummond picks up his copy of Darwin's book from the courtroom table. Then he spies his copy of the Bible lying there as well, and he picks that up too. As he holds the books in his hands, balancing them against each other, Leslie Uggams begins to sing the "Battle Hymn of the Republic," the first line of which proclaims, "Mine eyes have seen the glory of the coming of the Lord." Drummond seems to muse to himself, and then he places the Bible squarely on top of Darwin and carries both books from the courtroom. The music swells, and Uggams sings, "His truth is marching on."

Critics disagree about the meaning of this last scene. Some see it as the director pulling his punches in order to soften the beating that religion took throughout the movie. Critic Donald Spoto writes that the final scene was inserted "to counteract the anger of those who might consider the film irreligious" and "to broaden the film's appeal." He sees the ending as problematic because it "muddies the impact of what has just preceded."[28]

There is another way of looking at the concluding scene, however. During the actual Scopes Trial, Darrow called Bryan as a witness for the defense, and Bryan accepted the challenge; these were both highly original and controversial moves. (Bryan's testifying was so controversial that the judge in the case later had the lawyer's statements removed from the court record). Bryan took his place in the witness box, and the exchange that took place next was by turns humorous, illuminating, and testy. At one point Darrow pointed out that not all religious people take the Bible literally or believe that the world is only a few thousand years old: "You do know that there are thousands of people who profess to be Christians who believe the earth is much more ancient and that the human race is much more ancient?"[29] Bryan acknowledged this to be true, and later, he himself indicated that he did not adhere strictly to a literal interpretation. When Darrow asked him if he believed that the earth was made in six days, he responded, "Not six days of twenty-four hours."[30] (In *Inherit the Wind*, Bryan makes a similar response: "I mean to state that it is not necessarily a twenty-four-hour day.") This response placed Bryan in the camp of those who hold what is sometimes called a "day-age" theory, which says that the biblical days referred to in Genesis are not literal days but rather periods of indeterminate length. Such an interpretation brings the biblical account of creation closer to that of the evolutionists in that it acknowledges that creation may have taken a very long time to develop.

Perhaps, then, the final scene of the movie is not a capitulation to religion but rather a suggestion that one need not choose between science and religion. The truth of God that Uggams sings about need not mean simply factual truth. As Catholic novelist Andrew Greeley has pointed out, if God can write history, God can also write poetry. Perhaps the final scene means to say that what in the movie Drummond calls the "poetry of Genesis" has a rightful place alongside the science of Darwin.

Creationism, Intelligent Design, and the Dover Trial

If so, then the film resolves much more on screen than has been resolved in real life. In real life, clashes between evolutionists and creationists continue apace. Moreover, the battle has also recently been joined by yet another voice in the debate: Intelligent Design.

The Church of the Flying Spaghetti Monster

Strictly speaking, Intelligent Design (ID) has nothing to do with the story of Adam and Eve. ID is a theory that holds that the universe, or at least certain features of the universe, are too orderly to have been the result of random chance. It is different from creationism in that it is not biblically based, nor does it adhere to the claim that the world was created by God in six days. According to the Discovery Institute, one of the most prominent promoters of ID, "Unlike creationism, the scientific theory of intelligent design is agnostic regarding the source of design and has no commitment to defending Genesis, the Bible, or any other sacred text."[31]

This professed agnosticism has been tested, however, by a satiric movement that calls itself the Church of the Flying Spaghetti Monster. The church was founded in 2005 when the Kansas State Board of Education was holding hearings to determine whether or not ID could be taught in its public schools. A twenty-four-year-old man who had graduated from college with a degree in physics sent a tongue-in-cheek letter to the Board expressing concern that "students will only hear one theory of Intelligent Design." The letter explained, "I and many others around the world are of the strong belief that the universe was created by a Flying Spaghetti Monster. . . . We feel strongly that the overwhelming scientific evidence pointing toward evolutionary processes is nothing but a coincidence, put in place by Him."[32] The point of the letter, and of the Church of the Flying Spaghetti Monster, was to allege that proponents of ID are not in fact agnostic when it comes to identifying the Designer of the universe, but that they have the God of Christianity in mind. The official website of the church features a banner with a mock-up of the Sistine Chapel's painting of "The Creation of Adam." Instead of Adam reaching out to touch the hand of God, the newly created man reaches for the noodly appendage of the Spaghetti Monster.[33]

Both ID proponents and creationists are clear that their positions differ from each other. And yet at times the lines between the movements blur. For example, the video *The Creation Adventure Team: Six Short Days, One Big Adventure* (2003), which is designed to teach creationism to children, relies heavily on the same arguments made by ID. Though clearly biblically based, it supports its contention that God made the world by offering the same evidence on which ID depends. For instance, it points out that the sun is exactly the proper distance from the earth to support life without freezing or burning it to death, that the earth spins on its axis at just the right speed to keep its inhabitants alive, and that the atmosphere protects the earth from (most) meteors. The video concludes, "That's just a fraction of the many details that God designed specifically with a purpose."

Perhaps it is not surprising, then, that the judge in an important recent court case ruled that "compelling evidence strongly supports Plaintiffs' assertion that ID is creationism re-labeled."[34] The case in question concerned the school district of Dover, Pennsylvania, which in 2004 had passed a resolution that said, in part, "Students will be made aware of gaps/problems in Darwin's theory and of other theories of evolution including, but not limited to, intelligent design."[35] The resolution prompted a lawsuit, and in December 2005 a judge decided against Dover's school district, stating, "The evidence at trial demonstrates that ID is nothing less than the progeny of creationism."[36]

The Simpsons: "The Monkey Suit" (2006)

A few months after the end of the Dover trial, the satiric cartoon *The Simpsons* aired an episode entitled "The Monkey Suit" which skewered antievolution legislation.[37] *The Simpsons* is one of the longest-running shows on television, having debuted in 1989, and it is famous for its cutting critiques of cultural trends. The focus of the show is the Simpson family that lives in the cartoon town of Springfield. Homer Simpson, a balding middle-aged boor, works at the town's nuclear power plant. His long-suffering wife Marge is a homemaker who cares for the couple's three children: Bart, a ten-year-old terror; Lisa, a precocious second-grader; and Maggie, an infant who constantly sucks on a pacifier.

"The Monkey Suit" also features the Simpsons' neighbor, a Christian evangelical and all-around nice guy named Ned Flanders. In the episode, Flanders takes his two sons to the Springfield Museum of Natural History and discovers that it includes a wing called the "Hall of Man." Inside, Ned is horrified to see that nearly all of the exhibits are about evolution. When he confronts the museum's curator to ask how it is possible to explain human origins without mentioning the Bible, the man points to an exhibit entitled "The Myth of Creation." The installation shows an arm coming out of the sky, pointing at the ground, and causing animals, flowers, and people to pop up. As Ned stares at the display, the Doobie Brothers' song "What a Fool Believes" plays in the background. Ned is appalled: "My most cherished beliefs a myth?" he cries in anguish.

Concerned about what the children of Springfield are learning, Ned turns to his pastor, the Reverend Lovejoy. The minister is not very helpful, however, and simply advises Ned to take the Bible "with a grain of salt." When his wife points out that taking a stand on evolution would bring publicity to the church, though, Lovejoy agrees to take up Ned's cause, and the two men manage to convince the local school principal to teach creationism in Springfield's classrooms in addition to evolution. Thus the children in the second grade are shown a video entitled *So You're Calling God a Liar: An Unbiased Comparison of Evolution and Creationism*. In the film, the Bible appears bathed in a spotlight from above and crowned with a halo, while Darwin's *Origin of Species* appears with blood-red letters that drip into hellish flames. Darwin (described by the video as "a cowardly drunk") also makes an appearance and at one point engages in a passionate kiss with Satan.

Eight-year-old Lisa Simpson is appalled by what she sees in the movie, and she points out to her classmates that even Pope John Paul II believed in evolution. Her complaints go unanswered, however, and the anti-evolution curriculum prevails. Despondently, Lisa reports to her mother Marge, "Today we had a test and every answer was 'God did it.'" Marge responds, "Well, I think it's good to give both ideas a fair hearing. Maybe they can learn from each other. Lots of times two incompatible things can both be true." Lisa is not convinced by this argument and takes her concern to the town council: "Evolution and creationism cannot coexist, people! It is time to go back to teaching one single truth!" The town agrees, but not in the way that Lisa had hoped. As a result of her speech, teaching evolution is henceforth banned in Springfield's classrooms, and only Genesis may be taught.

Lisa decides to fight back against the new curriculum. She organizes a secret club consisting of "seekers of truth" who gather to read Darwin's book aloud. (On the blackboard she has written the club's motto: *Viva la Evolución!*) Before she can get past the first page, however, the Springfield police burst in and arrest her for "the teaching of non-biblical science." Her case goes to court as "God v. Lisa Simpson," with lawyers Clarice Drummond for the defense and Wallace Brady for the prosecution. Things look bad for Lisa, as the sympathies of the courtroom are clearly with Brady. Brady refers to Darwin's theory as "devilution" and blames evolution for all of the evils of the world, including the death of Bambi's mother.[38] At that point, however, Marge decides that she should actually read Darwin's *Origin of Species* in order to "see what all the fuss is about." When she finishes, she exclaims, "Wow, Darwin's argument is incredibly persuasive!" Ever the good mother, she devises a plan to help Lisa with her case.

The following day at the trial, the prosecution puts two witnesses on the stand. The first is a scientist who holds a PhD in "truthology" from "Christian Tech." He testifies that evolution cannot be true because it has not found evidence of any missing link between apes and humans, and he provides an illustration of what such a link might look like for the courtroom to see. The next witness is Ned Flanders, who also doubts that humans and apes could have anything in common. As his testimony proceeds, however, Marge hands her loutish husband Homer a beer bottle for him to open. Homer struggles with the cap, desperate for a taste of his beloved brew, but the bottle-top will not budge. At this point Homer begins jumping around the courtroom, grunting and howling like an ape. Finally his antics cause so much commotion that Flanders interrupts his testimony in the witness box and yells, "Will you shut your yap, you big monkey-faced gorilla?" The courtroom gasps because it has become clear to all that Homer, holding his beer above his head and bellowing with frustrated rage, looks exactly like the "missing link" that the professor of truthology had testified did not exist. As a result, the judge in the case repeals the law against teaching evolution, and Lisa goes free.

It should be pointed out that though the *Simpsons* episode clearly sides with Darwin, evolutionists come in for criticism as well. When Ned and his sons go into the museum's Hall of Man, one of the exhibits they see in support of evolution is a collection of dinosaur bones with the title "Indisputable Fossil Records." The cartoon's inclusion of the sign can be interpreted as mocking the pretension that science knows all and may not be questioned. The same point is made during the trial when defense lawyer Drummond puts local scientist Professor Frink on the stand. Frink is a nerdy character with thick glasses and a peculiar habit of muttering to himself. Drummond asks him, "So does this theory of evolution necessarily mean that there is no God?" and the professor replies, "No, of course not." He then adds, "It just says that God is an impotent nothing from nowhere with less power than the undersecretary of Agriculture." His arrogance is clear, and equally clear is the show's satirical presentation of science's hubris.

At the very end of the episode, some reconciliation between religion and evolution is suggested. Having won her court case, Lisa seeks Ned out and explains to him that she respects his beliefs but that, as she says, "I just don't think religion should be taught in our schools, any more than you'd want scientists teaching at the church."

This solution, though, is not really very satisfactory. When Lisa says that she respects Ned's beliefs, what she is really saying is that she respects his right to hold erroneous beliefs. She has not changed her view that one must choose between creationism and evolution or between religion and science.

The episode does try to give some nuance to the science/religion debate in the voice of Marge. Mrs. Simpson, easily the most sympathetic character on the show, often represents practical common sense. When Lisa complains that she is being taught a lot of nonsense by the creationist curriculum, Marge tells her that sometimes "two incompatible things can both be true." To support her point, Marge offers Lisa a few examples. She says that on the one hand, Homer has told her that he has gone off to work. On the other hand, a quick glance out the window tells her that he is not at work but is in the family's backyard jumping on a trampoline. What she seems to be saying is that even though she knows that Homer has lied to her, she chooses to ignore the evidence of her senses and thus can believe both statements to be true.

The problem with this example is that it equates religion with a lie. Marge's advice seems to be that it is better to accept an untruth in order to keep peace in the family than to confront what one knows to be false. This is not a very good argument for the meaningfulness or the truth of religion.

Marge does give Lisa another instance of two apparently contradictory statements, however, and this second example is perhaps more helpful. Marge cites two beliefs about her young son Bart. The first, which is indisputable to anyone who has watched even one episode of the show, is that Bart is a brat. The other belief that Marge holds, though, is that Bart is her "special little guy." The truth of that second statement is equally apparent to fans of the show, as no matter how badly Bart acts, Marge consistently sees the good in him. Marge offers this example of contradiction to Lisa as a way of illustrating, again, that two incompatible beliefs can both be true.

The problem with this example, though, is that these two beliefs are not really incompatible. Surely one can love a child and consider him special even if he consistently misbehaves. But if it is not really an illustration of incompatible beliefs, Marge's example does at least hint at a way out of the religion-versus-science debate. If we think of religion and science as both making scientific claims about the origins of the universe, then Lisa is correct that we must choose. The world cannot both have evolved over a period of millions of years and have been created in six twenty-four-hour days, any more than Homer can really be both at work and on the family's trampoline. However, if we think of religion and science as making different types of statements about the world, then their claims will not conflict. It is no contradiction to say both that Marge loves Bart and that Bart is a brat. Both statements are true. In a similar way, perhaps both religion and science can make true statements about the world even if those statements are quite different. Unfortunately, however, the possibility that religion and science might truly not conflict after all is not developed by the episode.

Reclaiming the Culture: The Creation Museum

If *The Simpsons* does not solve the question of how religion ought to relate to science, another cultural manifestation of the debate is equally conflicted. The Creation Museum in Kentucky is a monument to Fundamentalism that was designed to be "a rallying place, calling people back to the absolute truth of the Bible."[39] At the same time, though, it seeks to use scientific research to bolster its claim that the world was truly created in six twenty-four hour days.

When entering the museum, visitors are first presented with the opportunity to have their photographs taken with a life-size model of a dinosaur. Dinosaurs are, in fact, one of the museum's big draws and are featured prominently in its advertisements and promotional materials. A bumper sticker sold in the museum's bookstore proclaims "We're Taking Dinosaurs Back!" Though it does not say precisely from whom the dinosaurs are being recovered, the implication is that they are being reclaimed from secular science so that they can take their rightful place in a biblically based worldview. Dinosaurs, according to the museum, lived in peace in the Garden of Eden with Adam and Eve. Why does the Bible not mention them? According to the museum, dinosaurs were created in Genesis 1:25 when God made the beasts of the earth. The reptiles lived in harmony with the first people and, because they were vegetarians, with the other animals as well. When God decided to flood the world, representatives of the dinosaurs were taken aboard Noah's ark. All of those not on the ark died in the ensuing flood, which accounts for the many fossil remains that we find today. The dinosaurs that were aboard the ark, as well as their offspring, eventually died out due to disease and starvation after the Flood.[40]

After having their photographs taken with the dinosaur, visitors then pass through several exhibits meant to make the point that creation and evolutionary theory both work with the same set of facts but begin with different perspectives. For example, a sign explains that human reason says that the universe began with the big bang billions of years ago. God's word, on the other hand, says that God created heaven and earth in six days and that creation took place only thousands of years ago. Another sign shows that human reason says that humans evolved from an ape that lived twenty million years ago. God's word, though, says that "God created man in his image" six thousand years ago. "God's Word is True," proclaims a sign: "Forty authors, writing over two thousand years, spoke the SAME MESSAGE." The Bible has prevailed, says the exhibit, despite attempts to question, destroy, discredit, and criticize it. Numerous attacks on God's word are listed on a sign in the museum. Their perpetrators include, among others, the "infidel philosopher" Voltaire, modernist theologians such as Charles Emerson Fosdick, the novel by Dan Brown called *The Da Vinci Code*, and "atheist evangelist" Charles Templeton.

The result of questioning God's word is made clear in a section of the museum called "Graffiti Alley." Here visitors encounter a brick wall papered over with images of warfare, the Columbine school shootings, gay marriage, and right-to-die legislation. A sign on the adjacent wall explains that when Scripture is abandoned by the culture, the results are relativistic morality, hopelessness, and meaninglessness. As visitors continue their walk through this section of the museum, they are surrounded by videos showing what happens when society ignores a literal interpretation of the Bible: drug addiction and alcoholism invade homes, children disobey their parents, and churches lose their focus.

Museum-goers have ample time to watch these videos as they wait for the doors to open into the "Time Tunnel" that takes them back six thousand years to the dawn of the universe. The tunnel leads to a small theater in which a short movie portrays the six days of creation. Following the film, visitors exit the theater and enter the Garden of Eden, or at least the museum's version of what it believes the Garden of Eden to have looked like. A life-size Adam, with thick hair and a full beard, kneels under a tree with one arm around a lamb and the other reaching out toward a cougar. A penguin, a toucan, and a scaly striped dinosaur stand nearby, and a sign explains that Adam did not have to name every animal that existed but only "birds, cattle, and beasts of the field," the last of which probably referred to animals that had close associations with humans. Naming these few hundred animals would have taken a few hours at most, according to the sign.

A few feet away stands an exhibit in which Eve has been created by God from Adam's side. Like her man, she too has thick dark hair, and she wears it so as to cover her naked breasts (see fig. 7.1).

In one display, she and Adam stand in a pool below a waterfall with the lower parts of their bodies covered by pond lilies. They seem to look fondly at each other, and they gesture toward one another with what appears to be affection. A sign states that the creation of Adam and Eve "is the foundation for marriage: one man and one woman."

Figure 7.1

Answers in Genesis
Courtesy of creationmuseum.org.

However, sin then rears its ugly head, quite literally. The serpent as depicted in the museum is a devilish-looking reptile with red scaly horns and blazing green eyes. Much like those in the contemporary world who disavow a literal reading of the Bible, the serpent questions God's word by asking, "Has God really said you shall not eat of every tree of the garden?" The serpent convinces Eve to sin, and she convinces Adam to eat from the forbidden tree. What they eat is not an apple but a berry-like fruit that grows in clusters.

The result of Eve and Adam's actions is the world's first death, as God must kill an animal in order to make garments of skin for the couple. Ever since then, says the museum, humans have lived with pain and toil, and they have faced the inevitability of death. Before the first sin, signs explain, there was no burdensome work. As a result of sin, however, we all have to contend with weeds, blight, poor soil, labor pains, and natural disasters. All of this will be wiped away, however, with the advent of the Last Adam, Jesus Christ. A short film near the end of the exhibit, just before one reaches the museum's chapel, shows how Jesus is the answer to the destruction wrought by Adam and Eve.

What is remarkable about the museum's assertions is that throughout, they are supported not just with biblical passages but also with illustrations of rock formations and explanations of plate tectonics. One poster explains that the settling of the earth's rock layers after Noah's Flood is the cause of the earthquakes that we experience today. Another contends that the different nationalities and languages that we have on earth now are all the result of God's scattering of the citizens of Babel in Genesis 11:1–9. Still another demonstrates how God must have provided special tools to organisms after the Flood so that they could diversify rapidly. It is not clear what these quasiscientific considerations are meant to add. On the one hand, the museum consistently teaches that one should trust God's word over human reason. Why, then, bolster religious claims with appeals to that very reason?

The answer seems to be that the Creation Museum is well aware that there are many skeptics in the world who will want to have their reason satisfied. The museum's Mission Statement explains,

> Throughout this family-friendly experience, visitors will learn how to answer the attacks on the Bible's authority in geology, biology, anthropology, cosmology, etc. They will also discover how science actually confirms biblical history, and be challenged to consider how the first 11 chapters

of Genesis—the first book in the Bible—addresses modern cultural issues such as racism, same-sex marriage, and abortion.[41]

In other words, the appeal to science accomplishes several ends. First, it allows Christians to evangelize more effectively because the faithful will have answers to the questions that skeptics ask. Second, it provides ammunition for the war against what the museum sees as the evils of our culture, which include racial discrimination, gay marriage, and abortion. Third, the appeal to science seems to be a way to give credibility to the Bible—science, says the museum, "confirms biblical history." It is this last motive that remains puzzling. If one should always choose the Bible over reason, then why would one use reason to confirm the truth of the Bible?

This same dilemma arises in the 2006 film *Jesus Camp*, a documentary that follows the lives of several children as they prepare for and attend a Christian evangelical summer camp. In one segment, an appealing young boy with an open face and a charming manner discusses creationism with his mother. The mother tells him, "If you look at creationism, you realize that it's the only possible answer to all the questions." In other words, the Bible provides the most reasonable explanation for where the world came from. A few seconds later, though, the mother, referring to the creationist video that her son has been watching, asks, "Did you get to the part on here where it says that science doesn't prove anything?" Here, explanations derived from evidence about how the world works are dismissed as irrelevant. But if science truly cannot prove anything, then it is not clear why one would use scientific reasoning to bolster the credibility of the Bible. On the contrary, one would presumably want to hold that the Bible is correct even if it can answer no scientific questions at all, or if its answers are incompatible with scientific evidence. Or, as one of the boys in the movie says (in what we should note is an inaccurate portrayal of the historical figure), "I think personally that Galileo made the right choice by giving up science for Christ."

River Out of Africa

The thought of giving up science for religion would send shivers down the spine of Richard Dawkins. Dawkins, an evolutionary biologist who writes scathing critiques of religious belief, does not mince words when it comes to Fundamentalism: "Fundamentalist religion is hell-bent on ruining the scientific education of countless thousands of innocent, well-meaning, eager young minds."[42] Dawkins's book *The God Delusion* (2006) was on the *New York Times* bestseller lists for weeks, and the author has become something of an intellectual celebrity who promotes atheism on talk shows and websites.

Among the religious texts that Dawkins criticizes is the story of Adam and Eve. Reflecting on the Genesis story, he writes that the first couple's transgression against God "seems mild enough to merit a mere reprimand" but instead results in banishment and pain. What kind of a God would take such harsh action for a small indiscretion, Dawkins wants to know. Moreover, he finds the Christian teaching about original sin to be reprehensible: "What kind of ethical philosophy is it that condemns every child, even before it is born, to inherit the sin of a remote ancestor?" Especially odious to him is the idea that Jesus atoned for original sin through his crucifixion; this teaching he calls "morally obnoxious."[43]

If he has little use for the Bible, however, he recognizes that the text is pervasive in our culture, and he uses its imagery to explain how evolutionary biology accounts for our origins. Thus, for example, he uses the phrase "river out of Eden" to refer to the flow of DNA that has been passed on from one organism to another. That river, he says, has over the course of time developed three billion branches: the number of species that have populated the earth at one time or another.[44]

In thinking about human ancestry, Dawkins provides an explanation for our existence that is, he says, "more interesting, maybe even more poetically moving, than the myth" of Eden.[45] His discussion of human evolution is complex, but a short version goes something like this: A few decades ago, a team of researchers sampled the genetic material of 135 women from around the world, and they noted differences in the women's DNA. Using knowledge about how quickly genes mutate, the researchers were then able to project a family history for those women that led to a hypothetical common ancestor who probably lived in Africa more than 150,000 years ago. This ancestor they called "African Eve."

African Eve is, as Dawkins explains, "the most recent woman of whom it can be said that all modern humans are descended from her in the female-only line."[46] He uses the qualifier "female-only line" because the researchers were working with genetic material that is inherited solely from one's mother. This material is taken from the portion of the human cell known as the mitochondria, or the "power house" of the cell. For complex reasons, both men's and women's mitochondrial DNA comes from their mothers. Thus, the mitochondrial lineage of a boy leads back to his mother and then to his maternal grandmother, to his maternal grandmother's mother, and so on. Eventually, the researchers claim, if we traced everyone's mitochondrial history back, we would arrive at African Eve, also known as "Mitochondrial Eve."

The research to which Dawkins refers was done in the 1980s. More recently, the National Geographic Society, in cooperation with the IBM Corporation, has undertaken what it calls "The Genographic Project" in order to chart the genetic history of the entire human population. Since 2005, scientists have collected genetic material from men and women around the world in the hope of being able to trace which populations migrated to which areas at different points in history. Unlike the earlier researchers, who looked only at DNA that was traceable through the female line, the National Geographic Society is also looking at men's Y chromosome, which is a genetic marker passed only along the male line.

At the beginning of their genetic story stands "Adam," whom National Geographic describes as "the common male ancestor of every living man." This Adam lived in Africa, say the researchers, about sixty thousand years ago. He was not the first person in history, nor was he the only person alive in his time. Rather, the Genographic Project explains that "his descendants are the only ones to survive to the present day." In other words, Adam had parents and grandparents and may have had many siblings and cousins. For whatever reason, however, the genetic lineages of these other relatives (as traced through the male line) have died out.[47]

On the Genographic Project website, visitors can purchase DNA swab kits that they can then have analyzed to see how their remote ancestors descended from "Mitochondrial Eve" or "Y-Chromosome Adam." Along with the results they receive a video called *The Journey of Man* which explains the conclusions that have emerged so far. At one point in the video, a scientist explains to an Australian aboriginal artist that the man's ancestors originally came from Africa. The man disagrees. His tradition, which has been passed down for generations through song, says that his people originated right there in Australia. To the scientist's explanation, he says, "I don't believe that. Because if our stories aren't correct, if they are a myth, the way that you guys might believe they are, and we know they're not, why isn't it possible that the Africans actually come from us?" The scientist responds, "It's complicated to explain."

Seeking a way to connect his research to the aboriginal tradition, how-ever, the scientist continues,

> In a way, what I'd like you to think about the DNA stories we're telling is that they are that. They are DNA stories. That's our version as Europeans of how the world was populated, and where we all trace back to. That's our song line. We use science to tell us about that because we don't have this sense of direct continuity. Our ancestors didn't pass down the stories. We've lost them, and we have to go out and find them. And we use sci-ence, which is a European way of looking at the world, to do that. You guys don't need that. You've got your own stories.

The man agrees: "No, we don't need that. We know where we come from. We know about creation. We know we come from here."[48]

The scientist's attempt to portray scientific findings as simply one story among others, neither better nor worse, would make Dawkins cringe. Writes Dawkins, "Show me a cultural relativist at thirty thousand feet and I'll show you a hypocrite. Airplanes built according to scientific principles work. They stay aloft, and they get you to a chosen destination. Airplanes built to tribal or mythological specifications . . . don't." He contrasts science with religion this way: "Scientific beliefs are supported by evidence and they get results. Myths and faiths are not and do not."[49]

The Battle Continues?

One thing is clear: the conflict between creationism and evolutionary theory shows no signs of abating. Popular comedian Stephen Colbert regularly skewers creationism by pretending to be one of its most ardent advocates: "I say, if we're related to monkeys, why don't they send me birthday cards?"[50] In one instance, Colbert opened his mock news pro-gram by intoning, "Tonight: scientists say humans inherited empathy from the apes. Once again, I'm living proof that evolution does not ex-ist."[51]

But does the battle really have to continue? Is there no way to recon-cile science with religion?

As we have seen already in chapter 2, the twentieth-century Protes-tant theologian Paul Tillich thought that science and religion, properly understood, would not contradict. The assertion that both areas of thought can be true is also made by contemporary Catholic thinker John

F. Haught, who was the only theologian to testify at the Dover trial. Like the fictional Professor Frink, Haught has considered the question of whether or not the theory of evolution means that God cannot exist. His answer is worth quoting at length:

> The central idea of theistic religion . . . is that the Infinite pours itself out in love to the finite universe. This is the fundamental meaning of "revelation." But if we think carefully about this central religious teaching it should lead us to conclude that any universe related to the inexhaustible self-giving love of God must be an evolving one. For if God is infinite love giving itself to the cosmos, then the finite world cannot possibly receive this limitless abundance of graciousness in any single instant. In response to the outpouring of God's boundless love the universe would be invited to undergo a process of self-transformation. In order to "adapt" to the divine infinity the finite cosmos would likely have to intensify its own capacity to receive such an abounding love. In other words, it might endure what we now know scientifically as an arduous, tortuous, and dramatic evolution. Viewed in this light, the evolution of the cosmos is more than just "compatible" with theism. Faith in a God of self-giving love, it would not be too much to say, actually anticipates an evolving universe. It may be very difficult to reconcile the religious teaching about God's infinite love with any other kind of cosmos.[52]

Haught believes that an evolving world, rather than a static one, is best suited to receive and to express the ongoing and infinite love of God. For him, the universe is the site where humans can experience the self-giving of God toward all creation. If he is correct, then it makes sense that humans should take a closer look at the way we treat the natural world, which is the subject of our next chapter.

CHAPTER EIGHT

Back to Nature

In 1926, an exotic dancer named Beryl Halley was arrested for performing onstage wearing only a gilded fig leaf. The judge in the case, no doubt merely seeking to better inform himself regarding the allegation that the performance was "indecent," attended Halley's show at the Broadhurst Theatre. He then dismissed the charges against the woman, ruling that the costume in question was "not unlike what may be seen in paint, marble or bronze in nearly every art gallery." The *New York Times* summarized the proceedings with the headline, "Stage Eve is Cleared."[1]

Indeed, innumerable paintings and sculptures depict the nudity of Adam and Eve and seem to relish in the couple's nakedness. The famed Sistine Chapel of Michelangelo shows the couple being cast from Eden wearing nothing at all, despite the fact that Genesis says that God made clothing for the man and woman before driving them out. Lucas Cranach the Elder's "Expulsion from the Garden" does likewise, as does Masaccio's fifteenth-century fresco "Adam and Eve Expelled from Paradise." (The latter had been amended at some point in the seventeenth century so that Adam and Eve's genitals were covered by painted-on fig leaves; however, the leaves were stripped away when the artwork was cleaned in 1990.) [2]

Nakedness is fascinating. This is true in part because nudity can be equated with simplicity, and simplicity with innocence. When eighteenth-century Spanish Catholic priest Junipero Serra first met the

California Indians whom he had come to convert, he was dumbstruck by what he saw. He wrote, "I came out at once, and found myself in front of twelve of them. . . . I saw something I could not believe when I had read of it, or had been told about it. It was this: they were entirely naked, as Adam in the garden, before sin."[3] For Serra, the natives of California represented the possibility of starting over, of beginning history anew, of watching the development of civilization happen all over again. They offered him a kind of innocence that Europe could never hope to recover.

This dream of returning to, or of creating, a simpler, purer time recurs over and over in popular culture. In this chapter we will look at four different manifestations of the desire to recapture the natural environment of Eden. First, we will consider visions of the world in which technology no longer intrudes into our lives. Second, we will look at nudist movements that invoke the story of Adam and Eve in order to explain and/or promote their practice. Third, we will focus on healthy-lifestyle promoters such as the Christian Vegetarian Association and the Jewish Vegetarians of North America. Finally, we will look at how environmentalists use the Genesis text to support their vision of how humans ought to relate to the natural world. Groups as diverse as the National Association of Evangelicals and People for the Ethical Treatment of Animals see Genesis 1–3 as providing insight into the way humans should care for the environment.

The Serpent and the Cell Phone

Oftentimes, dreams of paradise conjure up a time before technology intruded into our lives. A *Frank and Ernest* cartoon, for example, has God looking at the earth and saying to nearby angels, "We'll go with the Tree of Knowledge for now and save the Internet for later." The implication is that the lure of the Internet is the same sort of dangerous temptation that brought about the fall of humanity. A *Mother Goose and Grimm* cartoon has an angel looking down from heaven and telling God, "She ate the apple . . . but now she wants a Blackberry."[4] Again, the suggestion is that a Blackberry (a handheld wireless telephone and web browser) holds the same potential for destruction as did the forbidden fruit of Eden.

The Twilight Zone (2002)
An episode of the 2002 television show *The Twilight Zone* makes the same point. The science fiction series, which lasted for only one season, was

a revival of the classic show that ran from 1959–1964. The episode in question is entitled "Sanctuary" and is a commentary on contemporary society's reliance on technical gadgetry, as well as on its hectic pace.[5] The setting for the story is a freeway outside of a major city. A fast-talking sports agent named Scott Turner has gotten a flat tire and keeps calling for a tow truck to come and fix the problem. After some time, he leaves his car and wanders into the bushes to relieve himself. Soon, however, Scott is lost in the woods and happens upon a mansion in the midst of a lovely stand of trees. There he meets Marisa, a real estate agent who is also lost. Marisa, who claims to know the area well, is puzzled as to where they are and about their inability to find their way back to the freeway: "This place shouldn't be here," she tells Scott, referring to the mansion.

Scott and Marisa soon discover that their cell phones no longer work. This means that Scott is about to lose a major client, and Marisa is about to lose the fiancé with whom she had just had a major argument. The mansion they have stumbled upon has no telephones, nor does it have a driveway or a garage. No power lines lead into the house, and the only sources of light are candles and a fireplace. It is as if the twentieth century had never occurred.

And yet, the mansion also offers abundant charms. Scott and Marisa find closets full of lovely clothes that fit them perfectly. They swim in a heated pool and enjoy delectable food. After some time, they come to love their new home, and they throw the traces of their old lives (including their wallets and cell phones) away.

As in every Adam and Eve story, however, a third presence soon intrudes upon the couple's bliss. A woman named Rikki stumbles into the garden and explains that she was just driving on the freeway and was thrown from her motorcycle. Oddly, her cell phone works perfectly. More oddly still, Rikki seems to attract dangerous creatures into the mansion. The first sign of her malevolent influence is a wasp that stings Marisa. Soon after, a scorpion appears, and Rikki's only response is to say, "Cool." Then a snake makes its way into the house, and when Scott attempts to kill it, Rikki begs him simply to take it outside instead.

Throughout her stay with Scott and Marisa, Rikki tempts the couple with the use of her phone. At first, the two resist: "If we let the world back in, then we will lose everything we have here," Marisa tells Scott. After the encounter with the snake, however, Scott gives in and borrows Rikki's phone in order to call the client he had been so afraid of losing.

At that point, Rikki reveals her real purpose. She says ominously, "This was your chance to be free. To live in innocence again. All you had to do was accept what you were being given. But you mortals always want it all, don't you?" Suddenly a storm hits, and Scott and Marisa are transported back to the freeway where their adventure began. Once again, human beings have failed to find contentment in the simple pleasures of life, and in reaching beyond themselves have lost hold of Eden. At that point, the narrator of the tale observes, "Most of us dream of Paradise at one time or another. Scott Turner actually found his. Unfortunately, he was unable to hold on to it and found himself back in the game of modern life."

Star Trek: Deep Space Nine (1994)

The story ends differently for the space travelers in an episode of the television show Star Trek: Deep Space Nine entitled "Paradise." The episode features two members of the "Deep Space Nine" satellite who discover a group of colonists living on a planet previously thought to have been uninhabited. The colonists, it seems, had landed on the planet by accident ten years ago. They had tried to resume their original course but were unable to do so because all of their equipment had failed.

At first, the two men from Deep Space Nine intend to enact a rescue operation in order to put the colonists back on their proper course. However, they soon find that their own equipment, like that of the people they had hoped to help, no longer works. The men must therefore content themselves, at least for the time being, with learning about life in their new environment, and so they willingly join the colonists in the daily tasks of farming with crude implements and weaving cloth made from local resources. The group's leader, a woman named Alixus, explains proudly, "We've rediscovered what man is capable of without technology."

The group has also, however, discovered how difficult life can be without electricity or modern medicine. One woman dies from a fever that could have been cured by a serum that is readily available on the space station but that is impossible for the colonists to obtain. Moreover, the group has had to struggle to maintain order in their small society and has enacted draconian measures in order to enforce its laws. For example, a young man who steals a candle is placed in a metal "punishment box" for a day, is deprived of food and water, and nearly suffocates in the hot sun.

All of this might be simply the story of people who have made the best of a bad situation except for one thing: the crash that stranded the colonists was no accident. Alixus, it turns out, had actually planned for the ship to be drawn off course and had secretly devised methods to prevent the ship's technology from working. When the two members of Deep Space Nine discover this, they dismantle the secret force field that Alixus had constructed and resume communication with their space station. They confront Alixus with their findings and explain to the other colonists that anyone who wants to return with them is now free to do so.

At this point, Alixus explains her motive for having deceived the group. In the world that they left, she tells them, in the world of technological comforts, they would never have discovered their hidden strengths: "Would any of you have learned who you really are at the core if you hadn't come here?" By giving up the soft life of gadgetry and space-age paraphernalia, they have become stronger and more inventive. True, some among them have died because of the harshness of their lives, but those sacrifices were necessary for the good of the group.

Viewers who have come to despise Alixus for her deceptions and her cruelty (at one point she forced the captain of the space station to stay in the punishment box until he nearly died) might see this explanation as a lame excuse for a despotic power trip. However, as the crew of the space station takes Alixus into custody and prepares to beam the other colonists back to civilization, they encounter a surprise: the colonists do not want to leave. Explains one, "We have found something here that none of us is willing to give up." At the end of the episode, the members of the space station take Alixus away but leave behind the other inhabitants of the planet. In the last shot, a small boy and girl stand staring at the metal punishment box.

What should we make of this ending? Perhaps the message is that even a harsh life is better than the artificial existence afforded by technology. Or perhaps the message is that longing for the "simple" lives of our ancestors is a fool's game, and that we have forgotten how brutal life in nontechnological societies can be. Or perhaps the message is both of these truths, and that whatever our lives are, we cannot help but wonder how they might have been different. In any case, this episode is distinctive in that its characters choose to embrace the "paradise" that they are offered rather than to reject it. As we will see in the next chapter, movies and television shows by and large display a great distrust of utopian ideals. Nearly always, though characters may flirt with notions of Eden, they reject them in the end. The plot of this *Deep Space Nine* episode is so distinctive that it has been included in this book despite the fact that the show contains no overt references to the story of Adam and Eve.

Naked and Unashamed

The colonists whom the crew of Deep Space Nine encounter in the episode "Paradise" all wear clothing. Apparently, they do not consider clothes to be part of the "soft life" that they must give up in order to live more authentically. Other interpreters of the Adam and Eve story, though, have urged their followers to take off their garments and to live as they think God intended. This position has not received universal acceptance. Ancient Judaism, for example, in contrast with Greco-Roman pagan practice, was uncomfortable with open nudity. The second-century Jewish text *The Book of Jubilees* tells the story of Adam and Eve and concludes that since God clothed Adam after Adam's transgression, "[T]hose who know the judgment of law prescribed on the heavenly tablets know to cover their shame. They should not uncover themselves as the Gentiles do."[6]

In Christian tradition, as we have already seen, Augustine thought that the moment that Adam and Eve realized that they were naked was also the moment when they became ashamed of their sexuality. For much of its history, Christianity has urged its followers to clothe themselves always and with modesty. Medieval penitential manuals, for example, prohibited monks from standing while they washed themselves in the bath, "unless through the need for cleansing dirt more fully." If a monk sitting in the bath exposed his knees or arms without cause, the "immodest bather" was prohibited from washing again for six days.[7] In 1935 Pope Pius XI issued a letter in which he criticized nudist movements, which he called an "amusement that is specifically and paganly immodest, with an immodesty that often exceeds that of ancient pagan life, inasmuch as it is addicted to what is termed, with a horrible word and horrible blasphemy, the practice and cult of nudity."[8] Twenty years later, a Catholic bishop in Spain warned that when girls were ice skating, they should wear bloomers that reached below their knees, and he instructed the faithful that "nudism in all its forms is the devilish effort of paganism."[9]

This attitude helps explain why, when the nudist movie *Garden of Eden* was produced in 1954, the New York Board of Censors at first refused to allow it to be shown.[10] The movie tells the story of a young widow named Susan and her daughter (who appears to be around four or five years old), who are living with Susan's domineering father-in-law, a curmudgeon named J. Randolph Latimore. Seeking to escape the old man's control of their lives, mother and child take to the road. Unfortunately, their car breaks down on an abandoned stretch of highway, and mother and daughter are forced to find refuge for the night at a nearby resort. The name of the resort is the "Garden of Eden."

At first, Susan does not realize that they have happened upon a nudist camp. When she wakes in the morning and finds that her daughter has shed her clothes in order to play with the other naked children in the resort, Susan is not upset: "I've never seen anything so delightfully natural," she says. And yet, when she realizes that adults at the resort go about nude as well, she is shocked. Adults, she believes, should not appear without their clothing. However, her newfound friend Johnny, a member of the resort, questions why the bodies of men and women are any less natural than the bodies of children. Everyone, he believes, should be able to "walk around as God made them in his image."

Eventually Susan is persuaded that Johnny is right, and she comes to love her new environment. Old man Latimore, however, takes some convincing. When he first comes looking for Susan and his granddaughter, he is outraged at what he sees. After a short time spent at the Garden of Eden, though, even he begins to see the virtues of nudism. He joins the resort himself and, as a result, his heart is softened. He becomes a philanthropist and commissions a series of murals depicting the first days of the biblical story of creation. "All I ever thought of was money," he reflects. "I was a hard-bitten, narrow-minded grouch." Casting off his clothes turns him into a kind and loving man—so much so that he even agrees to give the bride away when Susan and Johnny get married.

Garden of Eden marked something of a turning point in the public acceptance of nudity on-screen. When at first the New York censors tried to block its distribution, the movie's producers filed a complaint in court, and they won the right to exhibit the film. The Appellate Division of the New York Supreme Court, and later the New York Court of Appeals, ruled that "nudity in itself and without lewdness or dirtiness, is not obscenity in law or in common sense." This decision influenced similar cases in other states such as Massachusetts, Missouri, and Illinois.[11]

As we have seen, public exhibitions of nakedness have often received the disapproval of religious leaders. And yet it is nonetheless true that both Judaism and Christianity have fostered traditions that involve ritual nudity. Ancient Jews engaged in religious bathing in order to cleanse themselves from impurity, and many contemporary Jews continue the practice. American Orthodox rabbi Aryeh Kaplan explains that the waters of the *mikvah*, or ritual bath, find their ultimate source in the river that ran from the Garden of Eden: "The Torah tells us that God planted a Garden, and in it, the Tree of Knowledge of Good and Evil. With it, the possibility was created that man would sin, and be evicted from Eden. Thus, even before God placed man in Eden, He established a link between the Garden and the world outside, namely the river which emerged from Eden."[12] Immersing oneself in the *mikvah*, therefore, is a way of reestablishing one's connection to God's original will for human beings.

According to Jewish tradition, it is important that a person who is cleansing himself or herself in the *mikvah* be entirely nude. Orthodox Jewish women who engage in the practice after their menstrual cycles re-move not just their clothing but also all jewelry, dentures, contact lenses, nail polish, and makeup as well. A contemporary practitioner of the ritual explains, "It is considered extremely important that the waters of the *mikvah* touch every part of a woman's body; even minute particles of matter that prevent this from happening make the immersion invalid."[13]

Christians likewise have at times engaged in ritual nakedness. Very early on, at least some Christians baptized their members in the nude, a practice which the fourth-century thinker John Chrysostom explained by reminding initiates of the original state of humanity, "when you were in paradise and you were not ashamed."[14] Moreover, there is a long his-tory of small groups of Christians attempting to live as Adam and Eve did in the Garden—that is, without clothing. As early as the second century, a group called the Adamites formed a community which they named Paradise, the intent of which was to restore original innocence to its members. When the community gathered for worship, they prayed in the nude.[15] Over a millennium later, in 1421, seventy-five members of another Adamite sect in Bohemia were burnt at the stake as heretics. The group had apparently engaged in free love (on the principle that they should go forth and multiply) and spent a fair amount of time naked, including during the performance of ritual dances.[16] In the seventeenth century, a Londoner named John Robins claimed to be Adam reincarnate and promised to restore the world to Paradise. At least according to some reports, he and his followers doffed their clothing in order to more closely approximate the lives of Adam and Eve.[17] In contemporary society, the Christian Nudist Convocation (CNC) declares, "We humans are . . . created with bodies and we confess that the naked human form is good and wholesome. Believers in Jesus are called to imitate Jesus, to follow God's pattern for living as found in the Bible, and to live in a right relationship with God as Adam and Eve did in the Garden, including the freedom to be naked and unashamed before Him and others."[18]

One problem with this position is that in the Genesis story, once Adam and Eve had transgressed, God not only cast them out of Eden but also made clothes for them. This would seem to indicate that God now intends for people to cover themselves. The fundamentalist organization Answers in Genesis charges that Christian nudists are "ignoring the entrance of sin and its consequences on this world."[19] By way of an answer, the Fig Leaf Forum, which calls itself "a newsletter for Bible-believing Christian nudists and Christian naturists," contends that "God clothed Adam and Eve to protect them against physical harm and an unfriendly climate outside Eden: painful toil, thorns and thistles (Genesis 3:17–18); sweat of your brow, tilling the ground (Genesis 3:19, 23); cold and heat, summer and winter (Genesis 8:22)."[20] In other words, clothing was not part of people's punishment for sin but was an act of mercy on God's part. When clothing is necessary for practical purposes, people should wear it. Therefore, when it is not necessary, people are free to forego such coverings.

Few are willing to adopt the CNC's stance; the American Association for Nude Recreation boasts that nearly one in five people would find a clothes-free experience a "highly desirable vacation choice," but that still leaves 80 percent who would shy away.[21] Indeed, many continue to associate nudity with immorality. For example, a 1999 episode of the cartoon *The Simpsons* includes a segment in which Marge Simpson falls asleep and dreams that she and her husband Homer are Eve and Adam in Eden. In commentary that accompanies the DVD version of the piece, director Nancy Kruse explains that she worked hard to portray the nudity of the couple with discretion. Though most of the action in the segment takes place pre-transgression, Homer and Marge both wear fig leaves that cover their genitals, and Marge's trademark blue hair covers her breasts. Predictably, in the show it is Homer who violates God's commandment not to eat from the forbidden tree, and when Marge disapproves of his action, Homer's response is simply, "You're pretty uptight for a naked chick."[22] The underlying assumption is that anyone who would display her nudity would not shrink from disobeying a divine order.

Every Tree That Is Pleasant to the Sight and Good for Food

In the same episode of *The Simpsons*, Homer routinely eats meat. A pig, who speaks with an upper-class British accent, wanders around Eden and, when he sees Homer, rolls onto his back and allows Homer to peel strips of bacon from his belly. After all, this is paradise, right? And what could be better than having your pork willing and ready-to-hand?

The *Simpsons* episode is distinctive, if not unique, in portraying Adam as a meat-eater. In the first chapter of Genesis, God creates human beings and says to them, "See, I have given you every plant yielding seed that is upon the face of all the earth, and every tree with seed in its fruit; you shall have them for food" (1:29). In the second chapter, after God creates *ha-adam*, God says, "You may freely eat of every tree of the garden" (2:16). In neither of these texts does God say anything about eating animals. Virtually all interpreters, therefore, have concluded that Adam and Eve were vegetarians. It is not until after the biblical flood in the ninth chapter of Genesis that God institutes the practice of meat-eating. At that point, God says to Noah and his sons, "Every moving thing that lives shall be food for you; and just as I gave you the green plants, I give you everything. Only, you shall not eat flesh with its life, that is, its blood" (3–4).

There are at least two ways to interpret these two moments in the Bible. The first is to say that God originally intended people to eat only plants but, after the Fall, God commanded people to eat animals as well; therefore, eating meat is now part of God's plan for human beings. The second interpretation, though, holds that God only gave meat to Noah's family as a concession, and that the ideal should still be for people to return to the vegetarianism of Eden.

Biblically based vegetarianism has a long history. Several early Christian writers advised their followers not to eat meat so as to more closely imitate the life of Adam and Eve in paradise. Both Basil of Caesarea and Jerome, for example, told their fourth-century readers that though God has sanctioned meat-eating, if they wanted to live as if they were in paradise, they should eat only fruits and grains.[23]

In the seventeenth century, the English preacher John Robins declared that he was the Third Adam (Jesus having been the second) and that he would restore the world to its original perfection. Like several other prophets of his time, Robins required his followers to imitate the First Adam and eat a diet of only vegetables.[24] In 1817, a group called the Bible Christian Church established itself in Philadelphia, and its members took their direction from Genesis 1:29, in which God gives the first humans every herb that bears seed, and every tree that bears fruit, for food; therefore, they lived as vegetarians.[25] Soon after, a minister named Sylvester Graham, most famous as the inventor of the Graham cracker, began preaching that meat was injurious to the body and that the diet that God had prescribed in Eden, which was entirely plant-based, was "adapted to the highest and best condition of human nature."[26]

Today, the Christian Vegetarian Association (CVA) holds that "The Bible depicts vegetarianism as God's ideal" and that "Several prophecies, such as Isaiah 11:6–9, foresee a return to this vegetarian world, where the wolf, lamb, lion, cow, bear, snake, and little child all coexist peacefully."[27] While acknowledging that we are not innocent like Adam and Eve were, the CVA nonetheless asserts that we have a responsibility to strive toward the kind of world in which our biblical parents lived.

But what of God's instituting meat consumption in the ninth chapter of Genesis? The CVA notes that at that point the Flood had killed off all vegetation, and so God permitted the surviving humans to eat animals for a limited period of time. "Importantly," the organization adds, "this passage neither commands meat eating nor indicates that the practice is God's ideal. Indeed, eating meat came with a curse—animals would no longer be humanity's friends."[28] The "curse" to which it refers occurs in Genesis 9:2, when God says, "The fear and dread of you shall rest on every animal of the earth, and on every bird of the air, on everything that creeps on the ground, and on all the fish of the sea; into your hand they are delivered." Here, humans and animals no longer coexist peacefully in God's creation. Instead, they have become mortal enemies.

Like their Christian counterparts, Jewish vegetarians have found support for their practice in the Adam and Eve story. They have also, though, at times looked to the writings of Abraham Kook, who in 1921 became chief rabbi of what is now Israel. Early in his career, Rabbi Kook had authored a series of essays entitled A *Vision of Vegetarianism and Peace* which were published in 1903–1904 and reissued sixty years later. In his reflections on vegetarianism, Rabbi Kook observed that the first man, Adam, was not told by God to consider animals as food. The rabbi thus asked rhetorically, "Is it therefore possible to conceive that a virtue of such priceless value, which had at one time been in fact a possession of mankind, should be lost forever?"[29] Rabbi Kook urged a transformation in the way that humans viewed each other as well as in how humans looked at animals. As Israeli ethicist Y. Michael Barilan explains, Kook understood the utopian vision of vegetarianism as "a prerequisite to the implementation of peace. The use of animals is not a privilege human-ity deserves, but a transitional behavior which it needs; a behavior that calls for constant monitoring and restraint."[30] As long as human beings still desire to shed blood, meat-eating should be allowed, argued Kook. However, for those who have conquered their lust for blood, vegetarian-ism is a step toward a messianic age in which people and animals will live together in peace. The Jewish Vegetarians of North America agree. Like their Christian counterparts, they argue that since God did not permit Adam and Eve to eat animals, people today should refrain from eating meat.[31]

The Genesis story of creation is used in contemporary culinary culture not just to advocate vegetarianism, but also to promote the cultivation and consumption of healthful foods. The Eden Organic company, which produces EdenSoy milk as well as a variety of other natural products, includes among its corporate goals, "To provide the highest quality life supporting food" and "To contribute to peaceful evolution on Earth." Likewise, Modern Manna, which describes itself as "a Christ-Centered Health Ministry," explains, "We find that the organic raw foods, just as God served them in the Garden of Eden, are the most nutritious and life-giving. They are packed with vitamins, minerals, phytochemicals, enzymes, and life force!" The logo of the "Apple & Eve" juice company reflects the company's values "by evoking images of purity and goodness, with just a touch of temptation thrown in to make things interesting. It stands as a symbol of the many fresh and delicious fruit juices we pro-duce." Urges Apple & Eve, "We hope you find our delicious juices a bit tempting and simply irresistible!"[32]

To Till It and Keep It

A connection between the Adam and Eve story and humans' care for the natural world is increasingly being made by conservative Christians, though not without controversy. In 2005 the National Association of Evangelicals (NAE) drafted a policy stating that since God had put Adam in the Garden of Eden in order for him to take care of it, Christians have a responsibility to protect the environment and thus to fight global warming. The NAE's vice president of governmental affairs, Richard Cizik, argued, "Genesis 2:15 specifically calls us 'to watch over and care for' the bounty of the earth and its creatures. Scripture not only affirms this role, but warns that the earth is not ours to abuse, own, or dominate." In response, James Inhofe, a Republican senator from Oklahoma and an evangelical Christian himself, remarked, "You can always find in Scriptures a passage to misquote for almost anything."[33]

Despite such opposition, the "green" Evangelical movement persisted, and by early 2009, over two hundred Christian leaders, including Cizek, Rick Warren (author of the best-selling book *The Purpose Driven Life*, 2002), and Jim Wallis (founder of *Sojourners* magazine) had signed "An Evangelical Call to Action" that stated that "when God made humanity he commissioned us to exercise stewardship over the earth and its creatures. Climate change is the latest evidence of our failure to exercise proper stewardship, and constitutes a critical opportunity for us to do better (*Genesis 1:26–28*)." The statement called on the federal government to enact legislation to reduce carbon dioxide emissions and encouraged state and local governments, churches, businesses, and individuals to focus on developing and using energy-efficient technologies.[34]

Several organizations with no religious ties also have also used the story of Adam and Eve to call for reform in humans' treatment of the natural world. For example, in 2007 the People for the Ethical Treatment of Animals (PETA) released a publicity photo of models posing as Adam and Eve and holding a sign that says "Back to Eden. Close All Zoos. PETA.org." The man and woman in the photo, who wear only fig leaves, are surrounded by illustrations of various animals that include a large snake, a monkey, an orangutan, a giraffe, a tiger, and a toucan (see fig. 8.1).

Figure 8.1

PETA Anti-Zoo Advertisement.
Reprinted courtesy of People for the Ethical Treatment of Animals (PETA). All rights reserved.

PETA calls zoos "An Idea Whose Time Has Gone" and urges, "The zoo industry must transform itself from a prison to a refuge, where the rights and welfare of individual animals are given the highest priority."[35]

In order to promote better care for the world's plant species, an organization called the Eden Trust in 2001 erected several huge biomes (one of which is the largest greenhouse in the world) that contain millions of plants from thousands of different species. Their effort, called the Eden Project, is located in Cornwall, England, and attracted over four million visitors in its first two years of operation. It describes itself as "a place of beauty and wonder which is about creating a positive future in a world that is going to go through radical change."[36]

Likewise, an unrelated organization called the Eden Foundation was founded in 1985 in order to promote diversity in local agricultural habits. The foundation points out that most of the world's food comes from a very small number of plant types, many of which cannot grow in the climates of the world's poorest nations. Asserts the foundation, "We believe that the key to prosperity for the poor lie[s] in underexploited, edible trees and bushes—the lost treasures of Eden."[37]

The desire to recover those lost treasures—to return to or to create an environment in which humans, plants, and animals achieve an elusive harmony, is powerful and, apparently, inexhaustible. Particularly now, as the twenty-first century brings increased reliance on technology as well as increased awareness of the dangers that technology poses, the Garden of Eden holds out a shimmering vision of a different way of life. References to the story of Adam and Eve instantly call forth ideas about how life ought to be. They evoke a world in which lions shall lie down with lambs and humans shall cavort naked as jaybirds; in which people shall lay down their Blackberries and eat organic blackberries instead; and in which all of us, together, will save the earth from climate change that might result in global disaster. As we will see in the next chapter, this longing for a better world does not end with calls for humans to change the way they interact with nature. Going back to Eden seems to require that we change our interactions with each other as well.

CHAPTER NINE

Paradise Regained

An old American folk song laments that things have changed for the worse since the world first began: "Sing hey, sing ho, let people grieve/ For the good old days of Adam and Eve."[1] It is a sentiment shared by people throughout the ages who have longed for a better time and a better way of life. Theologians use the word "prelapsarian" to describe those good old days. A prelapsarian theology imagines how the world might have looked before the transgression ("lapse") of the first humans, often with an eye toward recreating that world. In the nineteenth century, dozens of groups in the United States intentionally tried to form communities based on their visions of Eden.

In thinking about utopian movements, both real and fictional, we might keep several questions in mind. First, what problem does the utopia hope to solve? What, specifically, do the founders find wrong with the world as it is? In the 1986 movie *The Mosquito Coast*, the problem is America's shallow consumerist society. In the 2004 movie *The Village*, the problem is crime, as all of the inhabitants of the woodland village have been scarred by violence. Determining what a utopian community is reacting against can tell us much about its character.

A second question to ask is what problems are created by establishing the utopia. As innumerable books and movies have shown, perfection can have its drawbacks. One need only think of the movie *The Stepford Wives* (either the 1975 original or its 2004 remake) to see that the pursuit of an ideal world can bring harmful consequences. In the fictional town of Stepford, Connecticut, the wives to whom the title of the movie refers become nothing more than mindless, soulless incarnations of the "ideal" woman.

Another question to ask when analyzing utopias is what constitutes the boundary between "inside" and "outside." What is the door that allows one to travel between the ordinary world and the ideal one? Does the door swing both ways, or must one make an irrevocable choice? In the 1954 musical *Brigadoon*, a Scottish village is miraculously preserved from the evil ways of the outside world because it appears for only one day every hundred years. When an outsider from New York accidentally stumbles upon the magical town, he must choose between the life he has always known and the life he yearns for in Brigadoon. Only true love is able to open the door between the two dimensions.

In other cases what separates insiders from outsiders is knowledge about the nature of reality, as in 1998's *The Truman Show*. In this film Jim Carrey plays Truman Burbank, an insurance salesman who from the moment of his birth has unwittingly been the star of a twenty-four-hour-a-day reality television show. The entire world has watched Truman's every move in the little town of Seahaven, but Truman himself is oblivious to this fact. The producer of the TV show, a character named Christof, has taken great pains to prevent Truman from ever leaving Seahaven or learning about the true nature of his paradisiacal environment. In an interview, Christof (i.e. "of Christ") says, "The world, the place you live in, is the sick place. Seahaven is the way the world *should* be." When Truman finally realizes that he can escape from his utopia, Christof intervenes and for the first time introduces himself to Truman, saying, "I am the CREATOR . . . of a television show." He continues, "There's no more truth out there than there is in the world I created for you. The same lies. The same deceit. But in my world, you have nothing to fear." Ultimately, Truman defies the creator by leaving Seahaven and entering the less safe but more authentic life that awaits him.

Finally, the most important question in any analysis of utopian visions is which world we would, in the end, prefer to inhabit. Given the choice, would we opt for paradise, or would we decide that such a life is not worth the price we have to pay for it? Again and again, movies, novels, and television shows reject the idea that humans were meant for Eden. With very few exceptions, popular culture flirts with utopia but in the end settles for the sadder, grittier, but ultimately more satisfying life of this fallen world.

The Shakers

None of the examples of pop-culture utopias given above makes any reference to the story of Adam and Eve. *The Truman Show* comes close, as the name of the main character suggests that he is in some way representative of all human beings (i.e. he is the "True-Man"). Still, *The Truman Show* does not contain any explicit references to the Genesis story. And yet throughout American history, there has been a persistent tendency not only to dream of ideal worlds but to attempt to construct them using Genesis as an inspiration. One of the most prominent groups to look to the story of Adam and Eve as a guide, if not as a blueprint, was the United Society of Believers in Christ's Second Appearing, better known as the Shakers.

The Shakers arrived in the American colonies from England in 1774. At first their numbers were quite small, but by 1850 the group comprised four thousand members, and over the course of its more than two-hundred-year history in this country the Shakers have counted at least twenty thousand congregants.[2] The Shakers were founded by Mother Ann Lee, who was born in 1736 and who as a child was noted for her spiritual gifts. In her twenties, Lee got married and then gave birth to four children, not one of whom survived. In 1770, she had a vision in which Christ appeared to her and revealed that the original sin of Adam and Eve had not been simply eating a forbidden fruit but rather had been intercourse itself. The way to reverse that sin, then, was to practice continence, or abstinence from sex.[3] Taking its cue from this vision, a Shaker hymn titled "The Fall of Man" explained that Adam had succumbed to the temptations of the flesh, and that "his lost state continues still/ In all who seek their fleshly will, / and of their lust do take their fill."[4] Another Shaker hymn titled "Old Adam Disturbed" argued against the belief that marriage was better than celibacy. Noting that the New Testament writer Paul did not wed, the Shaker song urged, "But he that would be truly good, / A woman will not touch; / This is the one that God will own, / And Paul himself was such." [5]

Based on their reading of Genesis, particularly the passage in 1:26–27 in which God created human beings in God's own image ("male and female he created them"), the Shakers came to believe that God was not only Father but also Mother. They taught that God's male nature had come to earth in the person of Jesus, but that God's female nature had been incarnate in the person of none other than Ann Lee. Lee was the second Eve, as one Shaker theologian explained: "The second Eve—*Ann Lee*—was taken from the flesh of the sleeping anti-Christian body, for a helper for the second Adam, Christ Jesus; and she is called the Mother of all living the higher, spiritual life."[6]

For more than a century the Shakers thrived, often establishing orphanages as a way to replenish their numbers. However, like that of the other utopian groups discussed in this chapter, the dream of the Shakers did not last. Membership gradually dwindled, and in 2006 only four Shakers remained.[7]

Harmony in America

Another attempt at creating Eden on earth arose in the early nineteenth century when the German preacher George Rapp brought a few of his followers to the United States. Rapp believed that the Second Coming of Jesus was imminent, and in order to prepare himself and his flock for Christ's arrival he founded a "Harmony Society," whose communities were located first in Pennsylvania, then in Indiana, then again in Pennsylvania, and which were founded on Rapp's vision of Eden. Since Adam and Eve did not carry weapons, for example, followers of Rapp did not bear arms.

One of the more distinctive of Rapp's teachings stemmed from the preacher's reading of the first three chapters of Genesis. As it was for the Shakers, the passage in Genesis 1:27 in which God created humankind "male and female" was key to Rapp's theology. Rapp, who was influenced by the thought of seventeenth-century German mystic Jacob Boehme,[8] taught that Adam had originally had no sexual organs but had contained both male and female elements inside himself.[9] After his creation, however, Adam became restless and discontented, and so God created animals to be the man's companions. This did not help matters, however, because Adam noticed that the animals were divided into separate male and female bodies, and he wished that he could be like the animals. He became so preoccupied with his longing that he exhausted himself and fell asleep, and it was only then that God created Eve.[10]

In Rapp's plan, since God's original ideal had been that male and female be contained within one body, the most dedicated members of Harmony should remain celibate even if they were married. Not everyone followed this directive but, as George Rapp's adopted son Frederick explained, some members were "so ennobled in their virtue that they voluntarily have renounced fleshly intercourse and are preparing themselves solely for Christ and His kingdom."[11] Like the Shakers, the Harmony Society did not last. It was dissolved in 1905.[12]

The Oneida Colony

One of the most interesting of American utopian movements was formed in Oneida, New York, in 1848 by a Christian named John Humphrey Noyes. Taking seriously Jesus's proclamation that in the Kingdom of Heaven there would be no marriage (see Matthew 22:23–30), Noyes preached that men and women should not enter into exclusive relationships. Such pairings would only encourage, he felt, the un-Christian vices of egotism and acquisitiveness.[13] Contrary to the Shakers and the Rappites, however, Noyes did not preach celibacy. Instead, he instituted what he called "complex marriage," in which men and women would engage in intercourse with partners of their choosing, so long as the relationships did not become exclusive. Sexual partners, like property, were considered to be available for the good of the entire community. In order to prevent unwanted pregnancies from the numerous unions that took place, members of the Oneida colony practiced a form of birth control that Noyes called "male continence" in which men refrained from achieving orgasm and ejaculation.[14]

To explain his unconventional approach to marriage, Noyes distinguished what he called the amative function of sex (from the Latin word for "love") from its propagative function. Amativeness, he said, "was necessarily the first social affection developed in the garden of Eden." After all, Eve was created by God not because she was needed for reproduction but because God saw that it was not good for the man to be alone.[15] Adam and Eve, theorized Noyes, would have enjoyed pleasurable sex in Eden but would not have been burdened by unwanted pregnancies. He observed, "The infirmities and vital expenses of woman during the long period of pregnancy, waste her constitution" and "The awful agonies of child-birth heavily tax the life of woman."[16] (It may be relevant to note that Noyes's own wife had given birth to five children, only one of whom had survived.) Once children are born, the demands of nursing them, caring for them, and earning enough money to sustain them put tremendous strains on parents, and thus these demands, thought Noyes, were best kept to a minimum.

Sexual intercourse, on the other hand, was something that he felt was a good to be engaged in frequently. According to at least one report, some women from the Oneida Colony had sexual relations anywhere from twice a week to once a day. One member who had accidentally conceived a child named four different men as the possible father of the baby, as she had had sex with all of them in the previous month.[17]

Noyes valued the act of intercourse not only for the pleasure that it gave people, but also because he viewed it as a form of worship. Enjoying sex, he thought, was a way of participating in the sweet love that God has for God's people. In Noyes's interpretation of Genesis, "Adam and Eve, while innocent, had no shame," and therefore "Sexual shame was the consequence of the fall, and is factitious and irrational."[18] Proclaimed Noyes, "To be ashamed of sexual conjunction is to be ashamed of the image of the glory of God—the physical symbol of life indwelling in life, which is the mystery of the gospel."[19] He saw sexual shame as a form of blasphemy that showed ingratitude for God's gift.

The Oneida Colony lasted for only a few decades. In the 1870s Noyes's health declined, and a crisis in leadership developed. In 1881, the religious community dissolved and was reconstituted as a joint-stock company. That company, Oneida Silver, boasts that it is now one of the world's largest marketers of stainless steel silverware and flatware.[20]

Giving Pain, Receiving Wisdom

There have been a number of other American utopian groups that have invoked the imagery of Eden in order to inspire their members. A community founded in 1851 claimed that it had found the Garden's original location in West Virginia. In the early twentieth century, a Theosophist society in Point Loma, California, collected plants from around the world in order to recreate the Garden, and in Los Angeles a group of farmers hoped to cultivate one thousand acres that they called "the Garden of Eden."[21] However, utopian visions have not only been the province of small isolated groups. They have also entered into the stream of popular culture, as a number of recent novels, movies, and television shows illustrate.

The Giver (1993)

One of these is Lois Lowry's Newbery Award-winning novel *The Giver*. The book, which is aimed at children and young adults, is one of the twenty most-frequently challenged texts of the last decade. That is, it is one of the books most likely to cause controversy when it is purchased by school libraries or included in school curricula.[22] *The Giver* imagines a society in the future in which all suffering has been erased, and only one man, designated as the Receiver of Memory, is permitted to recall such things as war, famine, loneliness, and death. The other people in the society have chosen to live in a state of "sameness" in which there is only here and now, and there is neither pain nor love nor color. When twelve-year-old Jonas is chosen by the community to be the next Receiver of Memory, he learns for the first time about humanity's past, and at the same time he learns about suffering.

The world in which Jonas lives has no hills and no sunshine. The hills were leveled long ago in order to make transportation more efficient, and the sunshine was blotted out so that the temperature in the community's environment could be perfectly controlled at all times. There are no animals in Jonas's world, nor is there snow nor love nor sexual desire. Jonas does not miss any of these things, however, since he has never known of their existence. Neither has he known pain or discord; such things are simply unheard of in the orderly and predictable society in which he has been reared.

Jonas's society is governed by a Committee of Elders which oversees everything from marriage and reproduction to choice of career. When they reach their first birthday, all babies are given a name and placed with a family. When they turn nine, all children are given bicycles. At age ten, all girls have their braids cut, and at age twelve, all children are assigned to the job that they will perform for the rest of their lives. Some of the children will grow up to bear new offspring for the community. Others will function as laborers or doctors or engineers, or they will be caretakers for the old people in the community or will function as teachers. Everyone in Jonas's society knows his or her place, and only occasionally does someone disobey the community's rules. Those rules are recorded in a thick volume that is one of only three books available to residents. The other two books are a dictionary (since "precision of language" is one of the community's primary values) and a manual that describes every building, office, and committee structure in the community

Jonas himself disobeys the society's rules early in the novel by taking an apple from the group's stores. The theft began innocently enough, as Jonas and a fellow eleven-year-old were playing catch with the apple during a recreation period. As his friend tossed the fruit back to him, Jonas caught a glimpse of something unusual. As he watched, the apple changed somehow, though Jonas could not put his finger on exactly what the difference was. Four times, as the apple flew through the air, Jonas noticed something strange about it. Finally, at the end of the recreation period, Jonas put the apple in his pocket in order to take it home and study it. The theft did not go unnoticed by the Committee of Elders, though—in fact, nothing was unnoticed by them. That evening the Committee issued a general announcement that food was to be eaten rather than hoarded. Jonas felt ashamed for having violated the community's rules, and yet he also felt intrigued by that apple.

What we learn eventually is that what Jonas saw on the day when he played catch with his friend was the color red. He had never seen color before, as normally, everything looked the same, and people had even lost the capacity to distinguish one hue from another. Jonas, though, had a gift, a gift to see what others could not. The apple became for him a gateway into another realm of knowledge and suffering and, ultimately, of wisdom.

Because of Jonas's rare ability, when the time came for him to be assigned a career, he was appointed by the Committee of Elders to be the Receiver of Memory. He was to study with the old Receiver who would instruct him in the knowledge of the past. He, and he alone, would carry with him all of the memories of human history, including its wars and its triumphs and its plagues. Moreover, he would not simply be told about the past but would actually relive it. The old Receiver, now known as "The Giver," would transmit into his very flesh all of the memories of sunshine and snow and animals and color and music and love and grief that humans had ever known.

Thus Jonas undergoes numerous sessions of memory-transmission. After enduring one particularly grueling memory, a recollection of piercing hunger and neglect, Jonas asks the old Receiver, "Why do you and I have to hold these memories?" The elderly man replies, "It gives us wisdom."[23] Jonas could, of course, decide that such wisdom is not worth the suffering that it entails. Many years ago, the novel tells us, a young girl who had been chosen to be the Receiver had done just that—she had preferred death over the pain of memory. And yet Jonas comes to believe not just that it is good that he acquire wisdom through knowledge, but also that he share that painful wisdom with the others in his community. Like the decision of Adam and Eve, his choice has repercussions for the whole human family.

What prompts Jonas to lead his people out of their pleasant stupor is an incident in which he sees his father, whose job is to care for infants, at his job one day. A woman in the community has just given birth to twins, and according to the society's rules, only one of the twins may be allowed to grow to maturity. Jonas's father is responsible for choosing which of the infants will be kept and which will be "released," which is a term that the community uses to refer to those who because of age or infirmity or disobedience are sent to "Elsewhere." Jonas has never given much thought to where Elsewhere might be, but on this day he learns the truth. As he watches in horror, he sees his father inject a needle into the baby's forehead, wait until the child stops breathing, and then throw the small limp body down a disposal chute.

Jonas's reaction to the event is both fury and despair. He rushes to the Giver for an explanation, and the Giver urges him not to blame his father or the rest of the community for what they do: "Listen to me, Jonas. They can't help it. *They know nothing.*" Jonas is unwilling to heed his words, but the Giver persists: "It's the way they live. It's the life that was created for them. It's the same life that you would have, if you had not been chosen as my successor."[24] The implication is that the people in Jonas's world cannot be held responsible for their actions because they truly have no knowledge of good and bad. They do what they are told to do without question because they do not have the freedom or the ability to do anything else.

In a speech given to the Ohio Educational Library Media Association in 2001, author Lowry acknowledged that the themes of *The Giver* are similar to those of the Genesis story. She quoted a letter sent to her by an adult reader of the novel who noted that in both her book and the biblical tale, "[E]ach human must confront the needs for creative disobedience, sexuality, and self-reliance, as well as the knowledge of mortality." In her response to the woman's letter, Lowry agreed that pain is a gift of great value: "It is what makes us human," she said.[25] In another speech,

Lowry discussed the relation between knowledge and independence and urged adults to share books with children: "It is very risky. But each time a child opens a book, he pushes open the gate that separates him from Elsewhere. It gives him choices. It gives him freedom. Those are magnificent, wonderfully unsafe things."[26] If Jonas, then, is the bringer of pain and sorrow to his carefully perfected world, he is also the one who ushers in freedom, knowledge, and wisdom.

If we analyze *The Giver* in terms of the four questions discussed at the beginning of this chapter, we see that the world of Jonas was established in order to solve the problems that plague our century and the last. Such problems include warfare, unstable climates, families in crisis, and economic hardship.

On the surface, it might appear that the utopia does not create any problems of its own, as everyone in Jonas's community seems to be happy and healthy. Only when readers look more closely do they see the cost of such stability and order. As we have already noted, there is no moral decision-making in Jonas's world since residents are not aware of alternative ways of thinking. Beyond this, there is also no love. When Jonas asks his parents if they love him, they scold him good-naturedly for not using precise language. The word "love," they say, is "a very generalized word, so meaningless that it's become almost obsolete." Instead, they tell Jonas that they enjoy his company and that they take pride in his accomplishments.[27] There is also, we learn, no sexual passion in the society. As children reach puberty, they begin to take a daily pill that mutes sexual stirrings.

The door that separates insiders from outsiders is memory, and with it the capacity to imagine different ways of being. When Jonas receives knowledge of the past from the Giver, he becomes aware that things have not always been as they are now and that people are capable of making choices about how they will construct their future. As for the final question, the question about which world is preferable, readers will have to answer that one for themselves. In writing the book, Lowry has made her position clear. Her protagonist chooses to leave the only world he has ever known both in order to find a new life for himself and to give the twin gifts of memory and imagination to the rest of his community.

Pleasantville (1998)

Director Gary Ross's 1998 movie *Pleasantville* comes to much the same conclusion as Lowry does regarding the importance of creativity, sexuality, independent thought, and knowledge of suffering. *Pleasantville* tells the story of two contemporary teens who, though twins, could not be more different. Jennifer (played by Reese Witherspoon) is pretty, sexually promiscuous, and utterly uninterested in schoolwork. David (Tobey Maguire), on the other hand, is shy and nerdy. His one passion is watching reruns of an early 1960s-era television program entitled *Pleasantville*, a saccharine family show that features the characters George and Betty Parker and their two children, Bud and Mary Sue. Episodes of the show, all of which are shot in black and white, focus on life in the small town of Pleasantville and include such events as Bud accidentally breaking the neighbor's window, children adopting a stray cat, and Mary Sue taking her father to a school dance after her date has backed out.

The answer to our first question about utopias is answered early in the movie. It is clear why David likes to escape into the world of Pleasantville, as in his own world, teachers lecture him and his classmates about joblessness, global warning, drought, famine, and the spread of HIV. Even David's own home does not offer respite from the complexities of modern life, as his parents are divorced and his father shows little interest in living up to his parental responsibilities. When David hears his mother arguing with his father on the phone, he simply turns the volume on the television up so as to tune out his parents and their problems.

No wonder, then, that David is eagerly looking forward to losing himself in a twenty-four hour *Pleasantville* marathon that will be aired by his favorite nostalgia-TV station. With his father absent and his mother away on a trip with her new boyfriend, there is nothing to get in the way of David's enjoying a full night and day of nonstop pleasantry.

The problem is that David's sister Jennifer has other plans for the television set. She has invited a boy over to watch music videos and has even prepared for the evening by buying and wearing sexy new underwear. She and David begin to fight over the television remote control, and in the struggle they manage to break the device. Within seconds, a TV repairman appears at their door. This mysterious stranger is played by Don Knotts, an actor much-beloved for his role as Deputy Barney Fife in the long-running 1960s television series *The Andy Griffith Show*. Both David and Jennifer are puzzled as to how he knew that their television was broken since neither one had called for service. The repairman does not explain his presence but instead begins to quiz David about details from the show *Pleasantville*. When it becomes clear that David's knowledge of the program is encyclopedic, the repairman produces from his toolbox a special remote that, as we soon learn, has magical powers. As soon as David presses its shining red button, he and Jennifer find themselves transported into the television landscape of Pleasantville. They have stepped into the roles of Bud and Mary Sue Parker and must figure out how to fit in to a world very different from their own.

In Pleasantville, the twins discover, nothing unpleasant ever occurs. Every time that the basketball team shoots, the ball swishes through the net. There are no fires (the fire department's sole responsibility is to rescue cats who get stuck in trees), and there is never any rain. There are not even any toilets, as human excretion is apparently much too messy to have a place in the television world. Most importantly, everything in Pleasantville is black-and-white or some shade of gray, including the flowers.

That begins to change, however, when Jennifer (now called Mary Sue) begins to stir things up. Mary Sue introduces her new boyfriend Skip to sexual excitement, and immediately afterward Skip spies a red rose growing in a neighbor's yard. He shares his discovery with his friends, and soon teenage couples who had been shy about even holding hands begin to explore carnal pleasures. As a result, the teens themselves begin to take on color. One girl is shown at her family doctor's office being examined by a physician because her tongue has mysteriously turned red.

Mary Sue shares her knowledge about sex not only with her classmates but also with her mother, who apparently never learned about where babies come from. Somewhat shaken by Mary Sue's explanation, Betty declares that her husband would never engage in such an act. In response, Mary Sue explains that Betty is able to give pleasure to herself without the assistance of a man. Eager to put her newfound knowledge into practice, Betty draws herself a bath and soaks in the tub. Gradually, she brings herself to an orgasm. As she reaches her crescendo, a tree outside of the Parker's home bursts into flame. Clearly, Pleasantville is undergoing a revolution that no one could have predicted and that not everyone will welcome.

Initially, Bud is one of those who opposes the changes that his sister initiates; he is furious with Mary Sue for disrupting the orderly and predictable world of his beloved television program. Gradually, however, he comes to realize that it is important for the people around him to be exposed to new ideas and to places beyond their small town. Thus the answer to the second question about utopias emerges: while it is true that Pleasantville erases all the ills of our contemporary world, what it offers in return is only banality. No one thinks deeply about anything. No one questions anything. As in the world of *The Giver*, there are no books in Pleasantville. Or, rather, there are books, but all of their pages are blank. One day Bud starts to summarize the plots of novels like *Catcher in the Rye* and *Huckleberry Finn* to his fellow teens, and the pages of those books magically fill themselves in so that everyone can read them. Soon the young people of Pleasantville are flocking not only to Lover's Lane but also to the town library. Even Mary Sue, who in her life as Jennifer would not have been caught dead with a book in her hand, discovers the joys of reading.

There are three scenes in *Pleasantville* that make clear the connection between the movie and the story of Adam and Eve. The first takes place after the owner of the local soda fountain, a man named Bill Johnson, shyly confesses to Bud that he loves to paint. Bud borrows a book about art from the suddenly bustling library and brings it to Bill to study. The first painting that the two look at together is Masaccio's "The Expulsion from the Garden of Eden." In commentary on that scene, director Gary Ross explains that the whole movie is a "bit of an Edenic allegory." Just as Adam and Eve were banished from Eden, the denizens of Pleasantville are being forced from the safety and triviality of their perfect world.

The second scene that evokes the Genesis story is, in the DVD version of the movie, titled, "From the Tree of Knowledge." It takes place after a number of the young people in the town have begun to appear in color, and Bud and his best girl Margaret Henderson drive to a nearby lake surrounded by pink-petaled apple trees. On the banks of the water, small groups of teens relax on emerald-green lawns and discuss poetry. When evening falls and Bud and his date are alone in the moonlight, Margaret approaches one of the apple trees and spies a bright red fruit hanging from its branches. She plucks the apple and holds it out to Bud, saying, "Go ahead. Try it."

The camera then cuts away to a new scene, so we do not know right away whether or not Bud accepts the girl's offer. This is remedied later in the movie, however, in the movie's third reference to Genesis. As the town becomes more and more divided over the changes that are taking place, Bud happens to walk past a store selling televisions. He hears the voice of the mysterious repairman calling to him, and when he enters the store, Bud sees the face of the repairman appearing on every TV screen in the shop. Not only is the repairman omnipresent, but he is wrathful. He accuses Bud of ruining Pleasantville, asking, "You think this is a toy? You think it's your own little goddamn coloring book?" When Bud protests that he has not done anything wrong, the repairman asks, "Oh, no? Let me show you something." The next thing on the screen is a picture of Bud taking a healthy bite of the apple that Margaret had offered him. It is almost as if God had planted a video camera in Eden in order to capture Adam's transgression. The repairman circles the scene and draws an arrow pointing to Bud's teeth sinking into the fruit: "Boom! Right there!" he exclaims. "What do you call that? You know, you don't deserve this place. You don't deserve to live in this paradise!" The repairman then threatens to exile Bud from Pleasantville and demands that he hand over the magical remote. Bud refuses and instead runs from the store.

By the end of the movie, Pleasantville is no longer the safe and happy world that it was before David and Jennifer entered it. Women have stopped slavishly cooking and ironing for their husbands, young people have discovered the pulsing music of Buddy Holly, and society has been forced to reckon with diversity in appearance, thought, and opinion. Meanwhile, David has learned that the comfort afforded by Pleasantville does not make up for its lack of depth and complexity. When Margaret asks him what life is like outside of the town, David/Bud answers that it is louder, scarier, and a lot more dangerous. To this Margaret replies eagerly, "Sounds fantastic."

For her part, Jennifer comes to realize that her previous promiscuity was not very fulfilling: "I did the slut thing," she tells David. "It got kind of old." She decides to stay in her new world and to nurture her burgeoning intellectual life by going off to college. The fact that she gets on a bus at the end of the movie and heads off to parts unknown shows us how much Pleasantville has changed. Previously, residents of the town never thought to ask what lay beyond the few streets on which they had lived all their lives. (The local high school teacher taught that the end of Main Street was just the beginning again). Now, street signs point to other cities, and television sets broadcast images of Paris, Egypt, and Hawaii. The claustrophobia of the here and the now has been broken, and even though Pleasantville is louder and scarier than it was, it is also, we come to realize, more fulfilling.

The movie ends, in fact, by rejecting the very idea of paradise. When David decides to return home, he discovers that only one hour has passed in his own world. (Director Ross explains in his commentary that since *Pleasantville* episodes aired once a week for half an hour, David's two-week experience as Bud lasted only one hour. Moreover, Jennifer's four years in college would amount to only "a long weekend" in normal time.) David also discovers that his mother, who had set off on a trip with her new boyfriend, has had second thoughts about her relationship and is now crying in the kitchen. He goes to comfort her, and she sobs that at one point in her life she thought that everything was perfect—she had the right house, the right husband, the right car, and the right life. Now, however, she is divorced and struggling financially. "It's not supposed to be like this," she cries. To this David, filled with the wisdom of his recent sojourn into paradise, replies, "It's not *supposed* to be *anything*." Life, in other words, is not something to be measured against an imagined ideal but is a messy, unpredictable process through which we muddle as best we can.

This is, in fact, writer/director Ross's answer to the fourth question about utopias: the question about which world he would prefer to inhabit. As he says in his commentary, "One of the things I think this movie says is that life isn't tidy, and life isn't neat, and life doesn't follow rules. And that's the good news. And that's what makes life beautiful and wonderful and open and exciting and thrilling and confusing and scary and danger-ous and lovely and all those things at once." Viewers of the movie may disagree with Ross about the desirability of our messy and unpredictable world. We, like David, might long to lose ourselves in Pleasantville. After all, we have chosen to spend two hours in the alternative reality of the cinema rather than to face the grittiness of our own lives. At least, how-ever, Ross has made the choice clear for us.

Less immediately apparent is the answer to the third question enu-merated above, the question about what constitutes the door between insiders and outsiders, or between those who want to remain in the safe and predictable world of Pleasantville and those who have grown beyond it. As the film progresses, more and more characters begin to change from black-and-white to color. Betty is able to see color for the first time during her adventure in the bathtub, and she herself becomes colorized shortly thereafter. And yet it is not simply sexual passion that brings about the change in people. Jennifer/Mary Sue has had, as she says, ten times the sexual experience of the girls around her, and yet she remains in black-and-white for much of the movie. Her transformation occurs only when she turns down a date with boyfriend Skip in order to stay home and read.

Bud, likewise, remains in black-and-white even after his girlfriend has transformed. His own blossoming into color occurs during a scene in which his mother is being harassed and threatened on the street by some of the town's black-and-white ruffians because of her color. Bud sees the danger that his mother is in and rushes to her rescue by punching one of the young men in the face. This punch causes red blood to flow from the bully's cut lip, and the thug and his friends run away in terror. In the next moment, we see that Bud has lost his gray pallor and has taken on color.

The answer to the question of what constitutes the door between utopia and the nonidealized world, then, seems to be a character's recognition of some truth that had lain hidden and unacknowledged. For Betty, the truth was repressed sexual desire; for Jennifer/Mary Sue, it was a dormant intellectual passion, and for Bud it was an awareness that he truly loves his mother and must begin to relate to her as an adult rather than as a sulky adolescent.

One of the final scenes in *Pleasantville* hints that perhaps the transformation of these characters is not merely accidental but is rather part of a larger plan initiated and overseen by the mysterious TV repairman. As David makes the decision to return to his own world, and as he presses the red button on the television remote, the movie includes a brief shot of the repairman. He sits in his truck and gazes at David's house, in effect looking almost straight into the camera and thus straight at the viewers. He offers a knowing and somewhat sad smile, and then he puts the truck into gear and drives off.

What shall we make of this scene? The repairman's smile might indicate that he is glad that David has left Pleasantville and that he can now set about restoring it to its original innocence. This interpretation is undercut, however, by a shot of George and Betty Parker sitting on a park bench in Pleasantville, now both fully colorized, and admitting happily that they do not know what will happen next. If the repairman intends to force the citizens of Pleasantville to return to their previous way of life, he will have his work cut out for him.

A better interpretation might be to say that the repairman had intended all along to insert David and Jennifer into Pleasantville with two goals in mind. The first goal was to change the two teens for the better. During the film, both brother and sister make a transition from adolescence into adulthood. Mary Sue learns that she has worth beyond her ability to engage men sexually, and David learns to accept life as it is rather than to continue chasing after an illusion of what it should be. Second, the teens' sojourn in Pleasantville allows the town itself to grow from innocent triviality into mature complexity.

In addition to being an interpretation of the Genesis story, the movie is a commentary on the tumultuous events that rocked America during the late 1960s and the 1970s. During those years, the civil rights movement challenged long-standing beliefs about race and power by demanding that people of all skin tones, ethnicities, and backgrounds have equal access to schools, job opportunities, and voting rights. The movie not-so-subtly reminds viewers of this struggle when it shows citizens of Pleasantville being harassed because they no longer look like everyone else. In one such scene, morning dawns in the little town. A shopkeeper arranges his wares on the sidewalk outside his store, a boy on a bicycle rides through the waking streets delivering newspapers, and a sign in a shop window proclaims, "No Coloreds." Director Ross explains that the sign was included because "palpably and instantly it expresses the absurdity of racism."

In a similar way the movie comments on the traditional role of women as mothers and housekeepers by following the transformation of Betty Parker. When David and Jennifer first enter Pleasantville, Betty finds her deepest satisfaction in cooking for her family and welcoming her husband home from work each day. As the movie progresses, however, Betty discovers her own sexual needs as well as her romantic feelings for the owner of the soda shop, Bill Johnson. These insights allow her to blossom into color, and though her growth is painful for both her and her husband (whom at one point she leaves to fend for himself in the kitchen), viewers come to see that she is now a much more interesting, complex, and, indeed, beautiful woman.

If this interpretation of the TV repairman's smile is correct—that is, if the repairman intended all along for Pleasantville to be liberated from its banality, then we must ask how this affects a reading of the story of Genesis. Is it plausible to contend that God likewise was secretly pleased with Adam and Eve's transgression, and that God willed for the couple to leave Eden?

Image Versus Likeness: God Isn't Finished with Us Yet

It may seem odd to read the Genesis story as suggesting that God intended for Adam and Eve to leave their garden. After all, in the story God explicitly warns *ha-adam* not to eat of the forbidden tree. And yet, an interpretation that sees God as planning for the first couple to leave Eden is not new. Philosopher John Hick suggests that it originates as far back as the second century with the ideas of Christian thinker Irenaeus of Lyons. Irenaeus, like several other commentators, noted that in Genesis 1:26, God says, "Let us make humankind in our *image*, according to our *likeness*." However, when God actually creates people, the text says, "God created humankind in his *image*, in the *image* of God he created them" (1:27). In other words, the text opens the possibility that though we were created in the image of God, we have not yet been perfected into the likeness of God.

As Hick sees the matter, then, we are still in the process of creation, and that process involves what he calls "the long travail of the soul-making process."[28] This soul-making cannot be accomplished in a world in which there is nothing to struggle against and nothing to learn. Rather, our characters, that is, the likeness of God, must be fashioned "in an environment whose primary and overriding purpose is not immediate pleasure but the realizing of the most valuable potentialities of human personality."[29] Using the analogy of childrearing, Hick notes that children who are protected from every disappointment and hardship will not be likely to grow into adults capable of unselfishness, compassion, courage, or true moral decision-making. Therefore, though our departure from Eden has meant untold pain and sorrow, it may have been necessary for our growth as creatures who were intended to be not just the image of God but also the likeness of God.

Rejecting Perfection

In this chapter we have looked at two popular interpretations of the Genesis story, *The Giver* and *Pleasantville*, both of which reject utopia for the wisdom that comes with pain. These two are not unique. Over and over again, novels, movies, and television shows flirt with the idea of perfection only, in the end, to reject it. In the book *This Side of Paradise* (winner of the Hal Clement Award for Best Science Fiction Novel for Young Adults in 2001), a character named Mr. Eden founds a community called Paradise which boasts no crime, no poverty, no illness, and no discord.[30] And yet to achieve his goal, Mr. Eden must risk everything, including the happiness and even the lives of his family. Ultimately, Mr. Eden's vision is repudiated by the other characters in the novel, and Mr. Eden himself is destroyed.

Likewise, in a 1967 episode of the original *Star Trek* series, also entitled "This Side of Paradise," the crew of the Starship Enterprise beams down to a colony where, curiously, everyone is happy.[31] The cause of the residents' bliss turns out to be a plant that, when its spores are inhaled, induces feelings of peace and love. Even the normally staid Mr. Spock falls prey to the influence of the spores, and as a result he falls in love with one of the colony's inhabitants and spends his days looking at clouds and rainbows. Only Captain Kirk remains unaffected by the plant, and he finds that he is unable to convince his crew members to abandon their newfound bliss and return to the ship: "I don't know what I can offer against Paradise," he muses. Finally, he manages to overcome the plant's effects by inducing strong emotions in the members of the crew. Once the officers of the Enterprise become angry, the effects of the spores wear off, and finally both the crew and the colonists decide to leave the affected planet. At the conclusion of the show, Dr. McCoy quips, "Well, that's the second time man's been thrown out of paradise." To this, Kirk replies, "No, no. This time we walked out on our own. . . . Maybe we were meant to fight our way through: struggle, claw our way up, scratch for every inch of the way. Maybe we can't stroll to the music of the lute. We must march to the sound of drums."

Nearly all of popular culture's recent forays into paradise come to the same conclusion, and one can only speculate as to why. Perhaps our suspicion of Eden is due to experience with the twentieth century's totalitarian regimes. Those regimes, like the fictional utopias we have been discussing, also promised a bright future in which the troubled days of the past would be left behind. For example, on May 1, 1938, Adolf Hitler addressed the youth of Germany in the Olympic Stadium and reminded them:

> For centuries, our Volk was torn and at odds with itself, and hence it was incapacitated in its outside dealings; it was unhappy, lacking means of

defense and a sense of honor. . . . And now Providence allows us to reap the fruits of our labor: Greater Germany! . . . Seeing you here, my belief in Germany's future becomes boundless and unshakable! For I know that you will fulfill all our expectations!

So on this May Day, I greet you in our new great Germany! For you are our springtime! Through you shall and must be accomplished what has been fought for by generations throughout the centuries: Deutschland![32]

As would soon become clear to the world, the establishment of Germany's "springtime" would depend upon ridding the nation of all "undesirable" elements, including all those deemed non-Aryan and anyone who disagreed with the government. A quick glance at history will reveal any number of other glowing presentations of the future that masked more sinister methods of attaining it. Perhaps it is the fear of how these promises were enacted that leads popular culture to distrust utopian visions.

And yet, those visions retain their allure. In the *Star Trek* episode just mentioned, Captain Kirk unequivocally rejects Eden. Human beings, he says, were not made for the soft life of paradise. However, Mr. Spock is not quite so sure. When questioned about his experience in the colony, he replies, "I have little to say about it, Captain. Except that for the first time in my life, I was happy."

CHAPTER TEN

The Final Frontier

In 1943, the British writer C. S. Lewis published a novel called *Perelandra* as the second installment of his space trilogy.[1] *Perelandra* was set on Venus and featured a protagonist named Elwin Ransom whose mission was to prevent the one woman on the planet from emulating Eve and disobeying God's orders. The timing of the book was not coincidental. As war raged throughout Europe, Lewis's meditation on the nature of sin was at the same time a lament for how human beings had strayed so far from what God had wanted for Adam and Eve.

Perelandra was one of many science fiction versions of the Genesis story. Though the twentieth century fostered a suspicion about utopias, it could not squelch the longing for them. Wars, pandemics, and the invention of the atomic bomb threatened the very existence of humanity, and in response many artists and writers turned their attentions heavenward, toward the furthest reaches of space. Perhaps, they thought, the human race could begin again, having learned from its mistakes and resolved not to repeat them. Thus a 1957 *New Yorker* cartoon (see fig. 10.1) portrayed an astronaut in a space suit running toward an extraterrestrial Eve (complete with antennae) as she was about to pluck fruit from a tree, yelling, "Miss! Oh, Miss! For God's sake, stop!"[2]

In fact, the longing to begin anew in another time and another place (not to mention another galaxy) has been so strong that it has given rise to a huge body of Adam-and-Eve-in-space stories. The *Encyclopedia of*

Figure 10.1

"Miss! Oh, Miss! For God's sake, stop!"

New Yorker Cartoon by Whitney Darrow, Jr.

Science Fiction notes that a "considerable fraction" of stories submitted to science fiction magazines is reputed to concern characters based on the Genesis story.[3] Science fiction novelist Brian W. Aldiss has even coined a term for the genre: the "shaggy god story." Writes Aldiss, "The shaggy god story is the bane of magazine editors, who get approximately one story a week set in a garden of Eden spelt Ee-Duhn."[4]

The list of such stories is long. By and large, it can be divided into two categories. The first category consists of stories in which intrepid explorers seek out or stumble upon an unspoiled world somewhere—usually in the farthest reaches of space. The second category contains narratives about a disaster that is about to take place or has already happened. In these stories, human society is in jeopardy, and civilization must build itself back up from the rubble. Included in this genre is a subset of stories in which the issue is not that the human population faces immediate destruction from an imminent catastrophe but rather that our world (whether the earth itself, the humans who live on the earth, or humans on another planet) has become infertile and is entering a gradual decline. These narratives revive the image of Eve as the "mother of all the living."

Of course, as we will see, the two categories are not mutually exclusive. Often a particular television episode or movie will contain references to space exploration as well as to the perils that face human society on earth. Still, dividing the large number of science fiction uses of Adam and Eve according to these two types is a useful way to begin our final chapter.

"Lookin' for the Good Land"

A Venetian mapmaker in 1442 faced the question of where to place the biblical Garden of Eden. He located it near India, but cartographers at various other times have speculated that Eden lay in Sri Lanka, or in China, or in Syria, or in Palestine, or in the Alps.[5] In 1999, British archeologist David Rohl claimed to have located the Garden ten miles from the Iranian city of Tabriz.[6] Meanwhile, decades of war have all but destroyed the town of Qurna in Iraq where locals still believe Adam once reached for the Tree of Knowledge. Tourists now no longer stop by to have their pictures taken next to the "Adam Tree." Comments a Qurna resident, "The last time I saw a tourist was 1980."[7]

Cartographers, archeologists, and travel agencies are not the only ones interested in the search for the Garden of Eden. In their novels *Chasing Eden* and *Beyond Eden*, S. L. Linnéa and B. K. Sherer play with the notion that the Garden still exists somewhere in the Middle East. The hero of their two books is an army chaplain named Jaime Richards who discovers that, far from being a myth, Eden is in fact a real place whose location is known only to a select few. Hidden from the rest of the world, Eden is populated by many of the world's greatest thinkers, teachers, and scientists, all of whom lend their support to "the one place on earth that exists for the good of its neighbors."[8] Because of her intelligence, faith, and courage, Jaime is chosen by the Edenites to be an ambassador from their world to our own. To prove herself, Jaime must thwart several plots in which evildoers attempt to capture Eden for their own nefarious purposes.

One senses that in these novels, Eden, though it is portrayed unambiguously as a physical place, is also a metaphor for an inner reality. Members of the Eden community, even when they are away from home and walking among us in this world, are portrayed as wise, intelligent, generous, trustworthy, and unafraid of death. They are committed to making the world a better place, but they are also mindful that life as we know it is not the only life there is. When one character is faced with the choice of revealing the location of Eden to a villain, or watching his young nephew Stefan be murdered, he refuses to give up his secret: "Be brave, Stefan," he tells the boy. "It is not so bad to die. I will die soon, myself. And what is on the other side is . . . wonderful."[9]

In this section we will examine several stories in which the search for Eden occurs not on earth but in the heavens beyond. In each case, the storyline will include a physical journey to another world, but often that journey will serve as a metaphor for some inward exploration as well. Nearly always, science fiction versions of the Adam and Eve story are just as suspicious of paradise as were the utopian stories we discussed in the last chapter. For example, in a 1976 episode of the television show *Space: 1999* entitled "New Adam, New Eve," an ersatz god named Magus attempts to lure the crew of Moonbase Alpha to what he promises will be a new Eden. When Magus is exposed as being nothing more than a bright magician who has learned the secrets of physics (and is thus not a deity, as he claimed to be), he pleads with the crew to help him breed a new and better version of humans. In the end of the episode, the heroes of the show reject Magus's imagined paradise and defeat his plan.[10] In a 1997 episode of *Sliders* called "The Last of Eden," a universe-trotting team of explorers happens upon a "perfect" world that, they soon discover, is about to be obliterated by an earthquake. The residents of the Edenic planet are convinced that they are safe and that if they leave, they will die. It is up to boy genius Quinn Mallory and his fellow travelers to save the residents from their dangerous paradise.

Star Trek: "The Way to Eden" (1969)

The original *Star Trek* series was particularly suspicious of utopian visions. *Star Trek* featured at least four installments that made reference to Adam and Eve and, in all cases, the characters on the show rejected the various Edens that were offered to them. The show's pilot episode, which was entitled "The Cage," is a case in point. "The Cage" first aired in September of 1966 and starred Jeffrey Hunter as Captain Christopher Pike. (Later episodes would, of course, feature actor William Shatner as Captain Kirk of the starship Enterprise.) In the story, Pike is captured by a group of aliens who plan to use him to breed a race of slaves. In order to tempt Pike to comply with their wishes, they create for him an illusory world full of any pleasures that he desires. He can choose a fantasy that looks exactly like his own home on earth, or he can choose an exotic locale filled with seductive dancing girls. Whatever he wants, he can have—everything, that is, except true freedom.

The script makes explicit reference to the Genesis story by describing Pike as an Adam and the female companion with whom he is supposed to procreate as Eve. Though Eve is lovely and the life that the aliens promise him would be full of beauty and pleasure, Pike ultimately rejects the aliens' paradise. He threatens to kill himself rather than submit to his captors' will. The aliens are astounded at his choice and are prompted to look more deeply at human civilization. They conclude, "We had not believed this possible. The customs and history of your race show a unique hatred of captivity, even when it's pleasant and benevolent. You prefer death." Life in Eden, they learn from Pike, is not worth the sacrifice of one's free will. In the end, the aliens judge humans to be unsuitable for their purposes, and Pike is allowed to return to his spaceship.

As we saw in the last chapter, *Star Trek*'s first season also included an episode called "This Side of Paradise" in which the crew of the Enterprise was tempted to abandon its mission in order to settle on an Edenic planet. And, as discussed in chapter 1, the show's second season included an episode called "The Apple" in which a race of innocents was suddenly exposed to both violence and sexuality. In both cases, paradise was rejected in favor of a life deemed more authentic.

However, perhaps *Star Trek*'s most memorable use of the Adam and Eve tale occurred in a 1969 episode called "The Way to Eden." The episode begins with the Starship Enterprise in hot pursuit of a stolen space-cruiser called the Aurora. When Captain Kirk and his crew finally manage to apprehend the stolen vessel, they beam the thieves aboard in order to interrogate them. What they find is that the bandits, led by a scientist named Sevrin, are peace-loving, flower-wearing, guitar-strumming humans/humanoids who stole the Aurora only so that they could use it to fly to the planet Eden. As one of the hippie-like characters, a folk-singer named Adam says, the group is "Lookin' for the good land."

Captain Kirk has little sympathy for Sevrin and his companions. When he hears what they have in mind, Kirk asks incredulously, "Do they really believe that Eden exists?" First Officer Spock replies, "Many myths are based on truth, Captain." Spock is actually sympathetic to the group's desire to search for a different way of life. He explains, "There are many who are uncomfortable with what we have created. It is almost a biological rebellion, a profound revulsion against the planned communities, the programming, the sterilized, artfully balanced atmospheres. They hunger for an Eden, where spring comes."

Because one member of Sevrin's group is the son of an ambassador, Kirk treats the travelers as guests rather than as prisoners. This latitude allows Sevrin and his followers to commandeer one of the Enterprise's shuttlecrafts in order to continue their journey to Eden. Once again, Kirk and his crew take off in pursuit, and they follow the shuttlecraft all the way to a previously uncharted planet. When they arrive they are stunned by the planet's fantastic beauty. Bright orange and blue flowers flourish, and a serene lake, surrounded by graceful trees, glitters in the sun. The branches of one tree in particular are heavy with tempting pear-like fruit. At the base of the tree, however, Kirk and his men discover the body of the young musician who had sung with such longing about his search for paradise. Next to him lies a piece of the fruit with a bite taken out of it. Filled with acid, it has caused his death. Spock stares at the young man and says solemnly, "His name was Adam."

This episode clearly reflects the cultural clashes that were gripping America in 1968–1969. When Sevrin and his group are beamed aboard, they at first refuse to speak and stage a sit-in instead. Kirk then attempts to order them to comply with his interrogation, and in response they call him a "Herbert," which, as Spock explains, is an unflattering reference to a minor bureaucrat "notorious for his rigid and limited patterns of thought." Sevrin refuses to acknowledge that Kirk has any power over him and asserts, "We recognize no authority save that within ourselves."

But if "The Way to Eden" mirrored the 1960s' clashes between students and politicians/police, it also found a curious relevance in the 2008 presidential election. In the beginning of the episode, when Kirk is unable to persuade Sevrin's group to cooperate, Spock approaches them and holds his hands in front of his chest. He places the tips of his thumbs together and the tips of his fingers together as well, so that his hands form a circle. He looks at the hippie-like group and says, "One." The travelers understand his gesture, and they turn toward him, peer at him intently, and make the same gesture in response. Sevrin says to Spock, "We are one," to which Spock answers, "One is the beginning." When they ask him, "Are you one, Herbert?" Spock answers, "I am not Herbert." Instantly, everyone in the group relaxes. Spock, they realize, understands them and their mission far better than Kirk does.

This gesture, and the intonation of the word "One," played a role in the 2008 presidential campaign when a Los Angeles creative agency designed a poster in honor of Barack Obama that featured two hands coming together to form a circle. At the top of the poster was the name "Obama," and at the bottom, the slogan "Sign of Progress." Rays of light emanated from the O formed by the hands.[11] At almost exactly the same time, Obama's opponent, Senator John McCain, released an ad poking fun at the near-religious fervor of some of Obama's supporters. The ad, entitled "The One," compared Obama to Moses and to a messiah.[12] It was perhaps inevitable, then, that Internet pundits began to comment on the similarity between the salute in "The Road to Eden" and the Obama salute. Depending on one's political preferences, Obama was interpreted to be either the one who would lead America to a true promised land or the one who would, in the end, offer nothing but poisoned fruit.

Even though "The Way to Eden" ends tragically, with Adam and Sevrin both dying and their companions watching their dream become a nightmare, the episode does hold out hope for the future. In a final conversation with one of the travelers, Spock says, "It is my sincere wish that you do not give up your search for Eden. I have no doubt but that you will find it, or make it yourselves." The last part of this sentence indicates that paradise is not merely a physical place but is also a way of living: humans in harmony with each other and with whatever natural world they inhabit.

Star Trek V: The Final Frontier (1989)

First Officer Spock's interest in finding Eden did not end with the 1969 episode just discussed. Twenty years later, Paramount Pictures released *Star Trek V: The Final Frontier*, in which Spock's half-brother Sybok embarks on a quest for paradise similar to that of Sevrin and his companions. Unlike Spock (the product of a Vulcan father and a human mother), who prizes reason above emotion, Sybok is convinced that passion is the key to self-knowledge. He kidnaps Kirk and his companions, commandeers their shuttlecraft, and plots a course through "The Great Barrier," a region of space that no one has ever penetrated before. There he hopes to find Eden, "a place from which creation sprang." He promises his crew, "For us that place will soon be a reality."

In order to win followers, Sybok invites people to remember their most painful moments and, using his extraordinary powers of empathy, he relives those moments with them. With Dr. McCoy, for example, he experiences the conflicted agony the physician felt when his father asked to be euthanized. With Spock, he undergoes the feelings of rejection caused by a father who did not accept his mixed-race son. Somehow, this process of reexperiencing the most painful moments of life brings calm and peace to the ones whom Sybok touches.

Captain Kirk, however, rejects the premise that emotional discomfort should be erased. Pain and guilt, he says, "are the things we carry with us, the things that make us who we are. If we lose them, we lose ourselves. I don't want my pain taken away. I need my pain." His decision not to undergo Sybok's palliative process is consistent with the rejection of utopias that we saw in the last chapter. Specifically, Kirk's steadfast willingness to endure the agony of memory bears a remarkable resemblance to Jonas's decision in Lowry's novel *The Giver* to suffer through the collective human history that everyone else has forgotten. In that story, after Jonas experiences a particularly grueling memory, he asks the Giver for medication that will relieve his pain. The Giver, however, refuses him; Jonas must endure not only the memory itself but also the anguish that accompanies it. To do otherwise, says the Giver, would be to rob the memory of its significance. Jonas must remember not simply events but also how the events affected the frail flesh and bones of living humans.

Commenting on the importance of memory, in one of her speeches Lowry recalled an incident in which her father, whose mental faculties had been ravaged by age and illness, looked at a photograph of his first child. "That's your sister," he said to Lowry happily. "That's Helen." But then, in a puzzled voice, he added, "I can't remember exactly what happened to her." In fact, the little girl had died very young of cancer. Observes Lowry, "We can forget pain, I think. And it is *comfortable* to do so. But I also wonder briefly: is it safe to do that, to forget?"[13] For Captain Kirk, the answer is no: no, it is not safe to forget. Forgetting, or at least forgetting the pain of remembering, has led to Sybok's reckless highjacking of a spacecraft in order to find Eden.

To Kirk's great surprise, however, it turns out that Sybok has been correct about at least one thing: it is indeed possible to cross The Great Barrier without perishing, and after they have done so, Kirk and his fellow hostages find themselves on a barren planet that is more desert than garden. Suddenly, the ground opens up and great stone pillars push up into the sky. A deep male voice booms, "Brave Souls! Welcome!" At first the stunned group simply stares: "Is this the voice of God?" asks McCoy. The voice replies, "One voice, many faces."

"God" then explains that Sybok and the crew of the Enterprise are the first ones to have found him, since he has been trapped behind the Great Barrier for so long. He asks if the space shuttle in which they arrived can carry him through the barrier, at which point Kirk becomes suspicious that the being is not, in fact, divine: "What does God need with a starship?" he asks. Kirk's impudence enrages the being, who immediately shoots lasers from his eyes and injures Kirk and Spock. McCoy then also realizes that they have found not God but a malevolent monster: "I doubt any God who inflicts pain for his own pleasure," he exclaims. A battle ensues, and Sybok is destroyed, while Kirk, Spock, and McCoy are beamed safely back aboard the Enterprise. In a final scene that actor William Shatner describes as the central point of the script, the three men discuss whether or not God really exists.[14] Kirk concludes, "Maybe he's not out there . . . Maybe he's right here." Pointing to his chest, he explains, "Human heart." Once again, the outward journey toward Eden has led to an inward journey of self-discovery.

We should note that Kirk's decision to retain the pain of his memories is not one with which everyone would agree. Recently, researchers have actually made the relief that Sybok offered a real option by discovering a way to alter a person's recollection of a traumatic event.[15] Normally, when people undergo some form of distress, they experience a surge in the hormone adrenaline. This surge, it turns out, affects the way that memories are stored in the brain: the more adrenaline, the stronger the memory. Thus, for example, if someone is attacked by a mugger, the resulting adrenaline surge will make it difficult in the future for the person to forget the experience. In some cases, people suffer so intensely from the inability to forget that they cannot live normal, happy lives. This condition, called post-traumatic stress disorder (PTSD), can be crippling.

Science however, may soon be able to help those who suffer from PTSD. A drug called propranolol, normally used to reduce high blood pressure, has been shown to block adrenaline's effect on the brain. One study, for example, looked at the effects of propranolol on a woman who had been in a terrible car accident. Three years after the incident, the woman still suffered from nightmares in which she continually re-lived the event. In their experiment, doctors asked the woman to sit down and to write out all of the details of her experience. They then administered the propranolol. A week later, the woman reported that her nightmares had stopped. She was able to recall the event, but the memory no longer affected her as it had before.

Did she regret having her memory altered? When asked, the woman acknowledged that it was strange to have had her very thoughts, which many people believe to be in some sense their "selves," changed by a pill: "This study has taken away a part of me that's been in me for so long, and that I find very weird," she said. However, she continued, "I have regained my identity. What was broken when I was twelve was fixed. They have given me back myself."[17] Perhaps Kirk can choose the pain of memory because that pain, like Kirk himself, is fictional. Those enduring the real pain of life in this world might not be so quick to endorse the value of suffering.

"I Hope Your New World Will Be Different"

So far in this chapter we have looked at how science fiction narratives update the ancient search for the Garden of Eden. Whereas medieval mapmakers imagined a terrestrial Eden, science fiction writers often look to the farthest reaches of space to find their paradise. We now turn to the second broad category of sci-fi uses of Adam and Eve: apocalyptic and postapocalyptic narratives in which human life is threatened and must find a way to rebuild itself.

Probe 7: Over and Out (1963)

A now-classic use of Adam and Eve in an apocalyptic setting can be found in an episode of the original *Twilight Zone* series entitled "Probe 7, Over and Out."[18] The program originally aired on November 29, 1963, roughly a year after the Cuban missile crisis and just one week after the assassination of President John F. Kennedy.

The premise of the episode is that a one-man space probe has crash-landed on an unknown planet. The ship has been damaged, and its pilot, an astronaut named Cook, has been injured. Unfortunately, Cook can expect no assistance from his home base. As he discovers when he radios for help, a massive (presumably nuclear) war has broken out in his own world, and billions of people have already died. Cook is told that before long, all radio contact between him and his base will cease and that no one will be left on the planet that he once called home. In his final transmission to the astronaut, the military leader responsible for launching Cook into space tells him, "I hope your new world will be different. I hope you'll find no words such as hate. I hope there'll be . . . [silence]."

Abandoned and distraught, Cook begins to explore his new environment. He ventures out from the probe and at first finds the area uninhabited. Eventually, however, he discovers that he is not in fact alone; a woman has been spying on him from a hiding place in the dense underbrush that surrounds his defunct spaceship. In his first communication with her he learns that she also is a refugee from another planet. Her spaceship has also crashed, and she alone survived. When Cook attempts to bring her back to his own ship, though, the woman becomes terrified of him and runs away.

Eventually, Cook manages to convince the woman that he means no harm. He explains using rudimentary words and gestures that he is going to move his belongings out of the space probe and that he intends to establish a home for himself in an area where he has found flowers and fruit trees growing: "Sort of like a garden," he says. The woman indicates a willingness to follow him, and the two of them realize that they will have to learn something of each other's language if they are to spend the rest of their days together. Cook thus introduces himself: "Adam Cook," he says, pointing at his chest. The woman reciprocates: "Eve Norda." Adam then takes a fistful of dirt and asks her what she calls it in her language. She answers, "Irth."

As the two head off into the woods, Eve stops to pluck a piece of fruit from one of the nearby trees. She hands it to Adam, and in a close-up of the fruit we see that it is in fact an apple.

The episode then concludes with this commentary from Rod Serling: "Do you know these people? Names familiar, are they? They lived a long time ago. Perhaps they're part fable. Perhaps they're part fantasy. And perhaps the place they're walking to now is not really called Eden. We offer it only as a presumption." The implication of the story is that Adam Cook and Eve Norda, both of whom came to earth from elsewhere, are in fact our first earthly ancestors.

This twist of the plot can be understood as both disturbing and reassuring. On the one hand, the story is a chilling reminder of the human propensity for violence. During the episode, when Cook first approaches the woman whom we will come to know as Eve, he finds that she is terrified of him. This prompts him to reflect on what he calls the "psychological makeup of man." Observes the astronaut, "He's a frightened breed. He's a very frightened breed. Must be a universal trait." Audiences watching the episode so soon after the missile crisis, in a time when school children were routinely taught what to do if a nuclear bomb exploded, could readily have identified with Cook's assessment. The end of the episode, at which point Serling makes it clear that the characters come not from our future but from our past, might have reinforced the audience's sense of the inevitability of violence and warfare. "This has happened before," the episode seems to say, "So why would you think it would not happen again?"

Or, to put it another way, imagine that there was no twist of the plot at the end of the story, and that Cook and Norda were simply characters from the future. As the man and woman walked off into their new lives together in an unnamed garden on an unnamed planet, audiences could have imagined that the world the two would create would be peaceful and gentle and would never know the horrors of warfare. That might have been a hopeful message to send in 1963. As it is, however, the episode offers no such hope. We know what the descendants of Eva and Adam will do. They will build the same violent world that their ancestors barely escaped so long ago.

At the same time, though, that thought might offer a perverse sort of hope. After all, a society faced with its own potential for annihilation might reason that worlds have been destroyed in the past, and yet the human race persists. Perhaps even if we do blow ourselves up in a nuclear conflagration, someone will survive. Perhaps a man and a woman will survive, and they will reproduce somewhere new, and human history will live on.

New Eden (1994)

This more hopeful message underlies the futuristic movie *New Eden* (1994), which stars Stephen Baldwin as a slave named Hevel Adams, and Lisa Bonet as Lily, the woman who purchases and eventually frees Adams. The movie takes place in the year 2237, after a Great War has devastated most of the world. Adams is a pacifist who has been convicted of sedition for opposing the ruling government, and, as the movie opens, he and his fellow prisoners are being transferred to a penal colony. One of the prisoners, a swaggering felon named Kyne, teases Adams that he is foolish to continue to believe in the goodness of human beings: "You're a 'rule boy,'" Kyne tells him. "You believe in society."

When Adams, Kyne, and their fellow convicts arrive at their new destination, they expect that they will be locked up. However, they soon learn that this is not their fate. Instead, they are told that the walls of the building in which they stand are not meant to keep them in, but rather to keep them out: "Yes!" they are told, "The expulsion from Paradise has begun . . . Go and sin no more." At this point they are cast out into the sands of a barren landscape. Immediately, they are set upon by a group of marauding sand pirates, and most of them are slaughtered.

Adams manages to survive the massacre, but soon afterward he is captured and sold as a slave to Lily. Lily and her young son Luke are members of a scavenger community that lives on its wits and on the refuse that others have left behind. When Adams, a former engineering student, shows the scavenger community how to filter their polluted water, he becomes a hero, and Lily frees him from his servitude. Lily and Adams then fall in love, and Adams asks for Lily's hand in marriage. Lily refuses, however, saying that in the desolate world in which she lives, people do not marry.

Adams holds on to his hopes, and he has grand plans for the scavengers' village: "We're gonna call it New Eden!" he exclaims. He shows the scavengers how to grow plants for food so that they will not be dependent on others, and he convinces them that they will be able to trade peacefully with their neighbors for the other things that they need. Soon crops grow and are harvested, and it looks as if Adams's optimism is paying off. However, the village's newfound prosperity has attracted the attention of the roving sand pirates. These pirates, now led by the criminal Kyne, raid the village, and all of the crops are lost.

At this point, Adams abandons his pacifism and learns to fight. He is emboldened by the courage of the scavengers, and they in turn support him by asking rhetorically, "We're a family, aren't we? We're building New Eden, aren't we?" When the sand pirates come again, Adams at first tries to avert a war by warning Kyne not to attack. When Kyne laughs off his suggestion, Adams then challenges Kyne to settle the matter in a fight between just the two of them. The conflict escalates, however, and soon a full-scale battle begins. The residents of New Eden defeat the pirates handily, and Adams kills Kyne. The movie ends happily with the marriage ceremony of Adams and Lily.

It is worth pausing here to take note of the names of the characters in *New Eden*. The name Lily, of course, evokes the character Lilith from the Jewish tale of Adam's first wife. In the Jewish story, Lilith did not want to be subordinate to Adam, and so she rejected him and flew off into the wilderness. In *New Eden*, Lily is a defiant, independent single mother who lives in the wilderness and who initially refuses Adams's offer of marriage.

The leader of the sand pirates, the one who mocks Adams for believing in the value of civilization, is named Kyne. According to Genesis 4:1, the name of Adam and Eve's first son is Qain, usually written in English as Cain but pronounced in Hebrew as Kīn. Adams's first name is Hevel, the same Hebrew name given to Adam and Eve's second son, which is usually written in English as Abel. (It is surely no coincidence that screenwriter Dan Gordon chose these names; Gordon speaks Hebrew and served in the Israel Defense Forces from 1973–1975.[19]) According to the Bible, Abel/Hevel was a shepherd, and Cain/Qain was a farmer. When the time came for the brothers to offer sacrifices to God, Abel's offering was accepted, but Cain's was not. In anger and distress, Cain killed his brother Abel.

In *New Eden* we have an inversion of this story. Unlike Lilith, who was created as Adam's first wife but who then rejected marriage, Lily rejects marriage at first but then becomes the wife of Adams. Unlike Cain, who was a farmer and who killed Abel, Kyne is a nomad and is the one who is killed. Unlike Abel, who is a shepherd and who is murdered, Hevel is a farmer and is the one who kills Kyne in a fair fight. Moreover, the movie, unlike the biblical story, ends happily. The scavengers successfully fend off their attackers, and they look toward the future with courage and optimism. They are creating, after all, a *new* Eden, and this time, suggests the movie, there will be no Fall back into the mistakes of the past.

Increase and Multiply

Among the apocalyptic and postapocalyptic narratives that refer to Adam and Eve, a subset focuses on the issue of fertility. In these stories the key issue is the ability of either human beings or of the earth itself to create new life. For example, in P. D. James's 1992 novel *The Children of Men* (which was made into a movie in 2006), an inexplicable epidemic of male infertility threatens the human population. The story takes place in the year 2021, and its premise is that across the world, men's sperm has mysteriously lost its potency. No children are being conceived, and the human race must grapple with the prospect of its own extinction. When a woman named Julian does become pregnant, the main character in the novel has a conversation with Julian's husband and says to him, "Julian's child will be hailed as a miracle. You will be hailed as the father of that miracle. The new Adam, begetter of the new race, the savior of mankind."[20] Here, as in most of the apocalyptic tales in question, the story of Adam and Eve is used not to underscore human sinfulness but rather to focus on the precious and precarious nature of human life. A similar concern arises in the Korean sci-fi/martial arts film *The Last Eve* (2005), in which, after a comet destroys much of the earth, only three people remain alive: Adam, Eve, and a priest, whose face is veiled and whose identity remains mysterious. In order to prevent humanity from regenerating itself, the narrator of the movie says, Satan has sent seven demons to destroy Eve. In the last scene of the vignette, Adam wanders into a field filled with flowers and hears the cry of an infant. With great joy he finds a baby among the flowers and clutches it to his chest. As the segment comes to a close, the following New Testament passage appears on the screen: "For God so loved the world that he gave his one and only Son, that whoever believes in him shall not perish but have eternal life.

John 3:16." Even though Adam and Eve were unable to produce children, the movie seems to say, God took pity on humankind and provided new life for them.

The Handmaid's Tale (1986)

One of the most prominent uses of Adam and Eve to explore the importance of fertility is Margaret Atwood's novel *The Handmaid's Tale*, which was made into a movie starring Natasha Richardson in 1990. *The Handmaid's Tale* takes place in the near future, after Christian fundamentalists have seized control of the United States and have renamed it the Republic of Gilead. Because of environmental pollution, fertility rates have plummeted, and the government has taken drastic measures to increase births. Women who have shown themselves to be capable of bearing children are kidnapped and forced into service as "handmaidens" whose job is to copulate with and bear the children of the most powerful men in the new government. These men are known as the "Commanders" of Gilead.

According to the novel, the biblical warrant for the government's actions is found in Genesis 30 which tells the story of Rachel's inability to become pregnant by her husband Jacob. Distraught at her barrenness, Rachel convinces Jacob to have sex with her maid Bilhah: "Go in to her, that she may bear upon my knee and that I too may have children through her" (30:3). In Gilead, any child born to a handmaiden is immediately taken from its biological mother and given to the wife of the handmaiden's Commander.

The government of Gilead controls every aspect of life, and its citizens are expected to participate in the rallies or "Prayvaganzas" that are held periodically. At one of these prayer meetings, the Commander in charge reminds the handmaidens that bearing children is their only route to salvation. To make his point, he reads from the New Testament's First Letter of Paul to Timothy (which, most scholars agree, was probably not in fact written by the apostle Paul but rather by one of his followers). The biblical letter gives a variety of instructions concerning how the disciples of Jesus should conduct themselves, and the text that the Commander reads (2:11–15) gives particular attention to the behavior of women. In this passage from Atwood's novel, the protagonist, a handmaiden named Offred, recounts the Commander's speech:

"Let the woman learn in silence with all subjection." Here he looks us over. "All," he repeats.

"But I suffer not a woman to teach, nor to usurp authority over the man, but to be in silence.

"For Adam was first formed, then Eve.

"And Adam was not deceived, but the woman being deceived was in the transgression.

"Notwithstanding she shall be saved by childbearing, if they continue in faith and charity and holiness with sobriety."

Saved by childbearing, I think. What did we suppose would save us, in the time before?[21]

In Atwood's novel, as in the New Testament passage itself, women are seen as sinful daughters of the sinful Eve who cannot be trusted with authority and whose only hope for redemption lies in their wombs. Even the process of childbirth itself is reminder of sin, as the women of Gilead are denied anesthesia during labor. The justification for this practice is Genesis 3:16, in which God says, "I will greatly multiply thy sorrow and thy conception; in sorrow thou shalt bring forth children."[22]

Last Exit to Earth (1996)

Characters in The Handmaid's Tale read the story of Adam and Eve solely as a reinforcement of women's subordination. Other narratives, though, focus more on celebrating Eve's powers of generation. For example, the low-budget film Last Exit to Earth, produced by Roger Corman in 1996, is a campy sci-fi thriller that makes Eve's ability to bear life the central focus of the plot.

The movie opens in the year 2500, "After the Great Feminine Revolution." As we soon come to learn, a conflagration occurred in the year 2110, during which the world was nearly destroyed. Humanity's only hope was for women to take control of the government, since men had proved themselves too aggressive to conduct the world's affairs peacefully. The women's government enacted several reforms, including a decree that the gene for aggression would be spliced out of all newborn males. What the Feminine Revolution did not anticipate, however, was that the process of removing aggression would also render males sterile. Thus, though society in 2500 A.D. is serene and stress-free, it will soon come to an end because no children are being born who can carry it on.

The women's colony has already tried several methods of repopulation, including cloning, but nothing has worked. One of the women trying desperately to find a way to save humanity is a scientist named Eve. Eve has set up a training camp for some of the sterile, unaggressive men whom the women refer to as "poodles." In some of the movie's most amusing scenes, Eve tries various methods to teach the poodles how to be "manly," with the hope that environmental training will stimulate the production of fertile sperm. For example, she shows the men gladiator movies that periodically flash messages like "You are potent" and "You are virile" on the screen. She gives one of them an ax and tries to teach him how to chop wood, and she surrounds the others with the paraphernalia of cowboys and warriors. Nothing, however, seems to help.

Finally, Eve decides to travel back in time (along with her daughter and two other women, one of whom is named Lilith) to kidnap men from the year 2100. These male specimens, since they are living before the Feminine Revolution took place, are presumably fertile, and the time-travelers hope to copulate with them in order to become pregnant.

The plot of *Last Exit to Earth* is complicated and involves intergalactic highjackers, petty despots, and biological warfare. The upshot of the action is that Eve and her crew do manage to bring three men back with them to the future. One of these is the handsome captain of a space shuttle whose name is Jaid Adams. The other two are criminals who seek to gain control of the women's society by threatening them with a deadly virus. When the leaders of Eve's world see that she has brought violence back with her, they banish Eve from their midst. Before she leaves, however, Eve offers one last piece of advice: "You can't just remove aggression from human beings. It's part of us. Maybe our purpose is to look at the darkness and be strong in the face of it."

As it turns out, Eve will not be alone in her banishment, as Adams, with whom she has fallen in love, decides to join her. Moreover, Eve's daughter and Lilith also leave their homes in order to share her fate, and they bring with them some of the men who have shown promise in their training. As the movie ends, Eve gives birth to Adams's son, and Eve's daughter announces that she too is pregnant by one of the former poodles: "I guess environmental conditioning works!" she concludes.

The most interesting aspect of *Last Exit to Earth* is its suggestion that violence is an inherent part of sexuality. When Eve and her crew are debating whether or not to travel back in time, they discuss the dangers of bringing a "sade" (as in the Marquis de Sade) into their civilization. The women are appalled by the violence of the past, but they are also intrigued by the aggressive aspects of copulation. Eve reflects, "That's what we've lost: the danger, the delirium." When her daughter asks her if that means that sex is supposed to be "dirty," Eve replies thoughtfully, "If it's done properly!" Later on, when she is being seduced by Adams and agrees to make love with him, Eve sighs with mock resignation, "Oh God. I guess there's no escaping the vile, dirty part of life!"

All of this calls into question the Christian thinker Augustine's contention that in the Garden of Eden, Adam and Eve would have had sex but that their intercourse would have taken place dispassionately. Augustine, recall, thought that sex would have occurred in much the same way that two people shake hands, or that a farmer puts seed into the ground. *Last Exit to Earth* dismisses the idea that dispassionate sexuality could be fecund. Though it recognizes the horrors of violence (the movie contains a considerable amount of gore), it also maintains that human beings could literally not sustain themselves without the aggressiveness of passion.

Wall-E (2008)

In the animated film *Wall·E*, it is not humans' fertility that is at stake, but rather the ability of the earth itself to sustain life. The movie takes place in the year 2810, seven hundred years after the planet had become so clogged with trash that humans were forced to evacuate it. A corporation named BnL (which stands for "Buy & Large") had become the leader of the world, and its CEO had devised a plan whereby people would live on a spaceship until the planet could be restored.

Left behind on earth was a small robot named Wall-E (an acronym for "Waste Allocation Load Lifter: Earth-class") who spends the first part of the movie doing exactly what he was programmed to do seven centuries ago: compacting garbage. Wall-E's life changes one day, though, when a robot named Eve (i.e. "Extraterrestrial Vegetation Evaluator") is dropped off by a space shuttle. Eve's mission is to sift through the rubble left on earth to see if anything is growing there. When she discovers a small scraggly plant pushing up through the trash, she places it inside herself and carries it with her back to the mother ship that sent her. Wall-E, who has fallen in love with Eve, hitches a ride on the shuttle and discovers a world he could not have imagined.

Living on the mother ship are the humans who left the earth behind. These pampered people spend their lives sitting in comfortable armchairs that glide around the ship without anyone's making the least bit of effort. They pass the time watching television on small screens that hover just in front of their eyes, and sipping the space age equivalent of Big Gulps. They are all obese, and they have the physical abilities of babies; they have never had to do anything for themselves, and so they have forgotten even how to walk.

When Eve arrives back on the mother ship, the captain of the vessel realizes that earth can once again sustain life and that he should re-turn home. The ship's robots, however, do everything that they can to prevent the humans from heading back to earth. In order to defeat the robots, the humans must learn to stand on their own two feet, literally, and to take control of the technology that they themselves invented. Together, and with the help of Wall-E and Eve, the humans awake from their comfort-induced slumber and pilot the ship back home. There they plant the seedling that Eve had nurtured and, as the movie ends, Eve and Wall-E gaze adoringly up at a tree that has grown from the sprout.

Like almost every other movie that explores a utopian theme, *Wall-E* ultimately rejects an easy life in favor of a more difficult but also more satisfying one. As the director of *Wall-E* says in his commentary on the DVD version of the movie, "It's gonna feel like paradise to have come back to the real world at the end of the movie; even though it's still dirty and it has trash everywhere, you kind of are happy to be back. It seems like you're not in this fakery anymore, and you're sort of free of it."[23]

Looking Back, Looking Inward, Looking Forward

Over the course of this book we have seen just a small sample of the enormous number of references to Adam and Eve in popular culture. These references accomplish a number of ends. In some cases, invoking the Genesis story adds moral weight to a person's position on social or political issues. In others, Adam and Eve are used as a kind of shorthand for what it means to be a true man or a true woman; they are enduring representatives of "what men are like" and "what women are like." Some-times the story is used to lament the current state of affairs or to induce or articulate a longing for a better way of life. Other times, the story is used as an explanation of why the world is a certain way and why it would be unwise to attempt to change it.

However it is used, the story of Adam and Eve has generated reflections and allusions in popular culture that continue to delight, amuse, and provoke. Moreover, the flood of references to the story shows no sign of abating. In June of 2007, *Variety* reported that Disney had purchased the rights to a script called *All About Adam*, the plot of which "follows the biblical Adam as he trails Eve to modern-day Gotham after they have a lover's quarrel. Adam discovers Satan was behind the breakup."[24] If all goes as planned, the movie will be released in 2010. At this writing at least two other projects are in the works that make reference to the Genesis story: a movie titled *Destination Eden* and a film version of Lois Lowry's novel *The Giver*. No doubt, many other uses will arise over the next few years in cartoons, advertisements, and television episodes.

The purpose of this book has been to give readers some insight into the history of interpretations of the Genesis story and to enable them to make sense of the bewildering array of allusions to it. If nothing else, readers at this point should have developed a healthy skepticism regarding any simplistic reading of the Genesis story, as at so many points, the meaning of the text hinges on the translation of a particular word or phrase. Do the words *ezer kenegdo* (Genesis 2:18—"It is not good that the man should be alone: I will make him an *ezer kenegdo*") mean "a helper as his partner" or "a companion in front of him" or "a power equal to him"? Does the word *imah* in Genesis 3:6 mean "with her" or "also"? That is, does the woman give the fruit to her husband *who was with her* as she conversed with the serpent, or does she give it to him *also*, that is, after the conversation was over, and therefore without his knowing where it came from? Vast differences in theological, artistic, and popular presentations of Genesis can hinge on tiny details such as this.

Moreover, differences in interpretation can hinge on whether one understands the couple's life in the Garden of Eden to be normative, or if one understands their life in exile to be the model for people today. Depending on the answer to that question, one might say that we should be nudists, or that we should always wear clothing; that we should be vegetarians, or that we should eat meat; that men and women should interact as equals, or that men should rule over women.

In sum, the vast diversity of depictions of Adam and Eve in popular culture is no accident. Those varying presentations stem from long traditions of translation and interpretation. The hope of this book is that readers will now be more informed about what those traditions are and what the implications might be of choosing one over the other.

Notes

Preface and Acknowledgments

1. For a useful work on utopian visions in film, see Wheeler Winston Dixon, *Visions of Paradise: Images of Eden in the Cinema* (New Brunswick: Rutgers University Press, 2006).

2. "ComScore Top 50 Properties (U.S.)," www.comscore.com/press/data.asp (accessed 18 November 2008); "ComScore Top Global Properties," www.comscore.com/press.data/top_worldwise_properties.asp (accessed 1 May 2009).

3. "Popular Culture," en.wikipedia.org/wiki/Popular_culture (accessed 10 April 2009).

4. See John Storey, *Cultural Theory and Popular Culture: An Introduction*, fourth ed. (Athens: University of Georgia Press, 2006), 4–11.

5. A photograph of the quilt can be found at www.ritasquilts.com/eve.jpg (accessed 18 November 2008).

Chapter 1

1. James Snyder, "Jan van Eyck and Adam's Apple," *Art Bulletin* 58, no. 4 (December 1976): 514, www.jstor.org/; Frederic G. Cassidy, ed., *Dictionary of American Regional English* (Cambridge, Massachusetts: Harvard University Press, 1985), s.v. "Adam," etc.; BBC-h2g2, "American Diner Slang," www.bbc.co.uk/dna/h2g2/A890589 (accessed 18 November 2008).

2. For those unfamiliar with the Bible, what this citation means is that the story of Adam and Eve appears in the first section or "book" of the Bible, the

book of Genesis. It begins in verse 4 of the second chapter and ends in verse 1 of the fourth chapter.

3. "The Apple," *Star Trek: The Original Series—Season Two*, DVD, directed by Joseph Pevney (original air date 13 October 1967; Paramount, 2008).

4. Louis Ginzberg, *The Legends of the Jews*, trans. Henrietta Szold vol. 1, *From the Creation to Jacob* (Baltimore: Johns Hopkins University Press, 1937, 1998), 75; vol. 5, *From the Creation to Exodus: Notes for Volumes One and Two*, 97, n. 70.

5. Hildegard Schneider, "On the Pomegranate," *Metropolitan Museum of Art Bulletin*, New Series 4, no. 4 (December 1945): 117; Ed Cray, "No Apples in Eden," *Western Folklore* 22, no. 4 (1963): 277, www.jstor.org/.

6. Snyder, "Jan van Eyck," 512.

7. Augustine, *The City of God*, trans. Marcus Dods (New York: Random House, 1950), 465, 467.

8. "Life of Adam and Eve," in *The Old Testament: Pseudepigrapha*, ed. James H. Charlesworth (New York: Anchor Bible, 1985), 2:262.

9. Theophilus, "Apology to Autolycus," in *Eve and Adam: Jewish, Christian, and Muslim Readings on Genesis and Gender*, eds. Kristen E. Kvam, Linda S. Schearing, and Valarie H. Ziegler (Bloomington: Indiana University Press, 1999), 129–130; Tertullian, "On the Apparel of Women," in *Eve and Adam*, eds. Kvam *et al.*, 132.

10. Margaret English Frazer, "Hades Stabbed by the Cross of Christ," *Metropolitan Museum Journal* 9 (1974): 153–161, www.jstor.org/; Jacobus de Voragine, *The Golden Legend*, trans. William Granger Ryan (Princeton, New Jersey: Princeton University Press, 1993), 1:277–284; Jeffrey M. Hoffeld, "Adam's Two Wives," *Metropolitan Museum of Art Bulletin*, New Series 26, no. 10 (June 1968): 431, www.jstor.org/.

11. John Chrysostom, "Homily 18," in *Eve and Adam*, eds. Kvam *et al.*, 147.

12. Henry De Vere Stacpoole, *The Blue Lagoon: A Romance* (McLean, Virginia: IndyPublish.com, 2002), 149.

13. Elaine Pagels, *Adam, Eve, and the Serpent* (New York: Random House, 1988), 127–150, 69.

14. On this point see Kvam *et al.*, *Eve and Adam*, 310–315 and 323–339.

15. See Kvam *et al.*, *Eve and Adam*, 483–502, as well as Ken Ham *et al.*, "What Is the Bible's View on Interracial Marriage and Racism?" www.answersingenesis .org/home/area/faq/racism.asp (accessed 18 November 2008).

16. The Talmud asks, "And why does the man lie face downwards and the woman face upwards towards the man? He [faces the elements] from which he was created and she [faces the man] from whom she was created" (Niddah 31b).

17. David M. Carr, *The Erotic Word* (New York: Oxford University Press, 2003), 32–33, 36–37.

18. Ariel Glucklich, *Sacred Pain* (New York: Oxford University Press, 2001), 183.

Chapter 2

1. Steve Hendrix, "Father Knows Best?", *Washington Post*, 16 June 2007, 1(B).

2. Frey's note appears in editions of the book published after 15 April 2006 and can be found at http://search.barnesandnoble.com/booksearch/isbninquiry .asp?isbn=0307276902&displayonly=ITV#ITV (accessed 18 November 2008).

3. Howard Kurtz, "Oprah Throws the Book at Herself," *Washington Post*, 27 January 2006, 1(A).

4. Ken Ham, "Answers . . . With Ken Ham: Study Guide," www.answersingenesis.org/cec/study_guides/answersSG1.pdf (accessed 20 June 2008).

5. "Teaching the Kids," *Friends of God: A Road Trip with Alexandra Pelosi*, DVD, directed by Alexandra Pelosi (original air date 25 January 2007; HBO Home Video, 2007).

6. Paul Tillich, *Systematic Theology* (Chicago: University of Chicago Press, 1957), 2:44.

7. Paul Tillich, *The Essential Tillich*, ed. F. Forrester Church (Chicago: University of Chicago Press, 1987), 51, 50.

8. Paul Tillich, *Dynamics of Faith* (New York: Harper, 1957, 2001), 59–60.

9. John Paul II, "Address of Pope John Paul II to the Pontifical Academy of Sciences (October 22, 1996)," pars. 3.2, 5, 6, www.newadvent.org/library/ docs_jp02tc.htm (accessed 18 November 2008).

10. Ken Ham, "Creation is Religion," par.9, www.answersingenesis.org/home/ area/the-lie/chapter3.asp (accessed 18 November 2008).

11. Ken Ham, "Myth-ing the Point," par.21, www.answersingenesis.org/ Home/Area/wwtl/chapter13.asp (accessed 18 November 2008).

12. Tillich, *Dynamics*, 101.

13. Hermann Gunkel, "The Influence of Babylonian Mythology Upon the Biblical Creation Story," in *Creation in the Old Testament*, ed. Bernhard W. Anderson (Philadelphia: Fortress, 1984), 44–45.

14. Barbara C. Sproul, *Primal Myths* (San Francisco: HarperSanFrancisco, 1979, 1991), 44, 215–216, 325.

15. Tony Hillerman, *The Shape Shifter* (New York: HarperCollins, 2006), 213–215.

16. Gary A. Anderson, *The Genesis of Perfection* (Louisville: Westminster John Knox, 2001), 11.

17. Christian E. Hauer and William A. Young, *An Introduction to the Bible*, fifth ed. (Upper Saddle River, New Jersey: Prentice Hall, 2001), 65–66.

18. Ginzberg, *Legends of the Jews*, 1:76.

19. Michael Barkun, *Religion and the Racist Right* (Chapel Hill Press: University of North Carolina, 1996), 152. See also David N. Livingstone, "The Preadamite Theory and the Marriage of Science and Religion," *Transactions of the American Philosophical Society*, New Series 82, no. 3 (1992): 6, www.jstor.org/.

20. Alexander Winchell, *Preadamites; Or a Demonstration of the Existence of Men Before Adam* (Chicago: S.C. Griggs and Company, 1890), 297–298.

21. Chester L. Quarles, *Christian Identity: The Aryan American Bloodline Religion* (Jefferson, North Carolina: McFarland, 2004), 81. See also Barkun, *Religion and the Racist Right*, 160.

22. Elizabeth Cady Stanton, "The Woman's Bible," in *Eve and Adam*, eds. Kvam *et al.*, 350, 351.

23. Avery Dulles, *Models of Revelation* (Maryknoll, New York: Orbis, 1992), 98–99, 199.

24. Anderson, *Genesis of Perfection*, 11.

25. Israel Finkelstein and Neil Asher Silberman, *The Bible Unearthed* (New York: Free Press, 2001), 12.

26. John Van Seters, *Prologue to History: The Yahwist as Historian in Genesis* (Louisville: Westminster John Knox, 1992), 128. See also Andre Lacocque, *The Trial of Innocence: Adam, Eve, and the Yahwist* (Eugene, Oregon: Wipf & Stock, 2006), 17.

27. Richard Elliott Friedman, *Who Wrote the Bible?* (San Francisco: HarperSanFrancisco, 1987), 87.

28. On this point, see Van Seters, *Prologue to History*, 118–129.

29. Harold Bloom, *The Book of J* (New York: Grove Weidenfeld, 1990), 32.

30. Author's photograph of display, taken on site 9 July 2008.

31. John Kaltner, Steven L. McKenzie, and Joel Kilpatrick, *The Uncensored Bible* (New York: HarperCollins, 2008), 7.

32. Kenny Chesney, "I Want My Rib Back," 1994, *Kenny Chesney: In My Wildest Dreams*, CD (BNA Entertainment, 2004).

33. Mary Phil Korsak, *At the Start: Genesis Made New* (New York: Doubleday, 1992), 11.

34. John Humphrey Noyes, *Male Continence* (Oneida, New York: Office of the Oneida Circular, 1872), 13; quoted in Maren Lockwood Carden, *Oneida: Utopian Community to Modern Corporation* (New York: Harper & Row, 1971), 51.

35. Tillich, *Systematic Theology*, 2:29.

36. Duane Olson, "Fall, Creation, and Redemption in Neil LaBute's *The Shape of Things*," *Journal of Religion and Film* 8, no. 1 (April 2004), par. 1, www.unomaha.edu/jrf/Vol8No1/ShapeThings.htm (accessed 26 November 2008).

Chapter 3

1. Martin Buxbaum, *Rivers of Thought* (New York: Books, Inc., 1960), unpaginated. Ellipses in the oiginal.

2. Sojourner Truth: "Ain't I a Woman? (December 1851)," in *Modern History Sourcebook*, www.fordham.edu/halsall/mod/sojtruth-woman.html (accessed 19 November 2008).

3. For example, see Benedict Carey, "Criticism of a Gender Theory, and a Scientist Under Siege," *New York Times*, 21 August 2007, 1(F).

4. Descriptions of these conditions can be found courtesy of the National Library of Medicine and the National Institutes of Health, www.nlm.nih.gov/medlineplus/ (accessed 13 February 2009).

5. For discussion of the terms "sex" and "gender," see Michael S. Kimmel, *The Gendered Society* (New York: Oxford University Press, 2000), 2–3.

6. Joshua Zumbrun, "The Sacrifices of Albania's 'Sworn Virgins,'" *Washington Post*, 11 August 2007, 1(C).

7. Sally Cressman, letter to the editor, *Newsweek*, 4 June 2007, 17. See also Debra Rosenberg et al., "Rethinking Gender," *Newsweek*, 21 May 2007, www.newsweek.com/id/34772.

8. Dave Coverly, *Speed Bump*, 17 January 2005 (dist. Creators Syndicate); Bob Thaves, *Frank and Ernest*, 13 December 2004 and 29 October 2007 (dist. Newspaper Enterprise Association).

9. Phyllis Trible, "Eve and Adam: Genesis 2–3 Reread," in *Eve and Adam*, eds. Kvam et al., 433. The original essay appeared in *Andover Newton Quarterly* 13 (March 1973), 251–258.

10. Robert Alter, *Genesis* (New York: W. W. Norton, 1996), 8; Korsak, *At the Start*, 5.

11. Phyllis Trible, *God and the Rhetoric of Sexuality* (Philadelphia: Fortress, 1978), 80.

12. Trible, "Eve and Adam," 433.

13. H. Freedman and Maurice Simon, trans. and eds., *Midrash Rabbah: Genesis* (London: Soncino, 1951), 1:54.

14. Ginzberg, *Legends of the Jews*, 1:49. See also 5:63.

15. Hilary Price, *Rhymes With Orange*, 4 November 2006 (dist. King Features Syndicate).

16. Trible, "Eve and Adam," 432.

17. William Gesenius, *A Hebrew and English Lexicon of the Old Testament*, trans. Edward Robinson (Oxford: Oxford University Press, 1952), 617b.

18. Freedman and Simon, *Midrash Rabbah*, 133.

19. Rashi [Shlomo ben Yitzhaki], "Commentary on the Pentateuch," in *Eve and Adam*, eds. Kvam et al., 209.

20. Augustine, "The Literal Meaning of Genesis," in *Eve and Adam*, eds. Kvam et al., 150.

21. Thomas Aquinas, "Summa Theologiae," in *Eve and Adam*, eds. Kvam et al., 227.

22. Carr, *Erotic Word*, 28, 32.

23. Susan T. Foh, "The Head of the Woman Is the Man," in *Eve and Adam*, eds. Kvam et al., 394.

24. Trible, "Eve and Adam," 437.

25. Twain's *Extracts from Adam's Diary* was published in 1904, and *Eve's Diary* in 1906. The two are published together as *The Diaries of Adam and Eve* (Amherst, New York: Prometheus, 2000).

26. John Milton, *Paradise Lost*, Renascence Editions, at http://darkwing.uoregon.edu/~rbear/lost/pl8.html (accessed 9 April 2009), Book VIII, lines 824–825, 827–829, 830–831.

27. Milton, *Paradise Lost*, Book IV, lines 479–480.

28. Alix Olson, "eve's mouth," www.alixolson.com/written.html (accessed 20 February 2009).

29. In medieval bestiaries, the salamander was thought to be toxic and to have the ability to poison wells and fruit trees. See Robert A. Koch, "The Salamander in Van der Goes' Garden of Eden," *Journal of the Warburg and Courtauld Institutes* 28 (1965): 324.

30. Freedman and Simon, *Midrash Rabbah*, 149.

31. Edith Hamilton, *Mythology* (New York: Mentor, 1969), 71–72.

32. Jean Cousin the Elder, "Eva Prima Pandora," can be found via the Louvre's website www.louvre.fr/llv/commun/home.jsp?bmLocale=en (accessed 13 February 2009).

33. On the question of translation, see Kvam *et al.*, *Eve and Adam*, 33.

34. Stanley Cavell, *Pursuits of Happiness: The Hollywood Comedy of Remarriage* (Cambridge, Massachusetts : Harvard University Press, 1981), 1–2.

35. Heinrich Kramer and James Sprenger, "Malleus Maleficarum," in *Eve and Adam*, eds. Kvam *et al.*, 244.

36. Kramer and Sprenger, "Malleus Maleficarum," in *Eve and Adam*, eds. Kvam et al., 247.

37. Marian Keane, "Commentary," *The Lady Eve*, DVD, directed by Preston Sturges (1941; Criterion, 2001).

38. National Film Preservation Board, "Films Selected to The National Film Registry, Library of Congress 1989–2008," www.loc.gov/film/titles.html (accessed 13 February 2009).

39. Frank Miller, "Pop Culture 101—The Lady Eve," www.tcm.com/thismonth/article/?cid=89379&rss=mrqe (accessed 13 February 2009).

40. American Film Institute, "AFI's 100 Years . . . 100 Movies—10th Anniversary Edition," connect.afi.com/site/DocServer/100Movies.pdf?docID=301 (accessed 13 February 2009).

41. Gary Carey and Joseph L. Mankiewicz, *More About* All About Eve (New York: Random House, 1972), 27–28.

42. Mary Orr, *The Wisdom of Eve*, rev. ed. (New York: Dramatists Play Service, 1994), 21, 83, 84.

43. Joseph Mankiewicz, "All About Eve: Script," www.imsdb.com/scripts/All-About-Eve.html (accessed 13 February 2009).

44. "All About Lisa," *The Simpsons*, season 19, episode 20, directed by Steven Dean Moore (original air date 18 May 2008). At this writing, the episode is not yet available on DVD. Other references to the movie occur in an installment of *Saturday Night Live* (season 33, episode 1, original air date 29 September 2007), an episode of *ER* entitled "All About Christmas Eve" (season 12, episode 10, original air date 8 December 2005), and *Harry Potter and the Prisoner of Azkaban* (Warner Brothers, 2004), in which a shrunken head refers to this from the movie: "Fasten your seatbelts . . . it's gonna be a bumpy night."

45. Augustine, *The Literal Meaning of Genesis*, in *Saint Augustine*, ed. John Hammond Taylor, Ancient Christian Writers (New York: Newman Press, 1982), 2:176.

46. Aquinas, in *Eve and Adam*, eds. Kvam *et al.*, 235.

47. Wiley Miller, *Non Sequitur*, 17 October, 2007 (dist. Universal Press Syndicate).

48. Mary Daly, *Beyond God the Father: Toward a Philosophy of Women's Liberation* (Boston: Beacon, 1973), 51.

49. Daly, *Beyond God the Father*, 52–54.

50. Daly, *Beyond God the Father*, 47.

51. Daly, *Beyond God the Father*, 67.

52. Charles W. Hedrick, "Introduction: Nag Hammadi, Gnosticism, and Early Christianity—A Beginner's Guide," in *Nag Hammadi, Gnosticism, and Early Christianity*, eds. Charles W. Hedrick and Robert Hodgson (Peabody, Massachusetts: Hendrickson, 1986), 1.

53. *The Hypostasis of the Archons*, in *The Nag Hammadi Library*, ed. James M. Robinson (New York: HarperOne, 1990), 165.

54. Sandra M. Stanton, "Eve," www.goddessmyths.com/Erzulie-Lilith.html (accessed 23 February 2009).

55. James B. Pritchard, ed., *Ancient Near Eastern Texts Relating to the Old Testament*, third ed. (Princeton, New Jersey: Princeton University Press, 1969), 100.

56. Sproul, *Primal Myths*, 169, 66, 185, 201.

57. Sproul, *Primal Myths*, 157.

58. Joseph M. Murphy, *Santería: African Spirits in America* (Boston: Beacon, 1988, 1993), 79.

59. Leslie S. Wilson, *The Serpent Symbol in the Ancient Near East* (Lanham, Maryland: University Press of America, 2001), 13.

60. Sigmund Freud, *Interpreting Dreams*, trans. J. A. Underwood (New York: Penguin Classics, 2006), 370.

61. This image can be found at www.beloit.edu/nuremberg/book/images/Old%20Testament/big/The%20First%20Family%20IXr.jpg (accessed 13 February 2009).

62. Harold Kushner, *When Bad Things Happen to Good People* (New York: Anchor Books, 1981), 121.

63. Robert Lentz, "Eve, the Mother of All," via www.trinitystores.com/ (accessed 13 February 2009).

64. Charles Boer, trans., *The Homeric Hymns*, second ed. (Dallas, Texas: Spring Publications, 1970), 126.

Chapter 4

1. Ginzberg, *Legends of the Jews*, 1:74–75.

2. Daniel C. Matt, trans., *The Zohar* (Stanford, California: Stanford University Press, 2006), 3:348, n. 252.

3. Michael L. Satlow, "Jewish Constructions of Nakedness in Late Antiquity," *Journal of Biblical Literature* 116, no. 3 (Autumn 1997): 447–448.

4. Augustine, *City of God*, 471.

5. Augustine, *City of God*, 465.

6. Augustine, *City of God*, 466–467.

7. That is, they did not have to remove any clothing, since they were naked.

8. Milton, *Paradise Lost*, Book IV, lines 739–743.

9. John Chrysostom, "Homily 17," in *Eve and Adam*, eds. Kvam *et al.*, 147.

10. Gregory of Nyssa, "On Virginity," in *Saint Gregory of Nyssa: Ascetical Works*, trans. Virginia Woods Callahan, The Fathers of the Church: A New Translation (Washington, DC: Catholic University of America Press, 1967), 46.

11. Recordings of this skit can be found in numerous places, including a CD entitled *Radio's Famous Blondes* (Great American Audio Corp., 1992).

12. "Mae West's Name Banned," *New York Times*, 25 December 1937, 11; "Mae West Sponsor Is Sorry for Skit In Garden of Eden," *Washington Post*, 18 December 1937, 3, http://proquest.umi.com/pqdweb?RQT=403&TS=12354260 87&clientId=5604.

13. Jill Watts, *Mae West: An Icon in Black and White* (New York: Oxford University Press, 2001), 153.

14. Watts, *Mae West*, 73.

15. "Mae West Departs from Workhouse," *New York Times*, 28 April 1927, 27; "'Diamond Lil' is Lurid and Often Stirring," *New York Times*, 10 April 1928, 32; "Raid Mae West Play, Seize 56 at Opening," *New York Times*, 2 October 1928, 1, http://proquest.umi.com/pqdweb?RQT=403&TS=1235426087&clien

tId=5604; Simon Louvish, *Mae West: It Ain't No Sin* (New York: St. Martin's Press, 2005), 184.

16. Hal Humphrey, "On Radio Anniversary: Charlie and Mae Together Again," *Los Angeles Times*, 12 November 1964, 3(C), quoted by Watts, *Mae West*, 231.

17. Dawn B. Sova, *Forbidden Films* (New York: Checkmark Books, 2001), 270.

18. Leonard J. Leff and Jerold L. Simmons, *The Dame in the Kimono* (Lexington: University Press of Kentucky, 2001), 48.

19. "FCC in Mae West Inquiry," *New York Times*, 19 December 1937;"Mae West Script Brings Sharp Rebuke from FCC," *New York Times*, 15 January 1938, 1, http://proquest.umi.com/pqdweb?RQT=403&TS=1235426087&clientId=560 4; "Radio Officials 'No Gentlemen,' Let Her Down, Says Mae West," *Washington Post*, 28 January 1938, 3, http://proquest.umi.com/login?COPT=REJTPTI2OGE mSU5UPTAmVkVSPTI=&clientId=5604.

20. Quoted in Emily Wortis Leider, *Becoming Mae West* (New York: Farrar, Straus and Giroux, 1997), 340–341.

21. George Gallup, "The Gallup Poll: Voters Oppose Radio Censorship, With Majority Seeing No Vulgarity in Programs," *Washington Post*, 11 February 1938, 2(X), http://proquest.umi.com/login?COPT=REJTPTI2OGEmSU5UPTA mVkVSPTI=&clientId=5604.

22. Steve Craig, "Out of Eden: The Legion of Decency, the FCC, and Mae West's 1937 Appearance on *The Chase & Sanborn Hour*," *Journal of Radio Studies* 13, no. 2 (November 2006): 232–233.

23. Alter, *Genesis*, 10.

24. Augustine, *City of God*, 469.

25. Muhammad Ibn 'Abd Allah Al-Kisa'i, "Tales of the Prophets," in *Eve and Adam*, eds. Kvam et al., 192.

26. Freedman and Simon, *Midrash Rabbah*, 1:63.

27. Quoted in Jeanne Thomas Allen, "*Fig Leaves* in Hollywood" in *Fabrications*, ed. James Gaines and Charlotte Herzog (New York: Routledge, 1990), 124, 128. At this writing the movie is not available for home viewing.

28. Unsigned review of *Fig Leaves*, directed by Howard Hawks, *Variety*, 7 July 1926, in *Variety's Film Reviews*, vol. 3, 1926–1929 (New York: R.R. Bowker, 1983), unpaginated.

29. Allen, "*Fig Leaves*," 124, 126–127.

30. Quoted in Allen, "*Fig Leaves*," 128.

31. Vito Russo, *The Celluloid Closet* (New York: Harper, 1987), 77.

32. "3 Feature Bill Today at Metro," *Washington Post*, 15 August 1926, 1(F).

33. *The Garden of Eden*, DVD, directed by Lewis Milestone (1928; Flicker Alley, 2002).

34. At this writing, a copy of the movie is available at www.youtube.com/watch?v=_OiYOQptljw.

35. The others are *Eve and the Internment Question, Eve's Burglar, Adam as a Special Constable, Eve Adopts a Lonely Soldier, Eve Goes to the East Coast, Eve Outwits Artful Adam, Eve Resolves to Do War Work, Eve as Mrs. Adam, Eve in the Country,* and *The Adventures of Eve*. At this writing, none is available for home viewing.

36. At this writing, none of these movies is available for home viewing.

37. Rush, "Bible Pictures," *Variety*, 22 December 1922, in *Variety's Film Reviews*, vol. 2, *1921–1925* (New York: R. R. Bowker, 1983), unpaginated.

38. Sova, *Forbidden Films*, 20. See also "Film Seizure Attacked," *New York Times*, 13 February 1958, 23; and "Philadelphia Halts French Film Again," *New York Times*, 7 March 1958, 17, http://proquest.umi.com/login?COPT=U0ZEPTI mU01EPTQmSU5UPTAmREJTPTFBQ0Q@.

39. Roger Vadim, *Bardot, Deneuve, Fonda*, trans. Melinda Camber Porter (New York: Warner Books, 1986), 26.

40. Daniel Boyarin, *Carnal Israel* (Berkeley: University of California Press, 1993), 45.

41. Irving Greenberg, *The Jewish Way* (New York: Summit Books, 1988), 141.

42. "Alphabet of Ben Sira," in *Eve and Adam*, eds. Kvam *et al.*, 204.

43. Gershom Scholem, *Kabbalah* (New York: Dorset, 1974), 359.

44. Director's commentary, "Inauguration of the Pleasure Dome," *The Films of Kenneth Anger: Vol. 1*, DVD, directed by Kenneth Anger (Fantoma, 2007). In the director's commentary for *Lucifer Rising* (1972), Anger says that Lilith was supposed to have been married to Lucifer but that he rejected her. See *The Films of Kenneth Anger: Vol. 2*, DVD (Fantoma, 2007).

45. Genevieve Oswald, "A Vision of Paradise: Myth and Symbol in *The Embattled Garden*," *Choreography and Dance* 2, part 3 (1992), 30.

46. Anna Kisselgoff, "Dance: Graham Revival," *New York Times*, 3 March 1984, 16.

47. "Report Pope Bans Film of Adam and Eve, Minus Clothes, as Pictured by Italian Firm," *New York Times*, 10 November 1920, 15, http://proquest.umi.com/login?COPT=U0ZEPTImU01EPTQmSU5UPTAmREJTPTFBQ0Q@.

48. "Notes for *The Private Lives of Adam & Eve* (1961)," www.tcm.com/tcmdb/title.jsp?stid=87214&category=Notes (accessed 24 February 2009).

49. Tube, review of *The Private Lives of Adam & Eve*, directed by Mickey Rooney and Albert Zugsmith, *Variety*, 18 January 1961, in *Variety's Film Reviews*, vol. 10, *1959–1963* (New York: R. R. Bowker, 1983), unpaginated.

50. Vladimir Nabokov's 1955 novel about a sexually experienced young girl also makes a connection to the character of Lilith. See Alfred Appel, Jr., ed., *The Annotated Lolita: Revised and Updated* (New York: Vintage, 1991), 20.

51. Sova, *Forbidden Films*, 247.

52. "Lilith Needs a Favor," *Frasier*, season 10, episode 13, DVD, directed by Sheldon Epps (original air date 4 February 2003; Paramount Home Video, 2007).

53. Judith Plaskow, "The Coming of Lilith," in *Womanspirit Rising: A Feminist Reader in Religion*, eds. Carol P. Christ and Judith Plaskow (San Francisco: Harper & Row, 1979), 206–207.

54. Judith Plaskow, "Lilith Revisited," in *Eve and Adam*, eds. Kvam et al., 426.

55. Associated Press, "Lilith Tour Blasted by Falwell Editor," *Boston Globe*, 20 June 1999, 12(A).

56. Eric L. Wee and Todd Shields, "Lilith Name 'Dangerous,' Falwell Newspaper Says; Editor Cites Tour Title's Demonic Links," *Washington Post*, 20 June 1999, 1(C).

57. *Big Eden*, DVD, directed by Thomas Bezucha (2000; Wolfe Video, 2002).

58. Roger Ebert, review of *Big Eden*, directed by Thomas Bezucha, 8 June 2001, rogerebert.suntimes.com/apps/pbcs.dll/article?AID=/20010608/REVIEWS/106080301/1023 (accessed 24 February 2009).

59. United States Conference of Catholic Bishops (USCCB), Bishops' Committee on Marriage and Family, *Always Our Children: A Pastoral Message to Parents of Homosexual Children and Suggestions for Pastoral Ministers*, section 4, "Accepting your Child," www.usccb.org/laity/always.shtml (accessed 24 February 2009).

60. USCCB, Bishops' Committee on Marriage and Family, *Always Our Children*, section 5, "Accepting God's Plan and the Church's Ministry."

61. Catholic Church, *Catechism of the Catholic Church*, Part III, section 2, chapter 2, article 6, section II, number 2357, www.vatican.va/archive/catechism/p3s2c2a6.htm (accessed 24 February 2009). See also III.2.2.6.II.2331–2336.

62. Catholic Church, *Catechism*, III.2.2.6.II.2351–2355.

63. Catholic Church, *Catechism*, III.2.2.6.III.2370 and 2376.

64. Aquinas, "Summa Theologiae," in *Eve and Adam*, eds. Kvam et al., 232.

Chapter 5

1. W. R. F. Browning, *A Dictionary of the Bible* (New York: Oxford University Press, 1996, 2004), s.v. "Curse," Oxford Reference Online: Premium, via GEORGE, the Library Catalog of Georgetown University (accessed 24 February 2009).

2. Phyllis Trible, *God and the Rhetoric of Sexuality*, 124. See also Terence E. Fretheim, "Introduction, Commentary, and Reflections," in *The New Interpreter's Bible* (Nashville: Abingdon, 1994), 363.

3. Al-Kisa'i, "Tales of the Prophets," in *Eve and Adam*, eds. Kvam *et al.*, 192.

4. Koch, "The Salamander," 323–326.

5. For discussions of lies, truth-telling, God, and the serpent, see R. W. L. Moberly, "Did the Serpent Get It Right?", *Journal of Theological Studies NS* 39 (April 1988): 1–27; James Barr, "Is God a Liar?", *Journal of Theological Studies NS* 57 (April 2006): 1–22; and Moberly, "Did the Interpreters Get It Right?", *Journal of Theological Studies NS* 59 (April 2008): 22–40, www.jstor.org/.

6. Soren Giversen and Birger A. Pearson, trans., *The Testimony of Truth*, in *The Nag Hammadi Library in English*, ed. James M. Robinson (Leiden: E. J. Brill, 1996), 455.

7. Philip Pullman, *The Subtle Knife* (New York: Random House, 1997), frontispiece.

8. Philip Pullman, *The Golden Compass* (New York: Random House, 1995), 325.

9. Pullman, *Golden Compass*, 248.

10. Pullman, *Subtle Knife*, 176.

11. Pullman, *Golden Compass*, 350.

12. Pullman, *Subtle Knife*, 283.

13. Philip Pullman, *The Amber Spyglass* (New York: Random House, 2000), 28, 366.

14. Pullman, *Amber Spyglass*, 408, 416.

15. "The Dark Materials Debate: Life, God, the Universe. . .," *Telegraph*, 17 March 2004, p. 2, par. 9, www.telegraph.co.uk/arts/main.jhtml?xml=/arts/2004/03/17/bodark17.xml&page=2 (accessed 27 May 2008).

16. Philip Pullman, interview by Peter T. Chataway, "Philip Pullman—The Extended E-mail Interview," (Blog) *FilmChat*, 28 November 2007, filmchatblog.blogspot.com/2007/11/philip-pullman-extended-e-mail.html (accessed 24 February 2009).

17. Pullman, *Amber Spyglass*, 286.

18. Pullman, *Amber Spyglass*, 396–397.

19. Moberly, "Did the Serpent Get It Right?", 2.

20. Gerhard von Rad, *Genesis*, trans. John H. Marks (Philadelphia: Westminster John Knox, 1972), 95. See also David J. A. Clines, "Themes in Genesis 1–11," *Catholic Biblical Quarterly* 38, no. 4 (October 1976): 490.

21. Henry Francis Lyte, "Abide with Me," in Robert Chambers and Robert Carruthers, *Chambers's Cyclopædia of English Literature* (London: W. & R. Chambers, 1876), 2:467.

22. Augustine, *City of God*, 441.

23. Augustine, *City of God*, 412.

24. Catholic Church, *Catechism*, I.2.3.11.1008.

25. Frazer, "Hades Stabbed," 153–161.

26. Jacobus Voragine, *The Golden Legend*, trans. William Granger Ryan (Princeton, New Jersey: Princeton University Press, 1993), 1:277–284.

27. International Commission on English in the Liturgy, *Christian Prayer: The Liturgy of the Hours* (Boston: Daughters of Saint Paul, 1976), 1676. The homily appears to draw from the apocryphal Gospel of Nicodemus which was written sometime between the fourth and sixth centuries. On the dating of the text, see Alan E. Bernstein, *The Formation of Hell* (Ithaca: Cornell University Press, 1993), 274.

28. Ginzberg, *Legends*, 1:102.

29. For background information on the film, see Mike Figgis, *The Loss of Sexual Innocence* (New York: Faber and Faber, 1999), vii–xiii.

30. Figgis, *Loss of Sexual Innocence*, 6.

31. Figgis, *Loss of Sexual Innocence*, xi–xii.

32. Carl Zimmer, "This Can't Be Love," *New York Times*, 5 September 2006, 1(F).

33. Tom Kirkwood, "The End of Age, Lecture 3: 'Sex and Death,'" BBC Radio 4: Reith Lectures 2001, par. 14, www.bbc.co.uk/radio4/reith2001/lecture3 .shtml (accessed 28 April 2008).

34. Kasi Lemmons, commentary on *Eve's Bayou*, DVD, directed by Kasi Lemmons (1997; Lion's Gate, 2003).

35. Augustine, *Opus Imperfectum Contra Julianum*, 6, 27. Cited by and trans. Elaine Pagels, *Adam, Eve, and the Serpent* (New York: Random House, 1988), 139.

36. Augustine, *City of God*, 422.

37. Catholic Church, *The New Saint Joseph Baltimore Catechism*, official revised edition no. 2 (New York: Catholic Book Publishing, 1962–1969), 34.

38. Bill Watterson, *Calvin and Hobbes*, 3 April 1993 (dist. Universal Press Syndicate).

39. Roger Ebert, review of *Young Adam*, directed by David Mackenzie, 30 April 2004, rogerebert.suntimes.com/apps/pbcs.dll/article?AID=/20040430/REVIEWS/404300301/1023 (accessed 4 June 2008).

40. Darren Aronofsky, interview by Peter Sciretta, 31 October 2006, par. 16, posted 21 November 2006, www.slashfilm.com/article.php20061121aron ofskyinterview2 (accessed 25 February 2009).

41. Julian of Norwich, *Revelations of Divine Love*, trans. Clifton Wolters (New York: Penguin, 1966), 103.

42. Aronofsky, interview by Sciretta, par. 16.

Chapter 6

1. Janice C. Simpson, Anastasia Toufexis, and Sue Wymelenberg, "Coping With Eve's Curse," *Time*, 27 July 1981, www.time.com/time/magazine/article/0,9171,949233-2,00.html (accessed 25 February 2009).

2. New Revised Standard Version, Douay-Rheims translation, and Revised English Bible (1992) translation, respectively.

3. Targum Neofiti 1, in Hanneke Reuling, *After Eden: Church Fathers and Rabbis on Genesis 3:16–21*, Jewish and Christian Perspectives Series (Boston: Brill, 2006), 41.

4. Al-Tabari, *Ta-rikh al-Rusul wa'l-Muluk*, 1:109, quoted in D. A. Spellberg, "Writing the Unwritten Life of the Islamic Eve," *International Journal of Middle East Studies* 28, no. 3 (August 1996): 314, www.jstor.org/.

5. Hildegard of Bingen, *Scivias*, trans. Columba Hart and Jane Bishop (New York: Paulist, 1990), 83. On the subject of Eve's curse, see also Peggy McCracken, *The Curse of Eve, The Wound of the Hero* (Philadelphia: University of Pennsylvania Press, 2003).

6. *Oxford English Dictionary*, s.v. "Curse, n.," http://dictionary.oed.com (accessed 25 February 2009).

7. Patricia Crawford, "Attitudes to Menstruation in Seventeenth-Century England," *Past and Present* 91 (May 1981): 49, www.jstor.org/.

8. "End of the Curse," *The Golden Girls*, season 2, episode 1, DVD, directed by Terry Hughes (original air date 27 September 1986; Buena Vista Home Entertainment, 2005).

9. Alice, "I Didn't Miss Them, MM," (blog) *The Sam Seder Show*, posted 25 March 2008, http://samsedershow.com/node/2723 (accessed 25 February 2009).

10. Anna Piontek, "Reversing the Curse," *Indiana Daily Student*, posted 17 March 2008, www.idsnews.com/news/story.aspx?id=59824&comview=1 (accessed 25 February 2009).

11. "Reverse the Curse: Don't Buy Midol," posted 30 April 2008, www.feministpeacenetwork.org/2008/04/30/reverse-the-curse-dont-buy-midol/ (accessed 25 February 2009).

12. Peter Damian, quoted in H. Diane Russell, *Eva/Ave: Woman in Renaissance and Baroque Prints* (New York: National Gallery of Art, 1990), 12.

13. Kramer and Sprenger, "Malleus Maleficarum," in *Eve and Adam*, eds. Kvam *et al.*, 244.

14. Pius IX, *Ineffabilis Deus* (Apostolic Constitution of Pope Pius IX on the Immaculate Conception), 8 December 1854, www.newadvent.org/library/docs_pi09id.htm (accessed 25 February 2009).

15. "Sounds of Silence," *CSI: Crime Scene Investigation*, season 1, episode 20, DVD, directed by Peter Markle (original air date 19 April 2001; Columbia Broadcasting System, 2003).

16. "Role Model," *House M.D.*, season 1, episode 17, DVD, directed by Peter O'Fallon (original air date 12 April 2005; Fox Network, 2005).

17. "The Whore of Babylon," *Californication*, season 1, episode 3, DVD, directed by Scott Winant (original air date 27 August 2007; Paramount 2008); "Fire/Water," *Prison Break*, season 3, episode 2, DVD, directed by Bobby Roth (original air date 24 September 2007; 20th Century Fox, 2008); "Gee Whiz," *Aqua Teen Hunger Force*, season 3, episode 4, DVD directed by Matt Maiellaro and Dave Willis (original air date 22 August 2004; Turner Home Entertainment, 2005).

18. *New Catholic Encyclopedia* (Washington, DC: Catholic University of America, 1967), s.v. "Virgin Birth" p. 695.

19. The Infancy Gospel of James, in *The Other Bible*, ed. Willis Barnstone (San Francisco: Harper & Row, 1984), 390.

20. Bonaventure (attrib.), *Meditations on the Life of Our Lord* (Paris, Bibliothèque Nationale MS Ital. 115), trans. Isa Ragusa, eds. Isa Ragusa and Rosalie B. Green (Princeton, New Jersey: Princeton University Press, 1961), 32–33, quoted in Maria Warner, *Alone of All Her Sex* (New York: Vintage, 1976), 45.

21. *New Catholic Encyclopedia* (Washington, DC: Catholic University of America, 1967), s.v. "Virgin Birth", 696. The second edition of the *Encyclopedia* (2003) omitted this passage.

22. The following discussions of *Hail Mary* and *Polish Wedding* are a revised form of commentary that appeared in my book *Celluloid Saints: Images of Sanctity in Film* (Macon, Georgia: Mercer University Press, 2002), 171–192.

23. For a shot-by-shot breakdown of the movie that includes the dialogue in both French and English, see Maryel Locke and Charles Warren, eds., *Jean-Luc Godard's* Hail Mary: *Women and the Sacred in Film* (Carbondale, Illinois: Southern Illinois University Press, 1993), 146–183 and 197–228.

24. Vlada Petric with Geraldine Bard, "Godard's Vision of the New Eve," in *Jean-Luc Godard's* Hail Mary: *Women and the Sacred in Film*, ed. Locke and Warren, 113.

25. Warner, *Alone of All Her Sex*, 77.

26. Catholic League, "Vile *South Park* Episode Pulled," www.catholicleague .org/catalyst.php?year=2006&month=January-February&read=1990 (accessed 25 February 2009).

27. Charles T. Wood, "The Doctor's Dilemma: Sin, Salvation, and the Menstrual Cycle in Medieval Thought," *Speculum* 56, no. 4 (October 1981): 721, www.jstor.org/.

28. Bryce Andrew Sibley, "Where Angels Fear to Tread," http://campus. udayton.edu/mary//questions/yq/yq195.html (accessed 19 June 2008). See also Deborah Winslow, "Rituals of First Menstruation in Sri Lanka," *Man*, New Series 15, no. 4 (December 1980): 618, www.jstor.org/.

Chapter 7

1. Josh Eiserike, "The Creation Museum: You Can't Darwin 'Em All," *Mad*, 20 January 2008, 32. The illustration that accompanies the article is by Hermann Mejia.

2. John T. Scopes, *Center of the Storm* (New York: Holt, Rinehart and Winston, 1967), 60.

3. For a summary of current legislation regarding the teaching of evolution, see the websites of the National Center for Science Education www.natcenscied .org/ and the American Institute of Biological Sciences www.aibs.org/public-policy/evolution_state_news.html (accessed 18 February 2009).

4. Survey: Jon D. Miller, Michigan State University, 2007, cited by "Trend Lines: Acceptance of Evolution," *Washington Post*, 16 January 2007, 2(A).

5. Smithsonian National Museum of Natural History, "The Process of Evolution: Statement of Scientific Understanding," www.mnh.si.edu/press_office/statements/evolution.htm (accessed 17 February 2009).

6. Jon Hurdle, "Philadelphia Set to Honor Darwin and Evolution," *New York Times*, 23 June 2008, 18(A); Jonathan Falwell, "Falwell Confidential: Explaining the Foundations of the Universe," June 1, 2007, www.falwell.com/index.cfm?PID=14229 (accessed 28 July 2008).

7. Ken Ham, "Answers Radio" www.answersingenesis.org/media/radio (accessed 28 July 2008).

8. "Partial Text of the Butler Law," in Jeffrey P. Moran, *The Scopes Trial: A Brief History with Documents* (Boston: Bedford/St. Martin's, 2002), 74.

9. Tennessee Governor Austin Peay, quoted in *Nashville Tennessean*, 24 March 1925, 1, quoted by Moran, Scopes Trial, 23.

10. Moran, *Scopes Trial*, 50–53.

11. Moran, *Scopes Trial*, 8.

12. Stephen Jay Gould, *Ever Since Darwin* (New York: W. W. Norton, 1977), 12–13, 34, 36, 13.

13. Moran, *Scopes Trial*, 20.

14. The History Channel, *In Search of History: The Monkey Trial*, DVD produced by Tom Jennings (A&E Television Networks, 1997).

15. PBS, "American Experience: Monkey Trial. People & Events: WGN Radio Broadcasts the Trial," www.pbs.org/wgbh/amex/monkeytrial/peopleevents/e_wgn.html (accessed 21 July 2008).

16. To hear a recording of "You Can't Make a Monkey Out of Me" and other songs about the Scopes Trial, see PBS, "American Experience: Monkey Trial," www.pbs.org/wgbh/amex/monkeytrial/sfeature/sf_music.html# (accessed 28 July 2008). For information about activities involving chimps, see Edward Caudill, *The Scopes Trial: A Photographic History* (Knoxville: University of Tennessee

Press, 2000), 48–49, and History Channel, *In Search of History: The Monkey Trial.*

17. Moran, *Scopes Trail*, 172; "Ape Halts Mock Trail," *New York Times*, 17 July 1925, "English Versifiers Contest on A Scopes Trial Limerick," Special Cable to the *New York Times*, 26 July 1925, 1, proquest.umi.com/pqdweb?RQT =403&TS=1235426087&clientId=5604.

18. For an illustration from George Hunter's *A Civic Biology*, the textbook in use in Dayton, Tennessee, at the time of the Scopes trial, see Moran, *Scopes Trial*, 120.

19. Scopes, *Center of the Storm*, 83.

20. Jerome Lawrence and Robert E. Lee, *Inherit the Wind* (New York: Bantam, 1955), preface.

21. Edward J. Larson, *Summer for the Gods: The Scopes Trial and America's Continuing Debate Over Science and Religion* (New York: Basic Books, 1997), 240.

22. Stanley Kramer, quoted in Donald Spoto, *Stanley Kramer Film Maker* (Hollywood: Samuel French, 1978), 223.

23. Stanley Kramer, *A Mad, Mad, Mad, Mad World: A Life in Hollywood* (New York: Harcourt Brace, 1997), 174.

24. Michael Kazin, *A Godly Hero: The Life of William Jennings Bryan* (New York: Alfred A. Knopf, 2006), 177, 45, 267–268, 278.

25. Kazin, *Godly Hero*, 274–275.

26. H.L. Mencken, "Battle Now Over; Genesis Triumphant and Ready for New Jousts," *Baltimore Evening Sun*, 18 July 1925, 1, in Moran, *Scopes Trial*, 169–170.

27 "Mencken Epithets Rouse Dayton's Ire," *New York Times*, 17 July 1925, 3, proquest.umi.com/login?COPT=U0ZEPTImU01EPTQmSU5UPTAmREJTP TFBQ0Q@.

28. Spoto, *Stanley Kramer*, 220.

29. "Transcript of the Scopes Trial," in Moran, *Scopes Trial*, 152.

30. "Transcript of the Scopes Trial," in Moran, *Scopes Trial*, 156.

31. Center for Science and Culture, "Top Questions: Questions About Intelligent Design," Question 4, "Is intelligent design theory the same as creationism?" www.discovery.org/csc/topQuestions.php#questionsAboutIntelligentDesign (accessed 31 July 2008).

32. Bobby Henderson, "Verbatim: Noodle This, Kansas," *Washington Post*, 28 August 2005, 5(B), www.washingtonpost.com/wpdyn/content/article/2005/08/27/ AR2005082700019.html (accessed 25 February 2009).

33. See www.venganza.org/ (accessed 18 February 2009).

34. John E. Jones III, "Memorandum Opinion: In the United States District Court for the Middle District of Pennsylvania, Tammy Kitzmiller, *et al.*, Plaintiffs

v. Dover Area School District, *et al.*, Defendants," 33, www.aclu.org/religion/schools/23137lgl20051220.html#attach (accessed 1 August 2008).

35. Jones, "Memorandum," 1.

36. Jones, "Memorandum," 31.

37. "The Monkey Suit," *The Simpsons*, season 17, episode 21, directed by Raymond S. Persi (original air date14 May 2006). At this writing, the episode is not yet available on DVD.

38. See the 1942 classic Disney cartoon *Bambi*, directed by David Hand, in which the fawn's mother is killed in a forest fire.

39. Answers in Genesis, "Creation Museum," www.creationmuseum.org/assets/pdf/creation-museum/cm-brochure.pdf (accessed 17 February 2009).

40. Aside from the exhibits at the museum, see also Ken Ham, "Dinosaurs and the Bible," www.answersingenesis.org/docs/2.asp (accessed 17 February 2009).

41. Answers in Genesis, "The Creation Museum: Main Theme and Vision Statement," www.alrcnewskitchen.com/creationmuseum/docs/vision_mission.pdf (accessed 17 February 2009).

42. Richard Dawkins, *The God Delusion* (Boston: Houghton Mifflin, 2006), 286.

43. Dawkins, *God Delusion*, 251.

44. Richard Dawkins, *River Out of Eden: A Darwinian View of Life* (New York: Basic Books, 1995), 8.

45. Dawkins, *River Out of Eden*, 33.

46. Dawkins, *River Out of Eden*, 54.

47. National Geographic Society, "The Genographic Project, Journey Highlights: Adam," www3.nationalgeographic.com/genographic/atlas.html (accessed 12 August 2008).

48. "The Journey of Man," *The Genographic Project*, DVD directed by Clive Maltby, DVD (National Geographic Channels International, 2002).

49. Dawkins, *River Out of Eden*, 31–32, 33.

50. Stephen Colbert, *The Colbert Report*, 16 June 2008, www.comedycentral.com/colbertreport/videos.jhtml?videoId=173859 (accessed 25 February 2009).

51. Stephen Colbert, *The Colbert Report*, 28 March 2007, www.comedycentral.com/colbertreport/videos.jhtml?videoId=84417 (accessed 25 February 2009).

52. John F. Haught, "Does Evolution Rule Out God's Existence?," final two paragraphs, www.aaas.org/spp/dser/03_Areas/evolution/perspectives/Haught_1995.shtml (accessed 1 August 2008). Haught's testimony at the Dover trial can be found at www.talkorigins.org/faqs/dover/day5pm.html (accessed 17 February 2009).

Chapter 8

1. "Stage Eve is Cleared: Magistrate Who Saw Show Rules Fig-Leaf Adornment All Right," *New York Times*, 15 May 1926, http://proquest.umi.com/pqd

web?index=1&did=98378492&SrchMode=2&sid=3&Fmt=10&VInst=PROD
&VType=PQD&RQT=309&VName=HNP&TS=1239297572&clientId=5604
(accessed 9 April 2009).

2. Clyde Haberman, "A Chapel in Florence Reveals Its Wonders Anew," *New York Times*, 9 June 1990, 11.

3. Junipero Serra, *Writings of Junipero Serra*, ed. Antonine Tibesar (Washington, DC: Academy of American Franciscan History, 1955) 1:63.

4. Bob Thaves, *Frank and Ernest*, 27 February 2008 (dist. Newspaper Enterprise Association), http://frankandernest.com/cgi/view/display.pl?108-02-27 (accessed 26 February 2009); Mike Peters, *Mother Goose and Grimm*, 14 June 2007 (dist. King Features Syndicate), www.cartoonistgroup.com/store/add.php?iid=17611 (accessed 26 February 2009).

5. "Sanctuary," *The Twilight Zone*, season 1, episode 20, DVD directed by Patrick R. Norris, DVD (original air date 20 November 2002; New Line Home Entertainment, 2004).

6. *The Book of Jubilees*, in *The Other Bible*, ed. Barnstone, 13.

7. *Penitential of St. Columbanus*, in *The Irish Penitentials*, ed. Ludwig Bieler (Dublin: Dublin Institute for Advanced Studies, 1963), 107.

8. "Pope on Nudism," *Time*, 18 March 1935, www.time.com/time/magazine/article/0,9171,748550,00.html (accessed 26 February 2009).

9. "Girls in Summer Dresses," *Time*, 13 August 1956, www.time.com/time/magazine/article/0,9171,865463,00.html (accessed 26 February 2009).

10. Sova, *Forbidden Films*, 144.

11. Sova, *Forbidden Films*, 144–145.

12. Aryeh Kaplan, *Waters of Eden: The Mystery of the Mikvah* (New York: National Conference of Synagogue Youth/ Union of Orthodox Jewish Congregations of America, 1976, 1982), 36.

13. Lis Harris, "The Mikvah," in *Total Immersion: A Mikvah Anthology*, ed. Rivkah Slonim (Northvale, New Jersey: Jason Aronson, 1996), 128.

14. John Chrysostom, "Baptismal Instruction," in *Ancient Christian Commentary on Scripture: Genesis 1–11*, ed. Andrew Louth (Downer's Grove, Illinois: InterVarsity Press, 2001), 72. Laurie Guy argues that "the assumption that it was standard practice for baptismal candidates, including women candidates, to be stark naked at the point of their baptism cannot be upheld." See "'Naked' Baptism in the Early Church: The Rhetoric and the Reality," *Journal of Religious History* 27, no. 2 (June 2003): 142.

15. *Catholic Encyclopedia*, (New York: Appleton, 1907–), s.v. "Adamites at http://www.newadvent.org/cathen/011356.htm7.

16. Norman Cohn, *The Pursuit of the Millennium: Revolutionary Millenarians and Mystical Anarchists of the Middle Ages* (London: Temple Smith, 1970), 219–220.

17. Tristram Stuart, *The Bloodless Revolution: A Cultural History of Vegetarianism from 1600 to Modern Times* (New York: W. W. Norton, 2006), 15–17.

18. Christian Nudist Convocation, "Statement of Faith," www.christiannc.com/purpose.htm (accessed 26 February 2009).

19. Answers in Genesis, "Clothing and Genesis," www.answersingenesis.org/home/area/overheads/pages/oh20010427_21.asp (accessed 2 September 2008).

20. Fig Leaf Forum, "Fig Leaf Forum Responds To 'Answers In Genesis,'" www.figleafforum.com/resources_critics_aig.html (accessed 15 August 2008).

21. American Association for Nude Recreation, "Nudist Experiences Begin Here!" www.aanr.com/ (accessed 17 February 2009).

22. "Simpsons Bible Stories," *The Simpsons*, season 10, episode 18, DVD directed by Nancy Kruse, DVD (original air date 4 April 1999; 20th Century Fox, 2007).

23. Teresa M. Shaw, *The Burden of the Flesh: Fasting and Sexuality in Early Christianity* (Minneapolis: Fortress, 1998), 197, 178.

24. Stuart, *Bloodless Revolution*, 15–20.

25. Philadelphia Bible-Christian Church Maintenance Committee, *History of the Philadelphia Bible-Christian Church for the First Century of Its Existence* (Philadelphia: J. B. Lippincott, 1922), 163. See also Karen Iacobbo and Michael Iacobbo, *Vegetarian America: A History* (Westport, Connecticut: Praeger, 2004), ix–x, 9–14.

26. Sylvester Graham, *Lectures on the Science of Human Life*, second ed. (London: Horsell and Shirrefs, 1854), 316. See also Iacobbo and Iacobbo, *Vegetarian America*, 15–70.

27. Christian Vegetarian Association, "Are We Good Stewards of God's Creation?: FAQ's; Does the Bible Support Vegetarianism?" www.all-creatures.org/cva/honoring.htm (accessed 13 August 2008).

28. Christian Vegetarian Association, "Are We Good Stewards of God's Creation?: FAQ's; Why Did God give Noah Permission to Eat Meat (Genesis 9:2–4)?" www.all-creatures.org/cva/honoring.htm (13 August 2008).

29. Yitzchak HaCohen Kook, *A Vision of Vegetarianism and Peace*, quoted in Joe Green, "Rabbi Abraham Kook: From *A Vision of Vegetarianism and Peace*," in *Rabbis and Vegetarianism*, ed. Roberta Kalechofsky (Marblehead, Massachusetts: Micah Publications, 1995), 3.

30. Y. Michael Barilan, "The Vision of Vegetarianism and Peace: Rabbi Kook on the Ethical Treatment of Animals," *History of the Human Sciences* 17, no. 4 (November 2004): 71.

31. Jewish Vegetarians of North America, "A Vegetarian View of the Torah," jewishveg.com/torah.html (accessed 9 January 2009).

32. Eden Organic, "Company Goals," www.edenfoods.com/about/goals.php (accessed 9 January 2009); Modern Manna, "Modern Manna News," par. 6, www.modernmanna.org/news.asp (accessed 7 August 2008); Apple & Eve, "What's in a Name?" www.appleandeve.com/about_us/name_logo.php (accessed 18 February 2009).

33. Amanda Griscom Little, "A Crisis of Biblical Proportions," *Salon*, 7 October 2005; Michael Janofsky, "When Cleaner Air Is a Biblical Obligation," *New York Times*, 7 November 2005,18.

34. Evangelical Climate Initiative, "Climate Change: An Evangelical Call to Action," http://christiansandclimate.org/ (accessed 12 January 2009).

35. People for the Ethical Treatment of Animals, "Zoos: An Idea Whose Time Has Gone," www.wildlifepimps.com/feat/zootime/future.asp (accessed 12 January 2009).

36. Eden Project, "What's at the Eden Project?" www.edenproject.com/visiting-eden/whats-here/index.php (accessed 9 May 2009); see also Doug Alexander, "Back to the Garden," *Globe and Mail* (Canada), 13 August 2003, 6(T).

37. Eden Foundation, "Eden's Philosophy," www.eden-foundation.org/index.html (accessed 12 January 2009).

Chapter 9

1. "The Good Old Days of Adam and Eve," in *America Singing: Nineteenth-Century Song Sheets*, collected by the Library of Congress. http://memory.loc.gov/cgi-bin/query/h?ammem/amss:@field(DOCID+@lit(as107360)) (accessed 7 January 2009).

2. Priscilla J. Brewer, "The Shakers of Mother Ann Lee," in *America's Communal Utopias*, ed. Donald E. Pitzer (Chapel Hill: University of North Carolina Press, 1997), 37.

3. Brewer, "Shakers of Mother Ann Lee," 40.

4. Seth Youngs Wells *et al.*, *Millenial Praises: Containing a Collection of Gospel Hymns, in Four Parts; Adapted to the Day of Christ's Second Appearing. Composed for the Use of His People* (Josiah Tallcott, Junior: 1813), 94. Original from the New York Public Library, digitized 21 July 2006, http://books.google.com/books?id=ozcPAAAAIAAJ (accessed 1 October 2008).

5. Wells *et al.*, *Millenial Praises*, 54.

6. Harvey L. Eads, *Shaker Sermons: Scripto-rational. Containing the Substance of Shaker Theology. Together with Replies and Criticisms Logically and Clearly Set Forth*, fourth ed. (South Union, Kentucky: The Shaker Manifesto, 1887), 101. http://books.google.com/books?id=mslPBawPDj8C (accessed 2 October 2008).

7. Stacey Chase, "The Last Ones Standing," *Boston Globe Magazine*, 23 July 2006, 24.

8. See Peter Erb, "Introduction," in Jacob Boehme, *Jacob Boehme: The Way to Christ*, trans. Peter Erb, The Classics of Western Spirituality (New York: Paulist, 1978), 20.

9. Karl J. R. Arndt, "George Rapp's Harmony Society," in *American Communal Utopias*, ed. Donald E. Pitzer (Chapel Hill: University of North Carolina Press, 1997), 60.

10. William E. Wilson, *The Angel and the Serpent: The Story of New Harmony* (Bloomington: Indiana University Press, 1964), 23.

11. Quoted in Karl J. R. Arndt, *George Rapp's Harmony Society, 1785–1847* (Philadelphia: University of Pennsylvania Press, 1965), 210.

12. Pennsylvania Historical and Museum Commission, Old Economy Village, "Old Economy Village: Historical Overview," www.oldeconomyvillage.org/ (accessed 17 September 2008).

13. John Humphrey Noyes, *History of American Socialisms* (New York: Hillary House, 1961), 624–626.

14. Carden, *Oneida*, 49.

15. Noyes, *History of American Socialisms*, 631.

16. Noyes, *History of American Socialisms*, 632.

17. Carden, *Oneida*, 53.

18. Noyes, *History of American Socialisms*, 633.

19. Quoted in Spencer Klaw, *Without Sin: The Life and Death of the Oneida Community* (New York: Penguin, 1993), 156.

20. Oneida, Ltd., "About Oneida," www.oneida.com/index.cfm/fuseaction/content.page/nodeID/45c80cd8-88a3-44a3-9569-0495196eba88/ (accessed 2 October 2008).

21. Dolores Hayden, *Seven American Utopias: The Architecture of Communitarian Socialism, 1790–1975* (Cambridge, Massachusetts: MIT Press, 1979), 15, 18.

22. American Library Association, "The 100 Most Frequently Challenged Books of 1990–2000," www.ala.org/ala/oif/bannedbooksweek/bbwlinks/100most frequently.cfm (accessed 3 September 2008).

23. Lois Lowry, *The Giver* (New York: Random House, 1993), 111.

24. Lowry, *Giver*, 153.

25. Quoted by Lois Lowry, "The Beginning of Sadness," 4, 6, www.loislowry .com/pdf/Beginning_of_Sadness.pdf (accessed 26 September 2008).

26. Lois Lowry, "Newbery Acceptance Speech," 9, www.loislowry.com/pdf/ Newbery_Award.pdf (accessed 26 September 2008).

27. Lowry, *Giver*, 127.

28. John Hick, "Evil and the God of Love," in *Exploring the Philosophy of Religion*, ed. David Stewart, sixth ed. (Upper Saddle River, New Jersey: Pearson Prentice Hall, 2007), 194.

29. Hick, "Evil," 195.

30. Steven L. Layne, *This Side of Paradise* (Gretna, Louisiana: Pelican, 2001), 190.

31. "This Side of Paradise," *Star Trek*, season 1, episode 24, DVD directed by Ralph Senensky, (original air date: 2 March 1967; Paramount, 2007).

32. Adolf Hitler, in *The Essential Hitler: Speeches and Commentary*, eds. Max Domarus and Patrick Romane (Wauconda, Illinois: Bolchazy-Carducci, 2007), 466–467.

Chapter 10

1. C. S. Lewis, *Perelandra* (New York: Macmillan, 1944).

2. Whitney Darrow, Jr., "Miss! Oh, Miss! For God's sake stop!" (cartoon), *New Yorker*, 9 March 1957, www.cartoonbank.com/product_details.asp?mscssid =MVR8C9HSP1DA8N3UU4B0EJD60BCH4EN0&sitetype=1&did=4&sid=42 574&pid=&keyword=adam+and+eve&section=all&title=undefined&whichpa ge=7&sortBy=popular (accessed 26 February 2009).

3. John Clute and Peter Nicholls, eds., *The Encyclopedia of Science Fiction* (New York: St. Martin's Press, 1993), s.v. "Adam and Eve."

4. This quote appears at http://en.wikipedia.org/wiki/Shaggy_God_story (accessed 14 April 2009) and lists Brian W. Aldiss (pseudo. 'Doc' Peristyle) as the author, citing the October 1965 edition of the British science fiction magazine *New Worlds*.

5. Alessandro Scafi, *Mapping Paradise: A History of Heaven on Earth* (Chicago: University of Chicago Press, 2006), 18, 366.

6. Tibor Krausz, "Paradise Found," *Jerusalem Report*, 1 February 1999, 38.

7. Anthony Browne, "War Takes Its Toll on the Garden of Eden," *New York Times*, 28 May 2003, 15.

8. Sharon Linnéa and B. K. Sherer, *Chasing Eden* (New York: St. Martin's Press, 2006), 309.

9. Linnéa and Sherer, *Chasing Eden*, 263. Ellipses in the original.

10. "New Adam, New Eve," *Space: 1999*, season 2, episode 6, DVD directed by Charles Crichton, (original air date: 8 October 1976, A&E Home Video, 2007).

11. Paul Bedard, "One Nation, Under a New Obama Salute," *U.S. News & World Report*, blog entry, www.usnews.com/blogs/washington-whispers/ 2008/08/07/one-nation-under-a-new-obama-salute.html (accessed 6 November 2008).

12. "TV Ad: The One," www.johnmccain.com/Informing/Multimedia/Player. aspx?guid=779c7d13-7d76-47a5-a4cd-e928e8f1f1d6 (accessed 6 November 2008). This site is no longer active; a copy of the ad appears at www.huffington-post.com/2008/08/01/new-mccain-ad-compares-ob_n_116414.html (accessed 25 February 2009).

13. Lowry, "Newbery Acceptance Speech," 4.

14. William Shatner, "Commentary," *Star Trek V: The Final Frontier*, DVD, directed by William Shatner (1989; Paramount, 2003).

15. "A Pill to Forget?", *60 Minutes*, www.cbsnews.com/stories/2006/11/22/ 60minutes/main2205629.shtml (accessed 7 November 2008), 1.

16. "A Pill to Forget?", 3.

17. "A Pill to Forget?", 3

18. "Probe 7, Over and Out," *The Twilight Zone*, season 5, episode 9, DVD, directed by Ted Post (original air date: 29 November 1963; Image Entertainment, 2005).

19. David Brinn, "From Hollywood to Dodging Hizbullah: Screenwriter Answers the Call to Help IDF," *Jerusalem Post*, 13 March 2008, 8.

20. P. D. James, *The Children of Men* (New York: Vintage, 1992), 166.

21. Margaret Atwood, *The Handmaid's Tale* (New York: Alfred A. Knopf, 1985), 251. This speech does not occur in the movie version of the story.

22. Atwood, *Handmaid's Tale*, 131.

23. Andrew Stanton, "Commentary," *Wall-E*, DVD, directed by Andrew Stanton (Walt Disney Video, 2008).

24. Michael Fleming, "Disney Nabs '*All About Adam*,'" 3 June 2007, *Variety*, www.variety.com/article/VR1117966184.html?categoryid=13&cs=1 (accessed 23 January 2009).

Additional Uses of
Adam and Eve in Film

Information about all of these movies can be found at www.imdb.com or www.tcm.com.

Eden (2008)
Awake and Ovulate (2007)
Edén (2007)
The Gardener of Eden (2007)
Eden (2006)
The Eden Formula (2006)
Eve and the Firehorse (2006)
Project: Adam (2006)
Adam's Apples (2005)
Biblical Adam and Eve (2005)
Edén (2005)
The Nun (2005, a.k.a. *La Monja*)
The Night Owl (2005)
Adam & Evil (2004)
Casa Eden (2004)
E:D:E:N (2004)
National Lampoon's Adam and Eve (2004)
Edén (2003)

Eden (I) (2002)
Eden (II) (2002)
Eve (2002)
The Story of Adam and Eve (2002)
Eden (2001)
Escape from Paradise (2001)
Wormwood (2001)
The New Eve (2000)
A Piece of Eden (2000)
Blast from the Past (1999)
Dogma (1999)
Eden (1998)
Great Expectations (1998)
Adam and Eve (1995)
The Garden of Eden (1994)
2002: The Rape of Eden (1994)
And God Spoke (1993)
Eden (1993)
Eve (1989)
Diaries of Adam and Eve (1988)
Adventures of Mark Twain (1985)
The Original Dirty Pair: Project Eden (1985)
Angyali Üdvözlet (1984)
Stranger than Paradise (1984)
Adam and Eve vs. Cannibals (1983)
Eden (1982)
Paradise (1982)
The Gardener of Eden (1981)
Anime Parent and Child Theatre (1981)
Diary of Adam and Eve (1980)
Saturn 3 (1980)
Ángeles y Querubines (1972)
Glen and Randa (1971)
Adam and Eve (1969)
Fruit of Paradise (1969)
Mormon Temple Film (1969)
Adam and Eve (1963)
Adam and Six Eves (1962)

Eva (1962)
Male and Female Since Adam and Eve (1961)
Bachelor in Paradise (1961)
Adan y Eva (1956)
Death in the Garden (1956)
Adam and Eve (1953)
Forbidden Fruit (1952)
When Worlds Collide (1951)
Adam and Evelyne (1949)
The Apple Fell (1949, a.k.a. *Original Sin*)
Il Miraculo (1948)
Adam, Eve and the Devil (1945)
Eve Knew Her Apples (1945)
Desirable Lady (1944, a.k.a. *A Fig Leaf for Eve*)
Garden of Eatin' (1943)
Ever Since Eve (1937)
Green Pastures (1936)
Ever Since Eve (1934)
Good Morning, Eve! (1934)
Seven Footprints to Satan (1929)
Adam and Evil (1927)
Eve's Love Letters (1927)

Index